The Formation of Character in Education

The Formation of Character in Education: From Aristotle to the 21st Century offers an introduction to the foundations, practices, policies and issues of character formation historically. Following a chronological order, it charts the idea of character formation in the Western tradition by critically examining its precursors, origins, development, meanings and uses.

The book is based on the premise that current conditions and debates around character formation cannot be fully understood without knowledge of the historical background. It introduces many of the debates character formation has generated in order to offer different perspectives and possibilities and uses Aristotle as a lens to gain a better understanding of some of these positions, particularly the theoretical goals of character formation. Chapters explore character education from the classical period through the medieval, early modern, enlightenment and Victorian eras to 20th century influences, ending with a discussion of contemporary policies and themes relating to character education.

This book will appeal to academics, researchers, and post-graduate students in the fields of character and virtue education as well as the history of education.

James Arthur is Professor of Education and Civic Engagement and Director of the Jubilee Centre for Character and Virtues at the University of Birmingham, UK.

The Formation of Character in Education

From Aristotle to the 21st Century

James Arthur

LONDON AND NEW YORK

First published 2020
by Routledge
2 Park Square, Milton Park, Abingdon, Oxon OX14 4RN

and by Routledge
52 Vanderbilt Avenue, New York, NY 10017

Routledge is an imprint of the Taylor & Francis Group, an informa business

© 2020 James Arthur

The right of James Arthur to be identified as author of this work
has been asserted by him in accordance with sections 77 and 78
of the Copyright, Designs and Patents Act 1988.

All rights reserved. No part of this book may be reprinted
or reproduced or utilised in any form or by any electronic,
mechanical, or other means, now known or hereafter invented,
including photocopying and recording, or in any information
storage or retrieval system, without permission in writing from
the publishers.

Trademark notice: Product or corporate names may be trademarks
or registered trademarks, and are used only for identification and
explanation without intent to infringe.

British Library Cataloguing-in-Publication Data
A catalogue record for this book is available from the British Library

Library of Congress Cataloging-in-Publication Data
A catalog record for this book has been requested

ISBN: 978-0-367-20602-4 (hbk)
ISBN: 978-0-429-26246-3 (ebk)

Typeset in Bembo
by Apex CoVantage, LLC.

It is character which builds an existence out of
circumstance . . . this is that in the same family, in the
same circumstances, one man rears a stately edifice,
while his brother . . . lives for ever amid ruins.
G. N. Lewes, *Life of Goethe* (1855)

In Memoriam
John Arthur
24th May 1931 – 3rd April 2019

Contents

Acknowledgements		ix
	Introduction	1
1	Definitions and models of character	8

SECTION I
Foundations 37

2	Classical foundations	39
3	Early medieval foundations	55
4	Early modern foundations	69
5	Scottish enlightenment foundations	85

SECTION II
Practices 99

6	The English public school and character formation	101
7	Victorian character formation	111
8	20th-century influences on character formation	125

SECTION III
Policies and issues 137

9	Contemporary policies and themes	139
10	Conclusion	160

viii Contents

References	175
Further Reading (History and Philosophy)	187
Appendices	192
Index	230

Acknowledgements

My grateful thanks to Aidan Thompson, David Lorimer, Professor Kristjan Kristjansson, Professor Andrew Peterson, Professor Gary McCulloch, John Spencer and Paul Watts for their reading and commenting on various chapters of this manuscript.

Introduction

The formation of character has been a perennial aim of education, and yet it does not lend itself to a single fixed definition nor to superficial analysis. In writing about character formation, we are dealing with a concept of enormous complexity; one which is more often than not discussed in an obscurantist form. The fact that there are multiple and contested definitions of character and character formation is a defining characteristic of contemporary pluralist Western culture, but character formation has also been called many things throughout history. We live in a pluralist and rapidly changing culture in which we should choose to positively construct our characters using a variety of resources. We take what we find and use what we have from the situations we find ourselves in to build our characters. While there is broad agreement about the importance of character formation, this does not extend to the content of what it is or how it ought to be taught, nor whether it should be part of the formal or informal school curriculum. There is similarly difficulty in measuring and quantifying character, say, when compared to the acquisition of knowledge via examinations and attainment measures. It is also the case that the goal of character formation does not of itself dictate specific decisions – it simply provides a way of thinking about what policies and practices might assist in achieving the goal. With these initial caveats and limitations, one might ask why it is so important that we study character. It has never been more important, in our time of exponential change, to build the foundations of good character in every human being, since character is who we are and what we do. The nurturing of character is not void of stable meaning for the future of society depends on people of good character.

The pioneer of contemporary analytic educational philosophy R. S. Peters (1986: 57) believed an individual's character

> represents his own distinctive style of rule-following. But it represents an emphasis, and individualized pattern, which is drawn from a public pool. Character traits are internalized social rules such as honesty, punctuality, truthfulness and selflessness. A person's character represents his own achievement, his own manner of imposing regulations on his inclinations.

2 Introduction

But the rules which he imposes are those into which he has been initiated since the dawn of his life as a social being.

Peters refers to a 'pool' from which rules are selected and self-imposed, so it is best to think of this 'pool' as expressive of the broader meaning of education which constitutes culture. Every culture and any school system favours certain ends or values and these are inherent in attempts at character formation. The narrower meaning of education pertains to schooling. Character formation is a positive, purposeful activity, often intentionally designed to bring about desirable changes in students through enculturation and schooling. However, these changes are sometimes not the ones planned by the teacher at the outset or predicted by society.

Definitions of character and its development reflect different theoretical approaches and traditions and in turn favour one or more pedagogical methodologies. Indeed, character has been constantly contested and reinterpreted by a wide range of ideological positions from left to right, throughout history. Clearly, character formation is not a simple concept. It has gone through several incarnations over time to such an extent that, today, it could be said to be overgrown with redefinitions and interpretations. It has also been open to numerous misrepresentations through exaggerating one or the other of its component features, or simply mistaking good behaviour for good character. Most histories of education are chiefly concerned with questions of institutional and structural development of schools and not so much about what we learn as opposed to how we learn, where and with whom. Character requires a deeper examination of context and culture, which are often assumed or taken for granted, or not articulated. We have lost the understanding that learning to read and write were originally intended as the essential prerequisites for character formation. The question of 'formation' also raises questions about 'what exactly takes form' and 'what gives it form'. This is why those with an interest in character formation, at any level, need to be aware of its historical context, as this forces attention on the specific features of the context in which ethical discourse operates and on how aims and objectives are realised.

This text considers the concept of character, as it has been variously used historically, in attempts at character formation. It follows a chronological order, in the most part, to chart the idea of character formation in the Western tradition: its precursors, origins, development, meanings and uses. The text introduces many of the debates character formation has generated in order to offer different perspectives and possibilities. My purpose is not to suggest a return to some golden age of character formation, but rather to provide a more coherent overall picture of how character formation developed in particular times and places, in response to changing ideas, economic forces and political circumstances. I recognise that the character formation of individuals, and the relations of cultural contexts to individuals' thought and actions have and can be approached in a variety of legitimate ways. I also recognise that any society, past or present, can contain many individuals of 'good character' who nevertheless hold differing views with respect to the great moral debates of their time. However, I likewise recognise that Leon Kass (2018: 10) is right when he said: 'Today we are supercompetent when it comes to efficiency, utility, speed, convenience, and getting ahead in the world; but we are at a loss concerning what it's all for. This lack of cultural and moral confidence about what makes a life worth living is perhaps the deepest curse of living in our interesting times.' Serious disagreements continue to surface in any attempt to define character formation in education. This text focuses on coherent expressions of the idea of character formation explaining why they arise when they do: tracing the history of the concept by examining emerging new concepts or new uses of old ones. This account is by no means exhaustive but seeks to show that ideas about human character are derived from our reflections from the history of ideas.

Historical and cultural context is vital in determining the meaning of character formation, as well as recognising the obstacles to its development. As Christopher Dawson (2010: 5) once wrote: 'A common educational tradition creates a common world of thought with common moral and intellectual values and a common inheritance of knowledge, and these are the conditions which make a culture conscious of its identity and give it a common memory and a common past.' People became educated simply by living their culture and therefore the key to character formation was to live the culture. Standards of behaviour were determined by the culture and you could be considered educated without ever having attended a school. This work is intended to inform contemporary discussion of character formation; it does take a position in the debate – a broadly theoretical, neo-Aristotelian lens is adopted, which views virtues as constitutive of the good life and envisions the goals of education as forming people so they can live well and live rightly in a world worth living in. This approach reflects the primacy of character and character formation. Aristotle saw a direct link between how people should live and how society should be structured to make such lives possible – he had an image of the ideal State. It is interesting that selected reading of his works, namely his *Ethics* and *Politics*, can be used to suggest degrees of change and continuity in Western moral philosophy and practice from his own time to the present.

The goal of education is the search for the good life and while it is always intended to be useful, the question is to what end. The idea of character, here, includes not only a focus on the moral and intellectual virtues, which ought not to be divorced from each other in the process of character formation, but also a concern for what makes a full and meaningful life – it is, therefore, concerned with the question 'How should we live?' Beliefs about how life should be lived are of course the subjects of ethics and character development. They have also been the subject of much contested debates throughout the history of philosophy; not exclusively rooted in Ancient Greece, but seen by many, this author included, as the birthplace of ethical discussions. Where this book takes inspiration from Aristotle, we need to assess Aristotle's claims in the light

4   Introduction

of contemporary 'philosophical theory, scientific research and practical experience, revise or reject them where necessary, and consider their application to . . . contexts not envisioned by him' (see Miller, 1995: 336). Aristotle offers real promise and possibilities, but we also need to look beyond Aristotle to a range of ethical and other theories. Character formation in the Aristotelian understanding is an overarching concept and gives a central role to character virtues. The main factor in whether a person is virtuous in their nature is governed by what we call character. Simply put, a virtue is a good habit and a habit is an abiding quality in a person that inclines them to feel and act in certain ways. Therefore, a virtue is a habit that inclines one to act in a good manner, both externally and intentionally, whereas a vice is regarded as a weakness in someone's character. By character we decide not just what we ought to do, but who we will be. It is our desire to intentionally acquire virtues through practice. Virtues can be both valuable in themselves as well as for the acts they produce and the idea of the human good consists both in virtuous actions and in being a person of a certain character. The good for the individual and the good for the community are both necessary parts of the good of humankind. Acquisition of the virtues is therefore necessary to live a flourishing life. How we live a good life forms an intrinsic part of how we act in society; requiring, as it does, a commitment to foster the flourishing of all human beings in order that we can fulfil our potential. Aristotle would have said it is in our self-interest to desire the good life and he believed that we can and ought to teach the intellectual and moral virtues for right action. As Meilaender (1984: 10–11) observes:

> the virtues do not just equip us for certain activities, or even for life in general; they influence how we describe the activities in which we engage, what we think we are doing and what we think important about what we are doping. Our virtues and vices affect our reaction to the events of life, but they also determine in part the significance of those events for us . . . our virtues do not simply fit us for life; they help shape life. They shape not only our character but the world we see and inhale.

In sum, he concludes that the virtues determine who we are and the kind of world we see.

Aristotle would have advocated that we must surround the child with all the positive influences which society deemed to be healthy while simultaneously training their intellect so that they will eventually be the critic of those influences. Authentic character has a clear potential to resist blind conformity and act in a counter-cultural way. However, simply desiring something does not make it good, rather we desire it because we think it truly good. In the end, even Aristotle bemoaned in his own era:

> In modern times there are opposing views about the practices of education. There is not general agreement about what the young should learn

either in relation to virtue or in relation to the best in life: nor is it clear whether their education ought to be directed more towards the intellect than towards the character of the soul. The problem has been complicated by what we see happening before our eyes, and it is not certain whether training should be directed at things useful in life, or at those conducive to virtue, or at nonessentials. All these answers have been given. And there is no agreement as to what, in fact, does tend toward virtue. Men do not all prize most highly the same virtue, so naturally they differ also about the proper training for it.

(*Politics* VIII, I, 1337a)

Character is often cited approvingly by teachers, parents, and politicians each with their own understanding, but one that is not necessarily related to each other. Diverse conceptions and assumptions about character have led to ambiguity and therefore character formation/education/development remain controversial terms because of the range and variety of what they could reasonably mean. The understanding of education used here is not the same as learning, training or schooling, but comprises instruction and formation with the latter closer to the essential definition. Any genuine education includes information, formation and transformation – it therefore suggests value and involves the entire person. My use of character formation and character education are effectively the same in this text. Any historical study of the formation of character is an ambitious undertaking but one certainly worth trying. The subject could fill a shelf of books, but this text offers a short outline account in order that we may become conscious of the carryover of character ideas and practices from the past into the present.

This book offers an introduction to the foundations, practices, policies and issues of character formation based on the premise that the current conditions and debates about character formation cannot be fully understood without a knowledge of the historical background. There are issues in writing about character and character formation as conceptual categories as well as in organising a book on these themes along historical lines. McIntyre distanced himself from his first edition of *A Short History of Ethics* when he wrote in his new preface in the 1998 second edition, because he no longer believed that the great philosophers were talking about the same kind of ethics such that one could see them as existing within a single ongoing tradition. He suggested in his corrections that they represented a number of traditions of 'moral enquiry', not all offering accounts of the same thing. This same line of thought could be applied to the idea of character and character formation since there never has been one universally held theory of what character formation is, nor how best to teach it. However, my chief purpose is not to study the philosophical aspects of character formation in this text. I also recognise that many empirical studies in the social sciences that purport to study character, too often than not, focus on narrow outcomes or more usually on a single specific dimension of character ignoring the fact that character formation consists in a much broader range of ideas, justifications, and outcomes. Many of the social scientific studies offer no clear conceptual account, leading to the impression of what Wittgenstein called 'language on holiday'.

The text will provide an analytical narrative of character formation within the Western tradition, with some particular insights from the British context. The key features will include filling the gap by covering a neglected area; combining narrative and analysis and offering critical, but selective coverage of the field. In particular, the book will examine some of the ideological conceptions of character formation from Aristotle to the present. Clearly there are other older educational traditions in Egypt, Samaria and China, but this text will focus on the Western tradition beginning with Aristotle. The book also provides examples of teaching materials that were used to help form character in the different periods covered. The text does not survey the extent to which the different ethical and moral ideals of character were actually embodied in the conduct, day-to-day behaviour of the peoples that professed them. Nor does the book examine higher education or the character initiatives developed in preparing for professional life. In summary, the book provides a wider background to understand how the concepts of character and character formation have undergone a number of significant transformations over the centuries while retaining significant elements of continuity.

This book began as notes for a module on the MA in Character Education that was established by the Jubilee Centre for Character and Virtues at the University of Birmingham in 2015. It is therefore written to help meet a perceived need and builds on my book *Education with Character: The Moral Economy of Schooling* that was published in 2003. While ambitious in breadth the book is not intended to be comprehensive, but rather selective and it offers no single account of what makes a virtuous character, although it endorses some basic Aristotelian assumptions. The first section addresses the theoretical foundations of character foundation by examining the contributions of the classical, medieval, early modern and Enlightenment periods. This is followed by a section on the historical practices of character formation in British society while the final section looks at contemporary issues and policies. Chapter 1 begins by clarifying definitions of what character and character formation mean and a number of models are outlined to help us understand how character formation has operated in different contexts. Chapter 2 reviews the Greek and Roman heritage of character formation while Chapter 3 examines the continuation of this heritage through the Christian Middle Ages. In Chapter 4 the Renaissance and Reformation are considered as a time of change and continuity for early modern conceptions of character formation. Chapter 5 looks at the Scottish Enlightenment views of character formation as a bridge to the modern world. There follows a chapter on the English independent school's role in viewing character formation as concerned mainly with manners, sport and social class and then a chapter on Victorian approaches to character formation. The final two chapters consider first, character formation developments in the 20th century, and second, a review of contemporary policy issues and controversial themes in character formation. The book ends with a conclusion and appendices which contain a valuable series of illustrations of the teaching materials used in character formation found in general Western culture and schooling from the time of Aristotle to the present.

The book seeks to provide the reader with an historical overview of where the various positions on character formation come from. It uses Aristotle as a lens to gain a better understanding of some of these positions, particularly the theoretical goals of character formation. Aristotle said that no wind is helpful to a ship without a destination. The reader will note that many who are opposed to character formation in schools have been formed by some of the less inspiring accounts of Western history, by opposing philosophical backgrounds, and by some psychological theories of personal formation. It is hoped that the reader will gain renewed insight from a reconsideration of the idea of character formation both from the mind-sets of the opponents and supporters of different models of character formation.

Chapter 1

Definitions and models of character

Introduction

The formation of character could be said to be the aim that all general education has historically set out to achieve. It is an aim that has often not been explicitly stated, instead it has simply been assumed because much of the school curriculum has been traditionally a prerequisite for character formation. The inculcation of character has been seen as a primary function of culture and schooling, particularly since schools first appeared and there has been a lively debate about character formation for centuries. Debates about character formation have pervaded the course of history and arise at different levels of generality. Character formation has proven to be a remarkably resilient idea seen in the endurance and reoccurrence of the concept. Multiple forms of character formation have also made the concept difficult to fully capture, particularly when character is often defined as a broad based and unspecific entity. Beliefs about the formation of character were regularly taken for granted; they were tacitly presupposed and involuntarily formed rather than formally expressed or argued for. These implicit philosophies of character formation have persisted over a long period of time and are more lasting than the concrete manifestations of character in any period in time.

The transmission of knowledge was traditionally secondary to character formation. What was taught by way of content was believed to have the potential to stir the imagination, pass on enduring values and disclose the motives that actuate human character. Indeed, the idea that certain virtues should be cultivated in children via formal and informal education can be found in numerous ancient texts or writings: Sumerian, Chinese, Egyptian, Indian, Israeli among others, but this study begins with the Western tradition in the thinking and practice of Aristotle (384–322 BC). However, it recognises that during the Axial Age (8th to 3rd centuries BC) there were many cultural developments that overlapped between major civilisations on beliefs, values, religion, social and political thought and ethics. For Aristotle and the ancient Greeks, the education of a child was in part a matter of transmitting information, but also a matter of shaping their normative outlook, i.e. what is the best way to live? Education

Definitions and models of character   9

in this sense is never intended to be neutral for as Chesterton (1950: 167) says: 'Every education teaches a philosophy; if not by dogma then by suggestion, by implication, by atmosphere.' After two thousand years of analysis and discussion we have failed in modern times to resolve or reach a consensus on questions about character formation.

It was well understood that teachers affect what their students value and therefore teachers help influence the character of their students. Aristotle discusses in his *Politics* whether the job of character formation is best done by the child's father or by the community. He recognised that the home is a private, not a public institution, and that any inequalities in parental nurturing will reinforce inequality in the community. However, he did not recommend the practice of Sparta which was for the State to take over the whole education and life of young boys at the age of seven. In Athens the State left parents free to make their own arrangements for the education of their sons. It can be argued that the educational thought and practices of Greece are the most important of all earlier contributions to our contemporary education. It is, for example, from Greek thought and practice that the modern conception of the school as the constructive instrument of the State arose.

Today, many modern educationalists believe that human autonomy is the ultimate end of education. This implies an orientation towards the future through a concern for ever increasing opportunities for choice by continually widening the range of options. This has led to doubt and uncertainties with the precise meaning of character open to diverse and often contradictory interpretations. Who today wishes to be virtuous? Who even uses the word? Yet there are hundreds of definitions of character. Character is often used interchangeably with personality, particularly as psychology from the 1930s has tended to treat many character qualities as features of a theory of personality (Nicholson, 1998). Indeed, character was effectively supplanted by personality, but did not entirely disappear (see Allport, 1921). The language of character and personality is a discourse about individual differences, but character has a much longer pedigree. Character has moral overtones and is connected intrinsically with a normative understanding of human conduct while personality is more descriptive concerning the non-moral aspects of people. Character is about who you are and refers to what is truly at the centre, your inner beliefs and feelings and therefore cannot be separated from the person. Personality, in contrast, is often about how you seem to be or how you present yourself to the world. We cannot therefore reduce character to a question of personality or life-style.

Character

Throughout human history scholars and people more generally have vigorously debated the purposes, desires, feelings and habits that guide human conduct. It was inevitable that discussions of character would become fraught with conflicting definitions and with endless personal and ideological battles. How

10 Definitions and models of character

we are disposed to think, feel and act is clearly open to argument and interpretation, but the powerful idea of character lies at the heart of this debate even if there is less agreement on what it means and consists of. The origins of the word are not surprisingly Greek, 'Kharakter', signifying an 'engraved mark' impressed upon a coin or seal – a kind of stamp impressed by nature or education which marks out individuality. Through the centuries this has come largely to mean the complex sum of ideas or qualities distinctive of individuals and which need to be understood within particular contexts, both historical and modern. Character is a multi-faceted aggregate of ideas and qualities that significantly vary between individuals – it is what makes us different from each other, and like 'personality' it constitutes our distinguishing attributes. Today, character is often conflated with personality or personal growth. Gaps in character formation clearly correlate to gaps in income, family function, education and employment. Character is also an evaluative concept for its use can be of a commendable or culpable nature. Character qualities in the popular mind are often viewed through a lens with descriptive adjectives in order to distinguish types of character: good or bad, stable or unstable, noble or base, strong or weak, high or low and odd or no character. This evaluation of someone's character qualities can suggest the existence or lack of admirable character qualities. Ultimately, the way a person reacts to a situation defines their character which is often associated with virtuous behaviour which is to act on virtue from some particular motivation.

In the *Republic*, which is dedicated to outlining the formation needed for true virtue, Plato emphasised that character formation should begin early: 'The beginning is the chiefiest part of the work, especially in a young and tender thing, for that is the time at which the character is formed and most readily receives the desired impressions.' A modern commentator, Hauerwas (1975: 203) is even more profound: 'Nothing about being is more "me" than my character. Character is the basic aspect of our existence. It is the mode of the formation of our "I", for it is character that provides the content of the "I". . . . It is our character that determines the orientation and direction, which we embody, through our beliefs and actions.' In this character and identity are the same thing. John Stuart Mill from his *On Liberty* emphasised the independence of character when he wrote: 'A person whose desires and impulses are his own – are the expression of his own nature, as it has been developed and modified by his own culture – is said to have character.' There is an endless range of commentary on what character is or might be.

What are the general components of character, particularly in how it ought to be used in the academic literature? I provide a brief survey of some of what I consider to be the essential inter-connected factors that character consists of. Indeed, my attempt is to outline the descriptive features of what character means and which distinguish it as a particular kind of normative guide. First, character involves change over time – it is not fixed, static or set, but is malleable and continuous, not immutable during life. Character is also visible in our conduct. Second, character is shaped within and by cultural and civic context and therefore is a social, not an entirely individual process. It has the potential to transcend social, religious and racial differences – character is not completely contingent on identity, it may surpass our divisions and allow us to share many common values. Character, I believe, ought never to be aligned to either the political right or left, nor must it be co-opted for narrowly sectarian causes. Third, it involves choice and autonomy – to freely choose a way of life is to ensure our actions are guided by intelligence and reason resulting in reasonable action. It requires an ability to evaluate reflectively the moral claims of others in a sensitive way. We need to deliberate about which actions to take when the principles and convictions we have formed do not adequately or clearly apply, but knowledge alone is not sufficient without motivation. Fourth, it involves a life dominated by principles and convictions, the ability to discover or define one's life mission and desired lifestyle without blind conformity to the convictions and actions of others. There cannot be character without principles and ideals which are the guiding standards of an authentic life. A person of character will need to remain true to deeply held commitments so that their behaviour and actions reflect their enduring and settled habits. These habits are often automatic behavioural responses to cultural cues, which develop through repetition of behaviour in consistent contexts. Fifth, it involves observable actions according to these principles, convictions, rules and life mission – in other words character always requires practical expression through a lived ethics that puts into place the fundamental convictions of life. It must also involve self-observation and/or self-criticism in order to refine these principles, but ultimately through attitudes that are expressed consistently in judgement and action. Sixth, it involves regularity of expression – which requires a certain stability in moral attitudes and a persistence of effort. Character involves habitual behaviour as it is shaped by our doing. Seventh, it requires will power and motivation as well as the ability to act on appropriate judgements – the will here is self-conscious activity by the power to act deliberately. The development of any of these components can be blocked or impeded, particularly by the lack of basic resources, both human and material.

All these components of character ought to be seen as having a degree of usefulness for the individual in demonstrating what character is in any life. Each one of us is in a sense a configuration of these components of character that need to be understood as supporting each other. However, even these seven characteristics of character are not sufficiently comprehensive enough to capture the full complexity of human character (see Besser-Jones, 2014: 76–93) and this is why speaking of character is always an act of interpretation. The danger of both advocates and critics of character formation is to reduce character to a single component and placing too much emphasis on that component. As Kamteker (2004: 460) rightly observes: 'the conception of character in virtue ethics is holistic and inclusive of how we reason: it is a person's character as a whole (rather than isolated character traits), that explains her actions, and this

12 Definitions and models of character

character is a more-or-less consistent, more-or-less integrated, set of motivations, including the person's desires, beliefs about the world, and ultimate goals and values.' Character is not simply how people act, but how they integrate their motives and values and how they reason. It is a mixture of cognitive and non-cognitive elements and in this thinking and feeling are not unconnected.

Acting deliberately requires constant effort on the part of the individual to seek out their own character development. As Goethe wrote: 'Character is best formed in the strong billows of the world' or as Heraclitus said 'Protracted and patient effort is needed to develop character'. Character needs social experience so that the habits formed promote moral character which in turn allows culture to perpetuate itself. We could say that character is formed in particular communities marked by fidelity to a normative story. Marx (1852) once said: 'Men make their own history, but they do not make it as they please; they do not make it under self-selected circumstances, but under circumstances existing already, given and transmitted from the past.' This raises the important point that there are things in life that we have no choice over and these will constitute the limits and possibilities within which any given character is formed. Our character is, as Bondi (1984: 207) says subject to the accidents of history: 'This occurs in three ways: (i) events which are beyond our control of any individual or group, (ii) circumstances in which we simply find ourselves, and (iii) the past, insofar as we cannot change what has already occurred' and he concludes that 'the accidents of history form the raw material of character.' What to do in any given situation demands more than knowledge of the law, certain rules or your role. Therefore, we need the capacity to deliberate well and possess the ability to perceive what is morally relevant in any situation. We need to be able to read social situations, to understand the other's perspective and simply gain experience of life itself.

All of these components outlined above need to be brought into harmony with each other since actions presuppose a choice which will determine the action taken and for which the individual is responsible. You could say that character is a set of personal traits or as Aristotle called them, 'firm and unshakable dispositions' that evoke specific emotions, inform motivation and guide conduct. The possessor of these dispositions, it is often argued, will regularly and reliably act in accordance with the virtues. However, character formation should not be reduced to moral education since character involves a much broader range of human excellences than simply those that are viewed as moral. Virtuous character involves both the intellect, the will and the rational and affective part of the self. The virtues of character within an Aristotelian lens require us to live according to reason and the virtues of thought enable proper exercise of reason itself. Taylor (1964) provides a good definition of the complexity of character when he defined it as concerned with dispositions, desires and tendencies: 'having steady and permanent dispositions to do what is right and to refrain from doing what is wrong, having morally desirable wishes, desires, purposes, goals; and having the tendency to respond emotionally towards things in the morally appropriate way.'

Any two teachers or parents who are generally sympathetic to character formation are likely to view it differently and disagree about what features are more important. Having character is sometimes defined as knowing (cognitive) the good, loving (affective) the good, and doing (behavioural) the good. We know that someone's character cannot be easily assessed and that such assessment attempts are often surrounded with controversy. Some nevertheless, emphasise habit over reasoning while others focus on the environment over the individual. Conservatives are often suspicious of 'soft' virtues which they take to imply social-moral relativism while progressives are concerned about a too narrow focus on the individual over the structural inequalities to be found in the education system and society. Others want direct instruction to inculcate certain virtuous behaviours while yet others seek inter-personal relationships and a greater focus on efforts for community cohesion. They encompass diverse approaches, but it can lead to defining it too narrowly or exaggerating it to such an extent that you provide a caricatured version in order to justify dismissing the whole approach.

Character needs to be defined broadly as Aristotle described it when he argued that the goal of human life is to develop its essential excellences, the potentialities that define and constitute it. Aristotle places before us a vision of the good as an ideal to make progress towards. For Aristotle acquiring the virtues in order to secure the standards of good character and virtuous action, in turn requires persistent effort with the virtues becoming the habit of right performance. We need to know what virtue is before we can acquire it and it is clear that there is more to being virtuous than good behaviour. Aristotle provides us with the most developed and historically influential idea of character. The Greek educational tradition understood that the teaching of virtue was not intended for students to give a good account of themselves or that they should defend the idea of their good character in debate. It was rather about doing the good as the virtues were expected to have some practical and beneficial effect. Virtue here was defined as the disposition to desire and to do the right thing. It was also understood that virtues would be shaped by different communities. Virtue was viewed as constitutive of human flourishing, not simply instrumental to it and that virtue is both intrinsically and instrumentally valuable to an individual.

In summary, the main features of character can be said to comprise the following:

1 Malleable over time even when it is difficult and requires great effort
2 Is the product of reason and freedom
3 Requires sustained effort of the will to act deliberately
4 Conforms conduct to convictions and desired lifestyles
5 Is a complex sum of beliefs, emotions and actions that varies between individuals
6 Is shaped within and by cultural context
7 Results in self-caused practical actions

14 Definitions and models of character

Some people have these qualities and potentialities to a greater or lesser extent than others. Character is the set of traits, good or bad, that makes someone the kind of person he or she is. Aristotle would say that we are partly responsible for our own character and that excellence of character results from habituation or repetition of actions which result in turn in the formation of settled habits. Character formation therefore must continue throughout adulthood. Aristotle of course has had his critics, from the left and right, from Hobbes to Mills, who say he is 'elitist', 'impractical', 'racist', 'sexist', 'naive', 'morally prescriptive', 'politically incorrect' and presents 'outmoded ideas'. It is not the intention of this text to address these criticisms only to say that Aristotle is not an easy philosopher to understand and he does not answer all our questions about character, so it is important that I do not exaggerate the extent to which his ideas are relevant to current debates about character formation. Others reject Aristotle's ethics completely, as Trianosky (1990: 104) writes:

> although one's attitudes, emotions, reactive capacities, and skills are or can to some extent be developed by will, no effort of will, however sustained, is *sufficient* for their development. Character is the product not only of voluntary action but also of the activity of temperament, along with upbringing, childhood experiences, social environment, peer expectations, and pure happenstance. And not only temperament but all of these things are not themselves the product of some exercise of agency, whether voluntary or non-voluntary. Hence, no Aristotelian account of responsibility for character can succeed.

Harman (1999: 316) questions the existence of character itself as he writes 'ordinary attributions of character traits to people are often deeply misguided and it may be the case that there is no such thing as character, no ordinary character traits of the sort people think there are, none of the usual moral virtues and vices'. There is a difficulty in giving an adequate account of why a person should live the good life in Aristotle's thinking as well as the apparent weakness in his largely theoretical account of addressing particular decisions in concrete cases. Bertrand Russell (1945: 195) is perhaps the most critical when he wrote harshly: 'The book (*Ethics*) appeals to the respectable middle-aged, and has been used by them, especially since the seventeenth century, to repress the ardours and enthusiasm of the young. . . . There is . . . an almost complete absence of what may be called benevolence or philanthropy. The sufferings of mankind . . . do not move him. . . . More generally there is an emotional poverty in the *Ethics*.' Copleston (1993) is more judicious and his *History of Philosophy* provides a classic account of the ethical theory of Aristotle.

Kristjan Kristjansson (2013) in an important, balanced and influential article argues that there are persistent myths about character formation and he challenges these misgivings while recognising that there are still some well-founded misgivings remaining. He divides these challenges into six categories: conceptual, historical, moral, political, epistemological, and psychological (2013: 269). For Kristjansson, and for this present text, character formation is best understood as any form of moral education that foregrounds the role of virtuous character in the good life. His challenges could be briefly summarised in the following way: first, the concepts of character and virtue are not ambiguous notions, but rather they continue to be used with considerable consistency in the academic literature. Second, character is not a redundant term overtaken by other more contemporary expressions, but rather it retains its power to communicate meaning for the good life. Third, character and virtue language are not old fashioned, but rather are contemporary notions, particularly with the rise of virtue ethics as the moral theory of choice of many. Fourth, character formation need not rely on religious justifications, but can be fashioned in post-religious language. Fifth, character formation cannot be paternalistic as excessive moralising from any source undermines the freedom of the individual. Sixth, character formation cannot be character formation if it denies the capacity for intellectual enquiry. Seventh, character formation should not be conservative in orientation as character ought not to be aligned to the political right or left but must retain its potential to be transformative of the individual and society. Eighth, character formation does not ignore living well in community and therefore cannot be individualistic in orientation. Ninth, character formation while grounded in a virtue ethics approach remains open to diverse interpretations, but this does not mean the concept is entirely relative. Tenth, character formation is not completely situation independent since behaviour is a function of both character and situations.

Character formation

Herbert Spencer's (1851: II: chapter 17) statement that 'education has for its object the formation of character' is often cited among educationalists, but there is no body of scholarly literature in which the meaning of this statement is used with any consensus. Much controversy surrounds the definition of character formation. Perhaps this is because schooling can never complete the formation of character since we cannot become fully educated or reach a terminal point in any of the stages of formal education, meaning schooling. Learning and education are life-long endeavours and it is only through the trials of life that someone can be considered to be educated in character. Learning is the process of change that occurs for the individual and it is an individual experience. Education is therefore the preparation of the young for membership in the human community. Schooling is merely the preparatory stage that assists in the forming of the habits of learning – the means for continuing to learn after school has ended (see Adler, 1982). Schools are also just one attempt to institutionalise an educative process. Schools can therefore never turn out fully educated human beings far less produce the fully formed character. Their mission is a limited one to educate the student to his or her capacity and to help enable them to lead good human lives. Teachers guide, assist and aid the learner which means supporting and empowering them. Teaching is a deliberate act to induce learning in another person. This is not carried out in a vacuum, but with vision and intention and located within a specific historical, social and cultural context. Learning requires engagement with social contexts. Some argue that education is powerless to modify the character of a student while others suggest that the school is exclusively about knowledge and that character is a family matter. Others say that part of schooling is simply about telling students about the difference between right and wrong and incentivising them to do what the school considers to be the right thing. The reality is that genuine education is not about information, but transformation – the test is not what a student knows at any particular point in schooling, but rather about who they have become in the process. A student can conform to standards set by the school without changing their character – it is a form of conformity to institutional rules without any interior engagement with such rules. Character formation can never be about confusing character with social conformity nor is it about being swayed by every current opinion or to be simply governed by circumstance.

Character formation is an umbrella term that involves all implicit and explicit educational activities that build the character of people. The range and diversity of what can be reasonably called character formation permits a great deal of variation in the content of character formation. The location for character formation includes educational institutions, but it also involves engagement with voluntary organisations, communities, society and the State. Character formation aims to nurture the ethical, intellectual, civic, social and personal development of individuals. However, the umbrella nature of the term has grown with it being used to describe teaching which is associated with well-being, positive education, moral education, citizenship, behavioural strategies, social and emotional learning, religious education, personal growth, health education, and mental health. It has become an overarching concept that is concerned with anything that involves a continuing learning process and that enables young people and adults to become good, healthy responsible citizens. Essentially it aims to help form people so that they can live well in a world worth living in. In this sense living well is treated as equivalent to flourishing (*eudemonia*) which requires the possession, according to Aristotle, of the virtues (*arête*). A life worth living is therefore a life lived in accordance with the virtues. Aristotle's focus is on the ethics of someone's character rather than on their actions and the best way to know what we should do is to think about how to behave virtuously as opposed to simply following moral rules. Virtues, and their formation, therefore give us a guide for living well without giving us specific rules to live by. To possess a virtue is an achievement, as it is about being good at living one's life. The overriding good of Greek ethics was the achievement of a flourishing life. Consequently, virtue can be defined as a state of character that reliably and predictably enables one to act well which leads to our flourishing. It means committing oneself to the aim of acting well and doing well by engaging in public life with care and respect for others. However, definitions of living well and virtue are disputed mainly because both involve normative claims about what is good and admirable.

Formation is a purposive and conscious process that brings about the development of an individual into a particular thing or shape. Like education, formation means 'to lead out', to form, to fashion, to forge, but not in a passive way as the student must be free, active and co-operative in the process. The absence of formation can also guide character, but is really incoherent, unplanned and random. Formation here is understood as an active concept, for character is never static or truly formed – it is never achieved as a homogeneous whole. True formation is a planned continuous process that involves the interplay between both knowledge and experience and is conducive to the good of the individual and society. This must be deliberately planned, chosen and employed to modify both the behaviour and thinking of the child that he may become different from what he would have been without character formation. Kupperman (1991: 17) offers a definition: 'X's character is X's normal pattern of thought and action, especially with respect to concerns and commitments in matters affecting the happiness of others or of X, and most especially in relation to moral choices.' Teachers clearly play a vital role as teachers are in a position to report on character even if they are unable to give a comprehensive analysis of a child's character. As Arnold-Brown (1962: 67) said: 'If discipline is imposed by those who command respect, it will be accepted, welcomed and reproduced.' It can lead to us being led or compelled through experience, particularly if we lack the will to forge ahead by ourselves.

Models of character formation

The generic models outlined below are constructed as helpful tools or lenses by which we can describe what character formation is or has been in historical reality. In this sense the models are intended as explanatory and therefore do not claim to be a complete description or explanation of character formation. Each model identifies variables that have a meaningful and significant relationship to the forms of character formation intended as an outcome in each model. Some of these models will overlap and conflict with each other as well as simultaneously employ similar or contrary pedagogical approaches. In each of these models I recognise multiple perspectives on character formation, but they tend to emphasise one aspect of character education in order to achieve an integrated understanding. They also stand in considerable tension with each other for they are linked to competing claims of ultimate authority over the form and function of character formation. We could easily subdivide these models into a battery of subtypes and hybrid types and any attempt to explain these models in action would necessitate a number of books. It should be emphasised that

18 Definitions and models of character

these models are my own early conceptualisations distilled from my reading of the historical evidence.

We need to consider the distinctions between context and content in each of these models by examining the historical detail of each model, particularly the content of character formation and the conceptualisations of character underpinning them. We are not born into an abstract moral universe, but rather into a concrete historical ethical context. These models are about worldview and the discourse in each is different, but it should be recognised that ordinary people will operate with multiple models even when they exhibit contradictory tendencies. Each model is largely descriptive but can be employed in a prescriptive way when applied to character formation. There are overlaps and similarities between these models which means they can sometimes be aligned with each other, but some conceptions of character are associated with particular communities which means there are a plurality of forms of character, because considerable cultural diversity is an enduring feature of being a human being. Classifying the different positions for each model has not been easy.

Each model can be placed into the following main categories with a short historical exemplar or ideal outlined for each.

Hegemonic

There are a range of hegemonic models of character formation that include fascist, Marxist, authoritarian and nationalist constructs, but I restrict this model description to the Marxist conception. This hegemonic model reinforces the existing elites, character formation understood as a class concept, reproduction of compliant or socially acceptable human beings which can relate to the Marxist idea of the ruling class that manipulates the value system and mores of a society so that their views become the worldview. Some would argue that imposing a conception of the good on children is always an act of hegemony and domination: schools which were seen as instrumental for the reproduction of capitalist or State social relations (Bowles and Gintis, 1976). Socialisation inevitably serves as an automatic process of character formation and in schooling the student participates in a series of interactions 'systematically structured in a way that preserves the functioning of society or the particular institution within it' (Pritchard, 1988). The typical language of the discourse in this model includes: coercion, hierarchy, aristocratic, indoctrination, authoritarian, prescription, materialist determinism, uniformity, docility and domination. Kit Christensen (1994: 70) makes the point: 'The "right kind" of moral character by itself will never be sufficient to bring about human flourishing-with-others, or any radical social change for the better, as long as class society exists. In fact, given the extent to which people's objective circumstances determine both "who" they individually are, and how the actual course of events will unfold for them independently of their intentions and desires, it must be assumed that personal character will most often constitute at best only a secondary causal factor in historical development.' The State, seen from this model, is viewed as an instrument of the ruling class who influence the way people think, their conception of reality, and their values.

An exemplar of this type of all-encompassing character formation could be the education provided during Soviet Russia from 1917 until the 1980s which viewed character formation as a means to radically change society. This was a totalitarian society, run by an elite which expected unquestioning obedience, and which controlled the forces of coercion, the media, and required conformity to its communist ideology particularly through training in character. The Soviet Union sought as the main aim of education, not knowledge in schools, but 'socialist morality'. This 'Vospitania' (often translated as character education) involved every institution in the Soviet State that a person would come into contact with from birth to death. Parents, for example, were expected to attend lectures on how to bring up their children, and hear lectures on the radio and later television on the same theme. In education it concerned the non-academic aspects of school life and gave heavy emphasis to the socialisation of students as good citizens. It was the Communist Party that determined what character formation would look like and this included the idea of a strong will, self-sacrifice for the sake of society, and the idea that 'morality had no meaning outside of the context of the collective' (Baker, 1968: 291). The authoritarian dimension of this model could be described as government by a centralized power structure which is neither limited by a working constitution or authentic laws.

Soviet authority used many of the common pedagogical methods to instill Soviet character by means of biographical accounts of great men and women so that children could emulate their deeds and thoughts, the use of physical education to teach solidarity and an extensive range of extra-curricular activities. Character training was provided in and out of school to produce well rounded individuals who were politically educated with the aim to create: a strong sense of patriotism and internationalism, communist consciousness, love of work, respect for others and for property. It was the idea of the 'new man' who would be critical of the 'I' of Western capitalist society. Teachers were key to forming this 'new man' and were expected to take an active role in shaping the character of the young – a character that was future orientated to perpetuate communism (Korolev, 1968: 35). There was a stress on dance clubs, theatre groups, choral membership and schools provided numerous opportunities for this kind of enrichment. There was a sense of 'unity of expectations' in that if everyone demanded the same of each other then all will eventually comply and social psychology was employed to this end (Lakobson, 1968). The idea was to form a collective character identity and Anton Makarenko was the leading light in Soviet character education with his widely accepted aims that character formation must help children with (1) the need for purpose in life, and (2) the need for security and a sense of belonging (Baker, 1968). In the end Soviet character formation was ultimately a form of revolutionary human engineering. Its

20 Definitions and models of character

teaching methods and tools varied from coercion, extrinsic inducements, and exhortations through to social-conditioning.

Theological

Once again there are a number of theological models of character formation including Jewish, Christian, Muslim and other religions, but the model described here restricts itself to the Christian idea of character formation. Theological and religious based character formation within the Western Christian tradition gives priority to the virtues of faith, hope and love with reason and revelation required for ethical decisions and actions. Character formation in this model is dependent on and inseparable from religion. The typical language of the discourse in this model includes: faith, spirituality, morality, holiness, conscience, revelation, sin, dogma and salvation. It is difficult to select one representative Christian model of character formation as there are historically numerous examples. Even within one tradition it may have changed considerably over time, but the one selected here is the Jesuit model contained in the *Ratio Studiorum* of 1599. This was a hugely influential pedagogical manual that survived for more than three hundred years in Europe and around the world which had the dual aim of educating Christian souls and propagating the Catholic faith. The Jesuits were a new religious congregation that saw educating youth as a founding aim with education seen as a special ministry. They set out to inculcate religious principles in boys combined with useful knowledge. In this they followed the conservative humanists of the Renaissance and offered a classical curriculum that the founder Ignatius Loyola believed teachers 'should make it their special aim, both in their lectures and when occasion is offered outside them, too, to inspire the student to the love of God our Lord, and to a love of the virtues by which they will please him' (Cueva et al., 2009: 13). The means to achieve this was to provide a liberal classical education that was a graduated programme of teaching the Greek and Roman classics in an effort to affect the identity and state of flourishing of the learner.

The *Ratio* was effectively a plan of action as it did not outline any educational principles, but was more concerned with method and organisation. Nevertheless, the Jesuits sought to use the classics in a traditional manner to assist boys to emulate the virtues of character in these writings. Classical wisdom was assumed to inherently promote Christian pietas and the Jesuits associated it with discernment based not only on factual knowledge, but on judgement and insight. Thus, those who lacked knowledge could also become wise. This humanistic Christianity saw in the classical writings the idea that man acts in a form of contemplation and so he thinks before he acts making the inner life the source of the outer life (Schwickerath, 1903: 6). This gave the Jesuits the idea that they must develop the soul – the inner life conforming to God in Christ first in order to develop a strong will and prepare young people to strengthen the wider Christian community through their sound Christian character. In this the Jesuits were extremely successful and their school system, because it was uniformly realised throughout all their schools, was the first educational system. Today, the Jesuit model is hardly recognisable as being of the same tradition. The aims of character formation are much more activist and relational – more concerned with doing justice and personality development or a capacity for 'loving'. There is a plurality of objectives with no order or priority given to them and there is less emphasis on developing the inner life. Their idea of human nature is not the same thing as what went before. The principal teaching methods and tools employed varied enormously in time from instruction, modelling traits, proselytisation through to coercion or even progressive teaching.

Another way to understand this theological model is to consider the purposes of a Church school from a virtue rich horizontal and vertical axis. The horizontal axis represents the natural virtues of compassion, courage, reasoning, gratitude, justice and so on that a Church school will attempt to inculcate in students in forming their characters. However, this horizontal axis of other-related virtues does not make the school religious or distinctive as other schools can claim the same natural virtues without any religious affiliation. The Church school requires a vertical axis of the supernatural or theological virtues of faith, hope and love. The belief in God and the practice of these theological virtues through prayer and worship are intended to work with the horizontal human virtues to strengthen, reinforce and enhance them. The State school would not have this metaphysical way of thinking which attempts to define and rationalise character using that which exists outside of the material, i.e. horizontal axis. The horizontal virtues are transformed by the existence of a God-related vertical axis and conscience is formed as a guide and provides a powerful reason to motivate the will to act on the human virtues. It is this idea of conscience that makes the Church school distinctive as a model of character formation.

For the Christian school the formation of conscience is essential because one cannot become a person of character if conscience is ignored. What is the difference between character and conscience if both enable an individual to become morally good? Gini and Green (2013: 26) explain it in the following way: 'If character is living out what we value, conscience is its inner counterpart, that part of us that makes judgments and evaluations about when, how, and with whom that value should or should not be applied. Conscience is frequently the first step in making a moral decision, the internal uneasiness that prompts us to ask ourselves some hard questions.' Ultimately, as Wright (2010) says, Christians do not live for the human-centered goals of virtue formation for the sake of happiness or even 'human flourishing', but as means to follow Christ. In this sense Christian's can follow Aristotle's ethics up to a point, but Christian character formation is more than anything Aristotle ever imagined. It has a richer notion of the human person who is called to goodness and attracted to the truth.

Liberal

In this model we are not speaking of a liberal education based on the medieval concept of the liberal arts, but rather we are describing liberalism that emerged during the Enlightenment. This Enlightenment liberalism has deeply permeated our ideas of education and schooling. Liberal virtues, such as civility, tolerance and open-mindedness, are essential for self-governing citizens and for a healthy Western democracy. Typically, liberal virtues are valued for instrumental reasons and for allowing freedom from interference in pursuit of good lives. Some liberals view virtues for their intrinsic worth. The typical language of the discourse in this model includes: justice, social responsibility, diversity, oppression, free expression, human dignity, egalitarian, collectivist, and equal rights. There are many meanings of the word liberal, some of which overlap with other models described in this text. People who say they are opposed to character virtues in school usually mean they are opposed to values other than their own. An exemplar of this kind of character model could be the United States during the latter part of the 20th century. As Callan (1997: 2) says, free and equal citizenship is about the kind of people we become and the kind of people we encourage or allow children to become. He goes on (1997: 3): 'What we seem to forget is that the vitality of the political order depends on an education that is dedicated to specific ideals of character.' There is a commitment to the good of the polity and a willingness to share the responsibilities of society in a liberal model. Respect for fellow citizens and their rights flows from this ideal and Callan believes we need to accept and internalise these same ideals of character. There is of course a debate about liberal societies and government on whether they ought to have a view on the good life and take a stand on opposing views about character formation. The idea that a liberal model should mandate a distinctive education for virtue seems wrong because the very conception of liberal, for some, is that it should be devoid of any ethical ideal or should allow the freedom to determine ethical ideals individually. However, this is not the case in practice when liberal societies wish to promote a loose and vague idea of diversity, encourage a sense of justice, tolerance, and respect – sometimes believing in the perfectibility of humankind through unlimited societal progress.

The liberal State seeks to be impartial and even neutral, but in practice it is not, even if the liberal worldview says that character virtues are subjective. The liberal State generally promotes egalitarianism and universalist notions of equality as well as individualist agendas. The liberal State faces challenges in its educational aims because of the diversity of moral, religious and philosophical views of the good life held by citizens. The principal teaching methods involved persuasion, discussion and openness: the liberal model allows a degree of choice over values with character grounded in freedom, autonomy and decision-making. Character formation within the liberal State claims not to advance any particular view of the human life without there being a consensus and Rawls described the kinds of educational goals that would be acceptable in such a state: 'the dispositions to co-operate with others on reciprocal terms and to accept that there are many sources of reasonable disagreement among citizens' (quoted in Victoria Costa, 2004). This provides the minimal approach for character formation as it recognises that thick virtues as part of an education programme do not sit well with contemporary liberal ideas. There are many schools that embrace what they consider to be popular liberal approaches to education which include multiculturalism, socially active civic engagement, experiential learning in the community, life skills, health education, democratic education and much else besides. The liberal mind-set is often predominant in Western societies and can be seen in the attitudes of teachers and textbooks in schools (Vitz, 1986: 1). It could be said that liberalism has become a hegemonic political language in educational circles and yet it produces an excess of liberalisms, so that it becomes difficult to identify a coherent character model.

Republican-liberal

Republican-liberal virtues, such as civility, tolerance and open-mindedness, are considered essential for self-governing citizens and for a healthy democracy in this model. Virtues are valued for instrumental reasons, but the crucial value is freedom from domination rather than freedom from interference. The typical language of the discourse in this model includes: liberty, sociability, civic virtues, civil society, democratic, rule of law, conventions, utilitarian, empathy, solidarity, and communitarian. An exemplar of this model could be 14th-century Florence, a City-State inspired by a classical conception of republican liberty, but fully inclusive of a Catholic faith (see Pocock, 1975). Young wealthy men, in other words less than 10 per cent of the population, were brought up to expect a share in the government of the City: to attend the assembly, speak in debates, judge the arguments, take sides and vote, serve as a magistrate or sit on a jury (Siedentop, 2014: 28). The public space was everything and you could not be indifferent to the political process which led to a participative citizenship which gave you status, power and position in civic society. The public space certainly trumped the private space. Character formation included the civic virtues and the focus was on the political formation of sons. As Peterson (2011: 79) argues, the civic virtues are central to understanding this model as they were understood as those dispositions and character traits which, in their social expression, enabled citizens to participate in the public affairs of their communities. Florence resembled the City-States of Greece in size of population and was the location of the emergence of the Renaissance producing a lay cultural elite which read books. The origin of this new humanism began in the 11th century when more lay nobility received some kind of education in the liberal arts producing a class of people with a good knowledge of Latin (Thompson, 1963: 55). Encouraged by the Church, many small villages and towns employed a school teacher and by 1339 between 8,000 and 10,000 boys in Florence attended

24 Definitions and models of character

a primary school out of a total population of 90,000. Between 550 and 600 would receive a grammar school education (Davis, 1965: 415). Each commune or town council would direct these teachers to teach good morals to the children and all would employ the Latin classics as the content of this education.

As Dagger (1997: 200) says: 'Republican liberalism contains a vision of the good society, but not of a perfect one.' Inspired by the civic humanism of the ancient Greeks Republican liberalism teaches that you can realise your human nature in a democratic society which is characterised by participation in public life. Such a society is concerned with the freedom to act independently and on your own terms, but it is action that ought to have the common good in mind. Virtues here are role-related and the role appropriate to civic virtue is citizenship. So the republican liberal will respect individual rights, value freedom, tolerate different opinions, play fair, cherish civic memory and take an active part in the community (Dagger, 1997: 196), but this was still restricted to the elite who made laws for others to obey. The methods of teaching included rewards and punishments.

Neo-liberal

Harvey (2005: 2) defines neo-liberalism as a theory of political economic practices 'that propose that human well-being can best be advanced by liberating individual entrepreneurial freedoms and skills'. Indeed, that the market is 'an ethic in itself, capable of acting as a guide to all human actions, and substituting for all previously held ethical beliefs'. In this sense character is an ideal that assents to behaviour that upholds the economic structure. It has traditionally been connected with the Protestant work ethic in that hard work is seen as a good builder of character and the lack of this ethic is reflected in a weakness of character. It was a form of moralism – through applying codes of behaviour. Early 19th-century American schools organised character courses of study around moral codes and one example was prepared by the National Institution for Moral Instruction which was a 'Code for Successful Workers' which included:

> I will educate myself into strong personality. I will develop force of character and have some worthy purpose in life. I will use my leisure wisely. I will be well informed, self-possessed, self-controlled, self-respecting, stable, open-minded and teachable, alert, observing. I will be quick to understand, and of good memory. I will use my imagination, and be ready to take responsibilities. I will gain knowledge of human nature, show sympathy, and take an interest in people. I will be friendly, cheerful, harmonious, and always tactful.

The intention was corporate in emphasis to make the students conform to the standards expected in employment (see Appendix K) – producing a type of character orientation that is rooted in seeing oneself as a commodity in the market place.

It could be said that many conservatives and liberals share an outlook across the political and philosophical spectra that consumerism and materialism, springing from capitalist practices, have eviscerated human character. Neo-liberal concerns competing private individuals with marketable competences, including their character traits. Virtue itself can be associated with a taste for luxury goods and a degree of conformity. The typical language of the discourse in this model includes: competition, consumer, private ownership, free trade, liberalisation, deregulation, choice, unregulated, risk-taking, and privatisation. Sometimes it is accompanied by a neo-conservative dimension emphasising hierarchy, obedience, order and control. George Orwell (1949) described something of this when he depicted the ruling elite in *Nineteen Eight-Four.* 'made up for the most part of bureaucrats, scientists, technicians, trade-union organizers, publicity experts, sociologists, teachers, journalists, and professional politicians. These people, whose origins lay in the salaried middle classes and the upper grades of the working class, had been shaped and brought together by the barren world of monopoly industry and centralized government'. Orwell is recognising the tendency of modern life toward scientific planning, central control and specialisation which potentially de-humanise an individual by making their character less than what it is meant to be.

It is often said that those who live in the West live in a 'neo-liberal' world and that this phrase is used pejoratively, describing any tendency that is deemed undesirable. We can say that neo-liberalism is a theory of political economic practices that emphasise human freedom and individual competition and there is an impression that such a system has little need of virtues or ethics as it promotes individual self-interest over the common good. Sennett (1998) in *The Corrosion of Character: The Personal Consequences of Work in the New Capitalism*, is extremely critical of the effect of this form of capitalism on character. He describes the life of a worker and says: 'He feared that the actions he needs to take and the way he has to live in order to survive in the modern economy have set his emotional, inner life adrift . . . his deepest worry is that he cannot offer the substance of his work life as an example to his children of how they should conduct themselves ethically. The qualities of good works are not the qualities of good character' (1998: 20–1). Sennett highlights the potentially corrupting features of capitalism on individual character and Sandel (2013: 7) also argues that markets can corrupt individuals and that unregulated they undermine morality. Essentially it places the ethos of unfettered competitiveness at the centre of social life. Testing, league tables, performance pay for teachers, school choice and competition are the ideas that permeate many schools today who internalise these neo-liberal commitments in their educational discourse and consciousness that it makes it difficult for them to think otherwise.

The worker in Sennett's example lacks life-long commitments and loyalties at work and struggles to maintain a sense of ethical integrity. Short-term

26 Definitions and models of character

gains are prioritised, there is 'no long-term', and an atmosphere of continued change results in the loss of community. This process removes meaning from the workers' lives and undermines their well-being. In terms of character it divides will from behaviour and through instability makes it difficult to form settled dispositions of character or a stable sense of the self. It therefore weakens character and the form of materialism it promotes overwhelms moral commitment and causes detachment from society. Education is seen as having no special role within neoliberal ideology, but rather is a commodity like any other to be traded in the marketplace. Heightened competition and intensified individualism are the result so that the individual consumer becomes fully responsible by their exercise of choice. This market approach to character formation means that those who develop good characters, responsible and resilient, will be best prepared to participate in the market and gain material success through their hard work and character traits. It is difficult to prove causation in this context and it may be more productive to focus on the correlational question of whether character tends to be eroded in societies with free markets. In contrast there are academics who take the opposite view in that the individual agent can influence the organisation through their virtuous character and ethical behaviour. They argue that the capitalist system can endorse and grow the virtues of friendship, trust and reciprocity (Baker and White, 2016: 229). Maitland (1997) reminds us that Adam Smith and other Scottish Enlightenment thinkers saw commercial society as a moralising force and not about the narrow pursuit of our own interests – he also argues that the market can strengthen moral character. The teaching methods revolve around learning to respond positively to incentives and competition. An example of this, which places responsibility for character formation on the individual, is seen in a poster from a school wall in England which reads: 'The golden opportunity you are seeking is in yourself. It is not in your environment, it is not luck or chance, or the help of others; it is in yourself alone' (see Kultz, 2017: 58). This portrays students as lacking the character traits for success.

Conservative

Conservative virtues maintain and promote traditions, traditional societal institutions and longstanding values (Arthur, 2014). Conservation is often a synonym for 'traditionalist'. There are many types of conservatism for it is not a universal theory. The typical language of the discourse in this model includes: character, virtues, discipline, self-reliance, individual responsibility, standards, authority, tradition, sacrifice, custom, truth, freedom, prudence, industry, patriotism, and hard work. Often those who are conservative character educators are eager or anxious to preserve or recover a social order and therefore wish to preserve the traditional curriculum in schools (see Tate, 2017). There is no single uniform model of conservative character formation as this model is one of degree and the idea has changed many times. It is more of a state of mind

Definitions and models of character   27

or type of character, but conservatives are generally concerned about character and virtues. Through customs, conventions and a sense of historical continuity that links generation to generation – a conservative view would view human nature as a constant. Moral truths are permanent and there is a strong sense of right and wrong and opposition to involuntary collectivism. Laws by themselves cannot make people virtuous as they merely compel outward conformity to rules, but not internal consent. Conservatives seek to cultivate the best in people, but believe that governments can be the tutor to people as well as a servant. Will (1983: 21) writes that all governments proscribe, mandate, regulate or subsidise behaviour in people and that they are concerned about the inner life of citizens. However, the conservative view does not believe in the perfectibility of human nature (Doyal, 1997, Giroux, 1987).

It is important to make a distinction between traditionalism and conservatism and Karl Mannheim offers us such a distinction (see Wolff, 1993: 260ff). Traditionalism he says is a subjective instinctive inclination to do things as they have always been done or to view things as they have always been viewed. Conservatism is 'conscious and reflective' – it is the decision to retain the old way of doing things when presented with a choice of a new way. The conservative views education as a moral choice and the teaching methods are essentially traditional teacher led with specified content. It is said that conservatives prefer teacher directed learning with a curriculum of names, numbers, dates and places. Michael Oakeshott (1962) summarised this in 'On Being Conservative' when he wrote: 'To be conservative, then, is to prefer the familiar to the unknown, to prefer the tried to the untried, fact to mystery, the actual to the possible, the limited to the unbounded, the near to the distant, the sufficient to the superabundant, the convenient to the perfect, present laughter to utopian bliss.' You could say this was about character being shaped by ordinary human affairs to enable the person to make the best of herself. Formation is meant to develop the individual human being, the person, rather than simply to serve the State. Oakeshott, who believed in the traditional idea of a liberal education, conceived of education as a morally transformative process in which a student would not be the same at the end of a course of education than he or she was at the beginning. For Oakeshott education was about the formation of character and the appreciation of a rich intellectual tradition (see Corey, 2013) which promoted the good politics of civil association. However, it is difficult to recognise in modern conservative politics what 'conservatism' means for character formation as they are preoccupied with parental choice, accountability, local control, and standards. One would have expected a more substantive view especially as many conservatives see good and bad values embedded in schools, meaning that they are not value-free spaces.

The ideal of a conservative school that promotes traditional character formation would be one that had a common curriculum (a body of established subject knowledge) for all which provided cohesion and stability for society

28 Definitions and models of character

and culture. It would intentionally bring students into an already established culture and would be careful not to promote excessive individualism or change. Therapeutic approaches or functions would be seen as weakening education. In answer to the question how shall we live, the conservative school would have an ideal of the 'good' that it believed can be known and towards which the school would strive.

Psychological

The psychological model involves various theories that describe behaviour and make predictions about future behaviour from cognitive developmentalists, behaviour modificationists to neuroscience (see Zigler, 1999). However, there is no unified model here since the only idea that is agreed is the assumption that character formation must be based on empirical facts about how character develops psychologically which has led to endless disagreements. Interest in applying behavioural psychology to character formation has ebbed and flowed since the 1900s, but generally it adopts a sceptical view of character formation preferring instead to talk about educational situations that may elicit certain behaviours. The typical language of the discourse in this model includes: behaviour, motivation, development, change, measurement, tests, innovation, brain and motor development, nature versus nurture, and cognition. Models of character from a psychological perspective, particularly the components that make up human character, have generated many controversies and research issues, not least a sceptical view of character from many psychologists. There have been strong determinist assumptions behind what some have called the science of character, which has attempted to offer a better understanding of this complex concept. However, the results in popular psychology have at best been inconclusive and at worse simply 'advocacy science'. Academic psychological findings, particularly from cognitive-developmental research, are often complex and theoretical and there is a tendency to apply these findings before they are fully understood. The first book on the modern psychology of character could be attributed to Alexander Bain in 1861 entitled *The Study of Character*, and this fed into the Victorian optimism that psychology would offer effective measures of character. More general views can be found in 1923 in the study by J.A. Hadley, *Psychology and Morals* followed in 1927 by A. Roback's book entitled *Psychology of Character*. Roback comments on the chameleon-like qualities of character and how its development has taken a kind of protean fashion. He attributes the ethical and pedagogical nature of character as the reason why psychology did not engage with it preferring a study of personality instead. Psychologists have questioned whether character even exists and say they are not much concerned with moral questions because psychology is essentially a descriptive science. It is why, even in studying personality, they attempt to remove it of all normative content. Popular psychology has also spawned a psychotherapeutic culture of self-improvement.

This is a character model driven by the need for measures of the non-intellectual traits with the individual viewed as 'a collection of discrete, stable, and general qualities or "traits", the sum total of which equaled his or her personality' (Nicholson, 1998: 2). In this view character is only useful if it can be weighed, measured or counted. It is the main reason why character almost disappeared from the goals of education in the late 1950s. However, more modern studies by psychologists Lapsley and Power (2005) write that important insights about character and character education will only be forthcoming when there are adequate advances in character psychology. They say that how we understand the moral formation of persons must be conditioned on what we know about personality and development and that how we manage the moral education of character must be conditioned on what we know about selfhood and identity. As a psychologist, Blaine Fowers (2005) is also more positive about the link between psychology and character as is the positive psychology movement which emphasises character strengths. Fowers (2005) rehearses four types of characters based on Aristotle's commentary in the *Ethics*, they are: first, *the continent character* – which is selfish, amoral or immoral human desires which a person is able to exhibit control over in order to be of service morally. Second, the *incontinent character* – a person who knows what is right or virtuous, but does not have the self-control or capacity to live these moral standards. Third, *the vicious character* – a person who feels no conflict between inclinations and moral duty because they have no moral sense and act selfishly. Finally, *the virtuous character* – a person also feels no conflict between emotional inclinations and moral duty because their emotions have been trained to be aligned with their moral inclinations and they desire to do the good. Fowers makes clear that a person can exhibit all four of these character types in a life-time. Fowers (2008: 649) added a fifth character type which he called the 'beastly character' – a person who is enslaved to their desires or habits that suppresses or destroys their basic human capacity to reason, make good choices, and engage in good relationships with others. He admits that these types are underdeveloped and that psychology's contribution to the study of character formation is fragmented. The range of teaching methods in this model therefore vary and can range from 'fixing' the kids to teaching through different cognitive stages of development.

Radical

Radical ideological models range widely from militaristic to progressive expressions of character education, it is about examining the ideological orientations of character education. It is not a coherent category and defining accurately the various sub-models within this spectrum of authoritarianism to progressivism, left to right, is a difficult thing. They are often associated with political power as Yu (2004: 2) says: 'The construction of virtue is always tied to privilege, power and control.' The typical language of the discourse in this model can include a broad and contradictory range of words and phrases: radical, ideology,

30 Definitions and models of character

nationalist, eugenics, feminist, sexual, left, right, green, utopian, passive, obedience, and de-schooling. It is often associated with the ideas of modernity and is a very flexible model – suggesting a vague future education. It can be associated with fascism, socialism, communism, and replaces the old or traditional, emphasising that which is 'modern'. I describe two sub-models, the militaristic sub-model which is often associated with physical hardship and strict discipline, and the progressive sub-model which is also not homogenous.

Helen Roche (2013) provides us with a detailed example of the sub-model of militaristic character in her examination of how German children were taught to model themselves on young Spartans. The Prussian army began to self-identify with Spartan youth as early as 1820 in the Royal Prussian Cadet Corp. Originally founded in 1717 as a nursery for the Prussian Officer Corp and to educate the sons of impoverished officers the military training entailed strict military subordination through self-denial, self-discipline, physical prowess, self-sacrifice, devotion to the State and the Monarch, and comradeship (Roche, 2013: 34–5). Articles written at the time compared the training to Sparta and it was this Spartan mindset that shaped the character of Prussian officers that was later followed by the Japanese. By 1900 there were at least eight preparatory schools with boys aged between 10 and 15, many connected with nobility, which built character through athletics and team games with gymnastics used to encourage courage, endurance, agility, and competition. The boys would be surrounded by the glories of the past and statues of German heroes together with rituals that promoted patriotic self-sacrifice. Beatings were common and ill treatment from teachers and peers was accepted by the policy not to complain. Remaining silent was the norm with bullying rife in dormitory accommodation. There are many similarities with Spartan education here that emphasised duty and the excellences of character after the model of Sparta (Roche, 2013: 94). Consequently, the teaching methods are strict discipline, training and brainwashing (see Appendix L).

These schools were closed in 1920 after the First World War (Roche, 2013: 36), but effectively re-founded in 1933 through the creation of the National Political Education Institutes with the ideal of Sparta as the model. These were boarding schools for boys of Aryan descent, irreproachable character, pure racial health, full physical ability and high intellectual prowess (Roche, 2013: 181). A strict timetable was imposed and racial kinship was encouraged by the new Nazi ideology to such an extent that the Spartan ideal became the claim that the ancient Spartans were their true ancestors. Roche demonstrates that from older children and teachers came images of Sparta designed to inculcate ideals of endurance, discipline and military self-sacrifice and the identification with Sparta was used to justify the domination of other countries. It is interesting that Rutherford-Harly (1934) compares English public schools with Spartan pedagogy. However, it cannot be sustained that English public schools were anything like the totalitarian education provided in Germany which was more about social conditioning than education. Rosenthal (1986) saw this militaristic model of character at work in Baden-Powell's scout movement, but he also identifies the more economically inspired model of character that concentrated on instilling the work ethic.

In contrast, the progressive sub-model of character formation is associated with experiential learning, critical thinking, active and co-operative learning, community service and child centered pedagogy. You could think of progressives such as Pestalozzi, Froebel, Montessori, and Steiner who emphasised the needs and interests of the child, the community of the school, autonomy and preparing children for social life (Stewart, 1972). It brought together diverse methods and practices, often not too dissimilar to those of other models, and which changed over time. In this model the progressive is interchanged with experimental and radical. The first progressive school in Britain was founded by Cecil Reddie in 1880 at Abbotsholme while John Haden Badley, arguably the real originator of progressive education, found Bedales School in 1893. These schools were founded as an alternative to the authoritarian approaches to schooling current in English boarding schools in the late Victorian period. Badley was a secular socialist who had abandoned his Christian faith at Cambridge University, but had retained strong moral standards grounded in reason and science (Arthur, 2019). He was a supporter and member of the Moral Instruction League, a progressive educational organisation that advocated for character education. Badley, (1905) as headmaster of his new school, outlined his philosophy in an edition of *The Elementary School Teacher* in 1905. He spoke directly of 'training the body, mind and character' and explained how the 'unconscious' environment of the child's surroundings helped form their character. Badley introduced co-education within five years of the school's foundation for he believed that girls and boys ought to have the same curriculum and be educated together.

Badley's school did not contain a chapel and Christian education was not offered. Character building appeared to replace Christian teaching in line with what the Moral Instruction League had advocated. The educational approaches adopted included: children discovering for themselves, group work, manual labour, community meetings, games and exercise. Experiential learning was also a key feature, but experience is not a morally neutral phenomenon, it is not random and children do not spontaneously unfold. Indeed, Badley insisted on cold water, Spartan rooms and windows kept open as well as regular hygiene inspections to produce healthy bodies – not too dissimilar to more authoritarian practices noted elsewhere. Bedales School retains its progressive and fashionable outlook and just as in 1893 it is an expensive education for the social elite in society; despite Badley's socialism and advocacy of social justice his school was inspired by the public school tradition. The teaching methods for progressive education focus on the issue of pedagogy itself – on the process rather than the content, a concern with form rather than substance.

Many progressives have throughout time, as Hunter and Nedeliskey (2018: 25) say, sought to find a scientific footing for moral character. People who are

32   Definitions and models of character

impressed by the scientific approach often believe that human actions are inescapably determined, which results in thinking about any weaknesses or faults being the responsibility of the body or even the teacher. Consequently, there is nothing to commend or blame. Progressive education also emphasised the scientific understanding of the child particularly in psychology and biology, which in some cases led progressives to advocate for various eugenic causes. Some progressives held that low moral character was something predominantly inherited and one solution was to sterilise the morally inferior and restrict marriage for the poor. The logic was clear: *biological inferiority = social inferiority = inferior moral character.* Some of them therefore followed the teachings of Francis Galton who believed that character was hereditary resulting in Nazi racial ideology as explained in the hegemonic model described earlier (Arthur, 2019). This is a view that is still prevalent today with the idea that much of our character is inherited and is part of our DNA. A good example of this thought, that helped prepare the way for the eugenics agenda in the early 20th century, was the writings of Furneaux Jordan (1886, 1896). Jordan was a professor and surgeon in Birmingham who proposed that moral character could be seen visibly in the faces and bodies of the people he examined in his Queen's Hospital, Birmingham. He observed these features in the curves of their spine, their flesh, their bones, their skeletal structure and even in their nervous system. The title of his 1896 book, *Character as seen in Body and Parentage*, clearly depicts his extreme approach. Astonishingly, he proposed that battered women essentially asked for such violence from their husbands because of their physical features. He attempted to provide scientific evidence for degenerate characters along psychiatric Darwinism lines. Of course, the better off were viewed as a more mentally healthy breed. The approach took away any sense of guilt for the suffering poor and was a precursor to full blown eugenics as seen in the Nazi era. An era that saw the twin aims of seeking racial perfection while simultaneously trying to eradicate 'human imperfection': aims that have a long history.

A more modern example of a progressive school is A. S. Neil's Summerhill School founded in 1921. Neil (1960) was a liberal educator who believed children are virtuous at birth and that 'No one is wise enough or good enough to mold the character of any child'. He rejected the Christian idea of original sin, as well as Freud's idea that aggression was inborn, together with the ideas of progressive education. Adults, he believed should not impose their views on children and so he established Summerhill with his message of freedom. The children in the school were free to form their own character as he said: 'There is no need whatever to teach children how to behave. A child will learn what is right and wrong in good time – provided he is not pressured' (Neil, 1960: 224). It raises the question of whether we can really choose our own character *ex nihilo*. The school attracted students from ages five to 17 from all over the world but never exceeded 200, with the current numbers around 90. The school also attracted a huge amount of international publicity as the most unusual school in the world, where students and staff had equal votes to change the school rules and students choose whether to attend lessons or not (Croall, 1983). Neil's progressive philosophy of education led to difficulties in the school community and it is interesting to compare his ideas with John Dewey's who remarked that 'The idea that goodness of character will come without attendance to the means of creating it is a relic of the belief in magic'. Neil was claimed as a progressive educator (Howlett, 2013: 163), but his ideas are more in line with utopian and Romantic ideas following the example of Rousseau.

Virtue Ethics

Virtue ethics concerns the classical emphasis on an individual's character as the key element of ethical thinking rather than on a concern for rules and consequences – an Aristotelian theoretical lens. It emphasises the character of the actor who must be encouraged to do those actions that further their formation as a human being. It can be prescriptive in that it often consists, depending on the advocate, in the advocacy of particular virtues as worthy of being inculcated because many feel that modern society is in crisis and believe that other modern ethical theories have failed. The virtues are understood as the qualities of persons and their lives. The typical language of the discourse in this model includes: practical wisdom, flourishing, traits, excellences, habits, virtues, reason, dispositions, purpose, formation, motives, the good life, intellectual, and will power. Virtue ethics is a branch of normative ethics based on the works of Plato and Aristotle, but encompassing many other thinkers over the last two millennia who considered the goal of human existence the pursuit of excellences or of virtues. The word virtue here derives from the Latin *virtus* meaning 'excellence'. It is a model of character formation that comes in many varieties, an umbrella term covering a plurality of theoretical approaches to ethics. This model fosters virtues as the aims of character formation, so that the virtues are the affective and intellectual states that make a life excellent and worth living. Kass (2018: 287) aptly summarises what character requires:

> It needs help from a sharp mind. Though the beginnings of ethical virtue lie in habituation, starting in our youth, and through the core of moral virtue is the right-shaping of our loves and hates by means of praise and blame, reward and punishment, the perfection of character ultimately requires a certain perfection of the mind. Aristotle's Ethics famously teaches the indispensability of prudence or practical wisdom (*phronesis*) for the supreme sort of ethical virtue. Strictly speaking, one cannot be ethically good unless one is practically wise.

Practical wisdom or prudence plays the central role in virtue ethics since it is practical wisdom that generates the other virtues that comprise our virtuous character and help us to behave in particular situations. It provides the ability to deliberate well about means to ends. The re-emergence of virtue ethics and

34 Definitions and models of character

its growing influence has generated a number of critics and Doris (2002) presents the typical case against character being based on a virtue ethics approach. However, as Walker and Ivanhoe (2007: 4) summarise: 'In general, virtue ethical views assess human character as a primary mode of understanding the rightness or wrongness of actions and the goodness or badness of lives lived, view traits of character as stable dispositions to act and feel in contextually appropriate or inappropriate ways, and understand the virtues and vices as the primary mode of assessing character.' While Hoof (2006: 48) argues that 'Virtue ethics does a better job at performing the four tasks of moral theory: to understand morality, to proscribe norms, to justify them and to describe how they fit into our lives'. Character plays a fundamental role for virtue ethics and it is often contrasted with utilitarianism and deontology because it is character based, rather than outcome or duty based. In a virtue ethic view of character, you demonstrate good character in word and deed. For Aristotle, to be truly good one's actions and intentions must also be good together with one's judgement. In other words, your heart and your mind should come together to form character. A key difference in this model compared with more utilitarian approaches is that it precludes doing wrong that good may come of it, while the utilitarian approach requires intentionally doing wrong whenever a greater good would come of it.

This text will return to the notion of virtue ethics throughout, but we can summarise the model using Hoof's (2006: 80) outline of what Aristotle understood to be a theory of virtue ethics which is in sharp contrast to a tradition of an ethics of duty: (a) it is concerned with what makes life worth living; (b) human beings have purposes built into their mode of being and the acquisition of virtue helps us achieve those purposes; (c) a distinction is made between 'virtue of character; and intellectual virtues, based on our moral abilities, where 'virtues of character' are developed by training and intellectual virtues by education; (d) it is a normative theory in that certain behaviours are regarded as not worthy of human beings; (e) wisdom is an intellectual virtue, but practical wisdom is the master virtue since it allows us to judge rightly what a situation calls for from us and to do it; and (f) the goal of virtue is to flourish and you cannot flourish without being good'. Virtue ethics offers us a telos, an end point, which is a movement from who we are to who we could be. Human nature as it exists to human nature as it could be – the transition from one to the other is through the acquisition of character virtues. This process occurs over a life-time and is lived in various contexts. Having a virtuous character and acting in accordance with it is what it is to flourish, which means virtue is inherently good for people and also instrumentally good. Virtue is its own reward in this view. Within education the teacher appeals not to abstract principles or human rights, but to thick virtue terms in their teaching. This mode of teaching was the principal approach employed all the way from the ancient Greeks through the Middle Ages and into the Renaissance and beyond to the early modern era.

The benefits of a virtue ethics model of character formation for contemporary schools and students are both numerous and significant. First, in our pluralist Western societies virtues ethics can be independent and yet complementary to religious belief. It can be presented in schools free of religious terminology making it more likely to gain acceptance within a largely secular context. Second, the model is practical in application and while it does not provide clear rules on how to act it does build the capacity of students to make decisions through careful discernment and allows them to consider the consequences of their actions. It also allows them to make mistakes and is flexible making it adaptable to multiple situations. Third, the model addresses what makes a good human being by encouraging students to think through their actions on what it means to be a human being. It takes the whole student into account and does not ignore their emotional side and it gives due recognition to the students' intrinsic motivation. Fourth, it provides a rich language which helps us articulate character commitments in a clear way that acts as a bridge between the moral life in theory and the moral life in practice. This language aids a purpose driven ethic and in turn living life well. Finally, the model allows variety in how virtues influence the formation of character, but the goal is always to help the student flourish. I acknowledge that there is much conceptual and empirical work that needs to be done before the full implications of this model for students becomes clear, but it represents, for me, the model with most advantages for character formation.

Commentary

In each model described I have attempted to outline its main elements and explain in a simplified fashion the components of the model. This may be oversimplified and open to contestation and I acknowledge they are certainly incomplete and they may even conceal particular unconscious assumptions. However, they are provided here as an aid to our understanding and have an exploratory function as well as identifiable supporters who take them to be what we should be like or even what we want to be. Discussions of ethical matters in many of these models range from utilitarian terms of weighing competing goods to moralist terms of rules, rights and duties. It is worth noting that the language of one particular model can be used, while the practices denote another model – models can be re-shaped or morphed into another model through changing ideological positions of the educator. It is also worth remembering that in each of these models both society and the school socialise and educate young people into the model's ethos of character. In each model the modern school has teachers who supervise children separate from their parents in a specific building, not their home. Schools standardise and organise the life of students through a process of scheduling lessons and events. Schools also lay down rules to control their movement and to determine what they do which leads to high degrees of conformity. In all of this process children have no

36   Definitions and models of character

choice, rather they have an obligation to obey. A school will have an educational plan that is not neutral, but clear about what moral values are being enculturated in the school. Society is also formative of character as each model operates within a societal context and is underpinned by various sets of interests, motives and normative commitments.

Each of the above models also use overlapping teaching approaches and Puka (1999: 131) helpfully summarises these teaching methods as I apply them to the models I describe above: (a) instruction in basic values and virtues; (b) behavioural codes established and enforced; (c) telling stories with moral lessons; (d) modelling desirable traits and values; (e) holding up moral exemplars in history, literature, religion, and extolling their traits; (f) providing in-school and community outreach opportunities (service projects) through which students can exercise good traits and pursue the virtues. There are clearly a wide variety of teaching methods that can be used in addition to those listed here, but it also depends on the degree of authority or force exercised behind these methods. Authoritarian teaching methods are simply an abuse of the teacher's authority and they can be employed in any of the models above. Indeed, proponents of these approaches may find themselves divided across, rather than along, model lines. As McIntyre (1969) observed: 'It has become increasingly plain that whether a man calls himself a Christian, a Marxist, or Liberal, may be less important than what kind of Christian, Marxist or Liberal he is.' Seeking one exclusive single model seems futile as they naturally overlap, but each model reflects the interests that caused them to arise. Each provides its own interpretation which attempts to direct our thoughts and actions in regard to character formation. For example, militaristic or hegemonic models are diametrically opposed to virtue ethics models while radical models are opposed to neo-liberal models. Conservative, liberal republican and virtue ethics models contain many common themes while liberal, progressive and neo-liberal models overlap in some significant ways. Ultimately, we need to acknowledge that there is no single optimal model that commands agreement, but only perhaps for some a preference for one. Human beings have limits on the formation of their character in each model and these are biological, social and psychological limitations and they are not independent of their ancestral or personal pasts, yet are not a slave to them either.

Section 1

Foundations

Chapter 2

Classical foundations

The ancient Greek idea of education was founded on the notion of *paideia*; that it was the responsibility of a society and its adults to educate young men in character. *Paideia* means education or culture and education for the Greeks meant character formation (Marrou, 1956: 146). Early Greek education also comprised a preparation for citizenship through military and political training. Schooling (from the Greek *Skhole*) was a specialist and partial form of education that contributed to the formation of some young people as it was only open to males of high rank or simply aristocratic young men of the ruling class who possessed *arête* (nobility). The school in Greek society referred to education and formation of intelligence or the development of skills that can be taught, more than it referred to forming will-power. Hadot (1995: 12) explains that through the idea of *paideia* these 'young men strove to acquire the qualities – physical strength, courage, sense of duty and honor – which were suitable for warriors, and incarnate in the great, divine ancestors taken as models'. The *paideia* process was designed so that the Greeks respected the Gods, the laws and the rules of society. This included respecting their elders and parents as well as respecting the position of others – effectively avoiding the vices. If a man lived by these rules he received honour in the community (see Further Reading).

In Greek society women were under the control of men and had to live in the background; as Siedentop (2014: 17), quoting Fustel de Coulanges in his *The Ancient City* (1864), reminds us, paternal control was almost complete in the subordination of women:

> The Greek laws and those of Rome are to the same effect. As a girl, she is under her father's control; if her father dies, she is governed by her brothers; married, she is under the guardianship of her husband; if the husband dies, she does not return to her own family, for she has renounced that forever by the sacred marriage; the widow remains subject to the guardianship of her husband's agnates – this is to say, of her own sons, if she has any, or, in default of sons, of the nearest kindred.

40 Foundations

There is some fragmented evidence that some girls did attend school, but generally it would have been domestic instruction for girls (Beck, 1964: 85).

Sparta and Athens

The overwhelming majority of the population were not trained for the responsibilities of citizenship, but rather narrowly trained for one or another particular job to earn a living. It would, however, be a mistake to think that the ordinary person remained completely uneducated. Education is often identified as a transitive process – something one person (the teacher) does to another (the pupil) to induce some outcome. However, the historical record indicates the primacy of self-education or experiential education. The teacher could be present, or present in a text, or more commonly present in a living tradition of individual voices transmitting an oral tradition of stories. Every individual was initiated into society through 'enculturation' – schooling in a sense was only one specific form of enculturation with specialised knowledge in successive institutional forms which accounted for one element of character formation. General 'enculturation' was a conscious and systematic process to create a common worldview with universal intellectual and moral standards. Each individual was initiated into modes of thinking, understanding and acting through learning a language, occupying a particular public space and being enculturated in a particular time and culture. This was largely acquired orally and practically by the common tradition, folklore, religion, rituals, art, architecture, and apprenticeships, all of which had the ability to become embodied in the life of the community. This kind of education through experience rests within the individual and does not require a formal teacher. The acquisition of speech takes place in the home before any form of schooling and so it was the home and family that the Greeks considered the centre of a child's education. The family taught the child manners, how to behave in public and moral discipline as a preparation and contribution to character building. Culture was therefore transmitted in the home and through participation in society according to one's social status. The informal association of community life provided education for the people as children associated with adults and learned much from that affiliation. However, there was also a dark side to Greek and Roman cultural practices. Both Sparta and Athens practiced eugenics and infanticide was common with a committee deciding in Sparta and the father in Athens whether a child is fit to live or die. Rome also practiced infanticide, but with the addition that the father was able to order the death of his children at any time after their birth.

Sparta sought to build up character according to a clearly defined ideal which entailed absolute patriotism and devotion to the State (Marrou, 1956: 22). As Barrow (2007: 10) says: 'The Spartan upbringing was unashamedly set on moulding a certain kind of character, one for whom the highest calling was to honor the state by the way one lived and died.' Consequently, obedience was the principal virtue to be taught and the standard of goodness was that which served the State. In Sparta young boys remained with their parents until the age of seven when they were compulsorily recruited to barracks and they began their professional training for war until the age of 21. The curriculum consisted largely of fighting, boxing, wrestling, running, the use of the spear, stealing, military drill, ball-playing and military music. The emphasis was on building resilience and grit, courage and endurance, perseverance and a laconic demeanor. Patriotism and loyalty were prized. Punishment for non-compliance was severe. This is the classic authoritarian State military model of character development. Sparta imposed character from above and people lived for the totalitarian State, as Jaeger (1939: 83) said it was like 'living in a perpetual armed camp'. Jaeger (1939: 83) identifies the central issue of how much control the State should have which Plato (427–347 BC) examines in his Republic: 'The great social problem of all later Greek educators was to determine how individualism might be repressed and the character of every citizen might be developed on one communal model.' All adults were considered teachers and each person was forced to submerge their individuality to the authoritarian and racist system.

The intellectual dimension in Sparta was limited to memorising the *Laws of Lycurgus* and some Homer in *The Odyssey*. Some children might be introduced to Aesop's fables, myths, legends of the Gods and possibly Homer's *Iliad* (see Appendix A). These poems and plays helped shape character and it could be said that Greek education in character originated in the Homeric epics which emphasised many of the preferred virtues of Greek culture – the characters Greek society wished to reproduce. Poems were used to motivate children and adults to do good deeds and provided standards to judge how good or how bad the consequences of a person's actions were. Children were taught not just to embrace the hero of these texts, but to hold the virtues displayed too, as well as extend their capacity for fellow feeling. They set the standards of the community to which children and adults were expected to conform (Beck, 1964: 32). Children were presented with an unambiguous moral prototype which was the ideal of the good person and this was inextricably linked with the ideal of the good society. The epics by Homer taught the Greeks about the great drama of human life and actions and that the actions of characters have consequences and affect others. Homer effectively created a perfect man hero – a soldier and aristocrat. In Sparta it was not about individual heroes, but rather about a whole collective of City heroes. Schooling was largely physical and the virtues prized were self-control, discipline, endurance, reverence, self-sacrifice, all necessary for gaining citizenship. The education provided in Athens in contrast was cultural rather than technical and clearly directed towards a different kind of character formation (Beck, 1964: 72).

Athens complemented military training with instruction in reading, writing, music and geometry and thus had a broader notion of education, with provision for greater individualism. Music in particular was thought to profoundly influence and shape character. Both Plato and Aristotle thought that music contained intrinsic elements that were conducive to moral harmony and that it

42 Foundations

aided the formation of the ethical mind. This idea was extended into the Middle Ages with Boethius writing that music was a character-forming device that infused into children character, ethical norms and good manners. Teachers in classical Greece were hired by parents for a fee and had to provide a room to teach in – they would take a number of students. The social status of teachers was low and they practiced a form of rote learning. Students might attend a number of teachers – one to teach athletics and another to teach writing. Civil society and State institutions were also educative through participation in the assembly, juries, theatre, public games, and the general civil society. *The Fables of Aesop* were repeated in oral form to highlight weaknesses of character and provided moral lessons as did other poems and stories of heroic figures. Greek poets were viewed as teachers and their poems in or out of school were read not so much for amusement, but for the moral correction or messages they offered. These poems and narratives communicated thought, feelings and attitudes towards life and were heard constantly and memorised repeatedly and they constituted the basic education for all Greeks whether they attended a school or not. It was an oral tradition and civic experience that shaped perceptions and understandings of the world. Knowledge and virtue were taught and fused together as the Greeks had a model in the epics to inform their own behaviour and by which to judge others. As the military dimensions of training became softer over time the Sophists claimed that they could train young men for a political career. The Sophists essentially helped with 'successful' living. This required the teaching of rhetoric and grammar which became more important over time for practical reasons.

At primary level (7–13) the teacher (*grammatist*) taught reading, writing, chanting and arithmetic. At the secondary level (13–16) the teacher (*grammatias*) taught geometry, drawing, music, grammar and rhetoric. Rhetoric was about developing arguments in speech that were plausible and persuasive while grammar was the ability to string words together in a meaningful way. The content of the teaching materials that were used for this education was essentially moral texts. Elementary schooling was essentially about moral training and Marrou (1956: 221) notes:

> the humble slave who was known as the 'pedagogue' was a more important person as regards the training of the child than the schoolmaster. The schoolmaster was simply a technician, and he only affected a limited area of the child's intelligence, but the pedagogue was with the child all day, he taught him how to behave, how to be a good boy, how to get on in life, in society – all more important things than knowing how to read. We have made the school the decisive factor in education, for the Greeks the decisive factor was the surroundings in which the child grew up – the family with its servants and friends.

The Greeks were concerned that education should inculcate ethical ideals or a 'system of moral values and a way of life in conformity with it' (Marrou, 1956:

221); in other words, with the whole person rather than equipping technicians for specialist jobs. The emphasis was on the formation of the person as a person and the value of tradition – a largely conservative model of character formation. Self-discipline was essential as many Greeks believed that increased wealth promoted a softness which would lead to cowardice. Aristophanes in *The Clouds* even suggested that the use of hot water to wash in was morally decadent.

Greek culture

The popular Greek literature was, for the ordinary Greeks, the source of moral guidance and character formation. It would be a mistake to think that the philosophies taught by Plato and Aristotle were manifested in the ordinary lives of Greek citizens (see Dover, 1974: 1). Character formation was not achieved through moral philosophy or abstract ethical concepts, but rather through the practices of ordinary daily life. People at this time were born into a particular social structure and there was little in the way of social mobility. Character formation was more likely than not to consist of bringing children to conform to the particular customs, rules and judgements current in Athens. At a popular level countless moral lessons can be found in the pages of plays and literature of the time which were memorised and re-called by children. It was generally believed that you could not essentially change your fate in life – that it had already been determined by the Gods. Stories were used for adults and children to create an attachment to goodness, for it was believed storytelling affects our environment and helps shape how we think about ourselves and others – in short it influences our character and shapes culture. The chief vehicle for this process was the common use of proverbs, fables, myths and folktales which were transmitted orally as common sense sayings that offered advice and were thought to help build character in the masses. Morgan (2007) describes a collection of Greek and Roman proverbs that were widely shared and used to build individual character within popular culture. For example, 'His friends get out of the way if a man is doing ill' and 'There is no straightening a crooked billet' for someone who is unable to do good. For people who exaggerate we have 'The owl says one thing, the crow another' and for those who ask for money, 'Get help from someone who does not know you'. The stubborn person would be 'The withered bramble is the most unbending' and for those who overreact to small things in life, 'The elephant is scared of the mouse' while for good friends, 'friends are a treasure'. The famous Cato was himself the author of such remarks as 'by doing nothing men learn to do ill', and 'buy not what you need, but what is essential; what you do not need is dear at a penny'. There were thousands of these sayings in popular discourse and together with, say Aesop's fables, which have been read and taught ever since, they conveyed the moral messages of the culture. As Jaeger (1945: 41) sums up: 'Myth and heroic poetry are the nations inexhaustible treasure of great examples, from it devices its ideal and its standards for daily life.' The aim was to integrate one's personal story with that of the community by hearing and learning the community's stories.

44 Foundations

There was an overwhelming belief in popular culture that Good would always prevail and that if you mistreated someone then the Gods would ensure you would be mistreated at some point in your life. The same if you were kind then, the Gods would be kind to you. Love of your family was emphasised in *The Iliad* as was respect for your elders. It is interesting that Greek literature associates unattractive physical attributes as a sign of negative character traits – an association that has perhaps continued until today. Take for example Thersites, a soldier in the *Iliad* who is unreserved and a slanderer – his unsightly appearance matches his spiteful character: 'He was the ugliest man of all those that came before Troy – bandy-legged, lame of foot, with his two shoulders rounded and hunched over his chest. His head ran up to a point, but there was little hair on the top of it. Achilles and Ulysses hated him worst of all, for it was with him that he was most wont to wrangle: now, however, with a shrill squeaky voice he began heaping his abuse on Agamemnon' (2.216–222). When the Greeks thought about virtuous character they were more likely to think about concrete examples of virtuous individuals than abstract principles or rules. These concrete types would be drawn from history and poetry, i.e. Achilles in the *Iliad* or Odysseus in the *Odyssey*. It is why they became the primary narratives in the education of children. Pericles' *Funeral Oration* also provided a standard for Athenians in its objectives for a good life – one motivated by love, committed to the truth, justice and beauty and having a special concern for the poor and weak.

The people in 5th-century BC Athens believed virtues were admirable and praiseworthy; that virtues are primarily about actions – something one does. They thought that virtues differed depending on the social role one had – so the virtues of children, women, slaves and free men would be different. They did not believe that the virtues were connected – they were separate entities and did not entail that acting virtuously in one way had any relation to other areas of life. Also, that virtues can work against a person's best interests – a soldier can lose his life by acting courageously. Finally, practical wisdom or knowledge is but one virtue among others and wisdom had no special role for the ordinary Greek. This popular thinking was to undergo radical changes, as Greek philosophers developed versions of a philosophical theory of the virtues. Indeed, this was a period of intense pre-occupation with the theory of education.

Homer's epic poem *The Odyssey* is the prime example of a character suffering from hubris and excessive pride – who compares himself to the Gods. This kind of arrogance was considered unacceptable in Greek society. These were not simply adventure tales, but they addressed motivations for particular acts, considered the role and limits of reason and how they inspired character formation. Children learnt by heart stories and poems which were intended to improve moral character, particularly sitting in the classes of the *gramatistes* as described in Plato's Protagoras: 'When the boys understand their letters and are on the point of comprehending the written word, the teachers set before them on the benches poems of good poets to read, and they are compelled to learn by rote these works, which contain many admonitions and numerous descriptions, eulogies and commendations of virtuous men of long ago, so that the boy out of a sense of jealousy imitates them and yearns to be this sort of man himself' (Protagoras, 325e-326a). We know that a wide selection of poems was employed for this purpose (Pritchard, 1915: 113). Homer was considered the 'educator of Greece' and as Marrou (1956: 10) says, his extremely influential poems contained 'a summarization of men's duties to the God's – more, a handbook of practical morality, illustrating precept by example, and beginning with good manners for children'. Conceptions of character were first established in poems, developed as dramatic literature and then subject to philosophical analysis at one of the philosophy schools.

Protagoras answers Socrates' (469–399 BC) question about differences of character between parents and children. Protagoras asked Socrates to imagine a State in which everyone would be required to learn to play the flute; differences of natural ability would occur 'but at any rate all would be good enough in comparison with someone who knew nothing of flute-playing at all' (Protag 327a-c). It gives an optimistic assessment of education and some Greeks even proposed that all citizens should be educated at public expense – at Thourioi (Muir, 1982: 20). Higher education began at 16 and the purpose of the various Greek philosophical schools was to train young men to live well. This meant first the ability to think and speak well. Second, to act well in the world and finally to relate to others well. Therefore, the curriculum they followed included logic or dialectics which was designed so that they could speak intelligently. They studied physics in order to learn to live well in the physical world and they studied ethics in order to relate well to others.

As democracy flourished in Athenian society there was a concern to educate citizens capable of participating in society. Hadot (1995: 12) notes: 'it was necessary to know how to persuade the people, and how to induce them to make specific decisions in the Assembly. If one wanted to become a leader of the people, one thus had to acquire a mastery of language.' The goal of education was not the teaching of practical skills, but rather the forming of boys into virtuous men. The Greek tradition is essentially ethical rather than religious and the virtues could be a gift of nature, or could be developed as a habit or could be taught. Practical wisdom was required to make judgements in the world of practical human affairs. The purpose of athletics was to foster homogeneity with a willingness to obey rules and undergo discipline while also promoting individual physical competition.

Character as understood in ancient Greece

The term 'character virtues' is a translation of *ethike arete* while intellectual virtue is *dianoetike* in classical Greek. The former is dependent on the latter because the primary activity of character is a form of practical reasoning whereby each person deliberates and then freely chooses what makes his or her life a good life.

46 Foundations

People were considered most human when they personally engaged in thinking that led to rational and intelligent behavior. Virtue ethics is about making intelligent decisions. The ancient Greek rhetorian, Isocrates (426–338 BC) believed that the teacher must not only know his subject, but be an embodiment of the educational goals he asks his student to attain. The teacher must therefore live and be a constant example of moderation, civic virtue, and prudent judgement. The student must emulate the teacher demonstrating that the teacher's best teaching aid is his own character. Isocrates describes what it would take to be a person who has good character in his *Panathinaikos* by providing a demanding list of character qualities:

> First, those who manage well the circumstances which they encounter day by day, and who possess a judgement which is accurate in meeting occasions as they arise and rarely misses the expedient course of action; next, those who are decent and honorably in their intercourse with all with whom they associate, tolerating easily and good – naturedly what is unpleasant or offensive in others and being themselves as agreeable and reasonable to their associates as it is possible to be; furthermore, those who hold their pleasure always under control and are not unduly overcome by their misfortunes, bearing up under them bravely and in a manner worthy of our common nature; finally, and most important of all, those who are not spoiled by successes and do not desert their true selves and become arrogant, but hold their ground steadfastly as intelligent men, not rejoicing in the good things which have come to them through chance.

And in the *Antidosis* he says: 'mark you, the man who wishes to persuade people will not be negligent as to the matter of character'.

Sophists were originally seen as wise men and even poets and musicians were called Sophists (Schiappa, 2003: 4). However, the word came to have distinctly pejorative connotations. Socrates disliked the Sophists for charging fees from the aristocratic sons of rich families – he called it 'intellectual prostitution'. The Sophists claimed to be able to train people for a political career. The Sophists also attracted negative attention because they generally came from humble backgrounds and they emphasised rhetorical skills irrespective of the merits of any case – the idea was to win the case or the debate at whatever cost – it was not particularly about building authentic character. It was essentially about becoming an active citizen and achieving success, especially in politics and in the judicial system. However, the Sophists appeared to have no coherent philosophy of education as this very much depended on the individual Sophist teacher. Aristophanes wrote a popular play at the time called *The Clouds* which accused the Sophists of teaching young men how to cheat and lie. *The Clouds* influenced popular culture and consequently demonstrated a degree of hostility to the Sophists from the people. Nevertheless, the Sophists, as teachers, were popular and in demand. While they had no coherent philosophy many of them did advocate a fundamental utilitarianism in education which saw knowledge as an instrument and a means to increased power and efficiency in active political life (Marrou, 1956: 58). In contrast, what most counted for Socrates 'is not merely to live, but to live right'. The Sophists faced the prejudices of an aristocratic class, who nevertheless still employed them, and since they travelled from place to place they consequently did not enjoy citizenship anywhere; this to some degree placed them outside the sphere of morality (Siedentop, 2014: 44). Both Plato and Aristotle attacked the Sophists and are largely responsible for the pejorative tones about them that subsequently emerged; as Grote (1851: 485) summarises the hostility: 'ostentatious imposters, flattering and duping the rich youth for their own gain, undermining the morality of Athens public and private, and encouraging their pupils to the unscrupulous persecution of ambition and cupidity. . . . Socrates on the contrary, is usually described as a holy man combatting and exposing these false prophets.' Grote believed that the Sophists were actually the first professional teachers and that they had a positive impact on Greek society.

Plato serves as the background to Aristotle's work on character, particularly his ideas about education and its connections with the nature of the State. Plato's early dialogues present Socrates' ideas on certain virtues through the eyes of particular conversations with different characters who exemplify these virtues: *Charmides* considers temperance, *Laches* focuses on courage and *Euthyphro* on piety. In *Protagoras* Plato discusses virtue as deliberating well, which is illustrated through Socrates discussing the nature of virtue and whether it can be taught. Socrates in the *Meno* argues that virtue cannot be knowledge, something teachable, since there are no teachers of it. However, he changes his mind with *Protagoras* and ends in the belief that virtue is knowledge and can therefore be taught. This was important because the popular conceptions of character virtues in Athenian life were variable, but Devettere (2002: 61–3) and Irwin (2003: 39) summarise the main features of these popular notions of virtue. In the opening section of *Protagoras*, a rich young man called Hippocrates approaches Socrates announcing that the famous teacher Protagoras of Abdera has arrived in Athens and that he intends to secure his teaching services. Socrates cautions Hippocrates and demonstrates the hostility that both Plato and Socrates showed towards the Sophists. We can summarise Plato's conception of the purposes of education from his works, as outlined by Aloni (2007: 16):

1   Nothing is more important to human beings than the concern for their human image and the nature of their character.
2   Life devoid of critical examination of the good, just, true, and beautiful is pointless and worthless.
3   Human virtue, superior to all others and all-embracing, is wisdom, and it is manifested first and foremost in knowing good and evil.

48 Foundations

4 Human freedom, morality and happiness are a consequence of expanding knowledge and therefore intellectual education should be at the core of Man's education.

5 Good human life depends on the power of wisdom to dominate the elements which are considered more inferior (such as drive, emotion, and imagination) and channelling them into the realization of aims that reason identifies as worthy.

Plato's *Republic* was the first work on the philosophy of education. It is concerned with educating people so that a just society is achieved. To have or to form a good character is also to become fully human. Socrates, the tutor of Plato, taught that virtue is knowledge of the good. Socrates made a sharp distinction between those who are good and those who are not – to be perfectly good needs a perfect knowledge of the good so the question arises, can a child who has no knowledge of moral principles be good? Plato did accept that there was a lesser goodness which was attainable on the way to the ideal of the good that could be produced by the right training. Plato realised that goodness depends on habit or dispositions together with intellectual apprehension of what the good is. The Greek word for habit or disposition is *hexis*, which means the holding fast of oneself, now and in the future – it concerns a firm bearing or posture towards fear, pain, anger, love and the use of money. It does not mean, like in our modern sense of the word, something mechanical or rote and it certainly does not mean something imposed, but is rather freely chosen. Annas (1981) believes that 'Plato was the first thinker systematically to defend the notion that education is a training of character rather than an acquisition of information or skills' and she rejects the idea that there is anything totalitarian about Plato's ideas about character formation. Aristotle, who was in turn Plato's pupil, agreed with him on many of the fundamentals of his theory of education, but developed the principles further.

Both the *Republic* and Aristotle's *Ethics* and *Politics* concern themselves with the question of how a good person should live. They are also about how society should structure itself to make this type of life attainable. Both construe education as being related to the activities of the State and conceived education as part of the art of politics. However, Aristotle reminds us that the study of ethics is not entirely speculative, but is rather about how we become good ourselves. Plato's *Republic* outlines how each individual is destined to play a specific role in a society which aims at the good. These books were addressed to an audience which today would be considered undergraduate: they were mainly aristocratic young men who had already developed a degree of maturity, self-control and order in their lives. They had already developed habits of action based on experience that had been formed early in their childhood. What they received from Plato and Aristotle was the final stages of the process of moral education. For the Greeks the attainment of the good life was the goal of human existence and the virtues were the qualities that made a life excellent, particularly the virtues of courage, generosity, honesty, and loyalty. The person who possesses the virtues leads the best life.

In modern discussions about character most writers tend to polarise this ancient debate. They argue that in Plato's case, if a person knows the good he will do it. In contrast, Aristotle says we become good by practising good actions. From Plato there is the idea that character education is about improving thinking skills, whilst in Aristotle it is primarily about practising right behaviour. In one there is an emphasis on moral reasoning without moral action, in the other, conformity without inner conviction. This is to overstate their differences. Both believed that character must be actively cultivated in the young. Both were concerned about whether ethical behaviour could be taught. They debated mainly in terms of virtue and the virtuous and morality for them was not about rules or principles, but the cultivation of character. Conformity to a set of moral rules was not their aim in the development of this character, but rather character development involved *being* a certain kind of person and not merely *doing* certain kinds of things. Plato and Aristotle believed that the virtues harmonised with society so that courage, for example of the soldier, helped defend the community.

In Aristotle's case, right moral conduct was not a matter for explicit teaching. For him there is rationality in every moral choice and this cannot be omitted from the process through which virtue is formed. The child requires direction as well as knowledge. Whilst children must eventually decide voluntarily how to act in a certain way, this is achieved gradually as they become freer to make their own decisions. According to Aristotle, virtues are developed by an individual over time and signify a specific excellence in them of some kind. He describes two kinds of virtues, moral virtues – which are qualities of character, and intellectual virtues – which are qualities of mind. Aristotle lists a total of 12 moral virtues, together with a number of intellectual virtues including wisdom, intelligence, and scientific knowledge. He recognised that a person may have the ability to think about the good without having the disposition to implement it. In contrast, it appears that Plato did not think that anyone willingly acted immorally, and explained that if they did so act then it was through ignorance of the knowledge of the good. Applied to education this would suggest that all the teacher needs to do is point out the error in behaviour and the child will act accordingly. Many of those who advocate character formation justify their position by appeals to virtue ethics. To understand their arguments, we need to know what virtue is, why it is necessary to be virtuous and what these virtues are today.

Aristotle believed that character formation was a concern for the community just as much as it was for the individual. Therefore, the inculcation of good character required that education ought also to be provided by the laws of the community, which is the political community. Aristotle made it the legislator's duty to legislate on education (see Curren, 2000). He recognised that these laws may not be perfectly rational but neither would they be wholly irrational if the members of the body making the laws had been brought up to be virtuous. It followed for Aristotle that human beings must desire the good in order to choose the good which was either intelligence operating through a longing or a longing operating through thought. We choose to act well or badly in accordance with the dispositions of our desires. Desires require habituation in order to make them obedient to right reason and some of this is provided by command and the law is the most authoritative command. This is not about abstract principles as Aristotle emphasised that when we learn how to develop our character we turn to serious role models and later so-called character friends – we trust in living or dead prototypes of virtuous character. The law in this reasoning is instrumentally good and intrinsically good as it seeks to reconcile the common good with moral virtue. In reality the law makers in Athens did not legislate on educational matters and schools remained in private hands on a purely commercial basis. In the end Aristotle insists on the role of others, parents and teachers in forming character, but we are also responsible for our own character (Ott, 2006: 74).

To summarise, Aristotle's thought on character is challenging, but we can say that Aristotle's normative virtue theory of character focuses on a person's character and not on the actions they may or may not undertake. It is a theory that is not based on religion, but rather is naturalistic in the sense that character formation develops or fails to develop along certain natural lines. Aristotle displayed a confident and optimistic view of human nature believing that each individual has the potential to find his own flourishing (*eudaimonia*) and he sets a high standard for the formation of character. Indeed, that each individual has in-built direction (*telos*) in being human to become virtuous. His justification for the theory proceeds along empirical grounds – the accurate observation of people. In this theory most people are found to be neither totally bad nor totally good, but instead somewhere in between. Aristotle insisted that the moral virtues must be cultivated by habit while the intellectual virtues should be cultivated through instruction. He names 12 moral virtues which he says fall between two vices – the vice of excess and the vice of deficiency. So, for example, the virtue of modesty falls between the excess of shyness and the deficiency of shamelessness. He recognised that it was necessary to have knowledge of the virtue of modesty, but that this is not sufficient for a person to act with modesty. Modesty can only be formed in a person by repeated actions which means developing habits – the constant expression of modesty in real contexts; 'we are what we repeatedly do'. He moves to the intellectual virtues which comprise five main virtues and four ancillary or secondary virtues. The main intellectual virtues are (1) technical skills (*techne*) which is simply the skill to make something, (2) scientific knowledge (*episteme*) – which is the knowledge of empirical facts, (3) prudence or practical wisdom (*phronesis*) which is the meta-virtue that helps balance the other virtues and aids decision-making, (4) intelligence or intuition (*nous*) which is the ability to think and finally (5) wisdom (*sophia*) which comes with experience and age. The other four minor intellectual virtues he refers to are all related to the above five main virtues and are good deliberation, deep understanding, judgement, and cleverness. Character is the practice and development of certain virtues and the avoidance of certain vices over a life-time and it is directed by a complex fusion of intention, motivation, thought, feeling, action, intuition and emotion. Both the moral and intellectual virtues play vital and indeed indispensable parts in the formation of character and represent the foundation of the entire structure of Aristotelian character. Finally, Aristotle taught that we have a purpose and the function of life is to attain that purpose through the acquisition of virtues and that the value of these virtues resides in the state of *eudaimonic* character – virtues as constituents of our happiness.

Theophrastus was Aristotle's favourite student and succeeded him as head of the Lyceum. Theophrastus's treatise on 30 *Characters* outlines the vices and weaknesses of character of ordinary Athenians, but he also wrote many works on the subject of ethics. His book is simply called *Characters* and is a series of lively and humorous ethical stories concerning the manners of Athenian society that forms a picture of his time around 319 BC (Pertsinidis, 2016). These stories are highly realistic and serve as a guide to appropriate conduct. Each character is the possessor of a virtue or vice and is portrayed by means of his distinctive 'style' or 'way of life' (Walker, 1989: 356). They are detailed literary portraits of generic male character types with negative behavioural attributes of speech and conduct. The purpose of these sketches of the character traits of the average Athenian citizen was to convey ethical teaching in a practical way (see Appendix B).

The reform of the popular notions of character virtues by Plato and Aristotle are summarised by Devettere (2002: 63–5) as follows:

1   Virtues are admirable and praiseworthy.
2   Virtues are psychological states comprising dispositions, habits, and character – denoting the kind of person we are.
3   Virtues are based on our common humanity – as a set of virtues relevant to everyone regardless of social role.
4   Virtues are unified and cannot be separated from each other.
5   Virtues are always in the person's best interests.
6   Practical wisdom is the foundation virtue as it leads to the other virtues because we need to see what the goal of life ought to be.
7   Virtue requires human freedom to be authentic.
8   Living in accordance with civic virtues was equated with conduct approved by God.

However, popular notions of the virtues continued in Athenian society. Plato in the *Laws* believed children needed to be educated because they knew so little, were immature, were easily persuaded, and unreliable judges. Plato and Aristotle emphasised the importance of training and environment for the formation

52 Foundations

of good character and citizens. They believed that nurture and nature worked together and that education was an end in itself. That playing games as a child had the purpose of being able to follow rules. When Aristotle speaks of the excellences of character he does not mean that you necessarily follow moral rules as virtuous character involves having an overarching purpose in life – a high principle. Excellent character for Aristotle was the ability to pursue happiness through a disciplined life. Isocrates (436–338) in *Antipodes* also spoke strongly about virtuous leadership. In summary, personal character and conduct was governed by traditional morality based on the virtues of justice, courage, self-restraint and wisdom (Kitto, 1957: 133). As Harman (1999: 19) notes: 'Greek ethical theorists seem to have agreed on one point: they believed that non-legal restrictive influences on behaviour were in a sense deeper and more fundamental than statutory laws.' Laws were in written form and clear, while thoughts that were not uttered were implicit and belonged to the realm of habit.

Rome

Rome never produced philosophers of education of the calibre of Socrates, Plato and Aristotle, but it did freely adopt Greek educational theory and practices as its own. Rome effectively appropriated the legacy of Greek thought, but adapted it by selection of the parts it liked, downplaying those it did not, and adding its own perspective. Colish (1997: 5) makes clear that the area in which there was most consistency between Greeks and Romans was in the theory and practice of education. The main thinkers on education it produced were Cicero, Quintilian and Plutarch. In the Roman period character became more something that is fixed – given at birth. It is not surprising therefore that Rome began the nature (genes)–nurture (environment) debate about the two sources of individual character. The good life for the Greeks and Romans was a life well lived – one that achieved happiness. They believed that developing a virtuous character was necessary to lead a good life and that in Rome the highest goal in life was the attainment of material success. Training in Rome was practical for imperial service, but character formation was still the chief goal. Part of this education was to cultivate respect for ancestral customs and is why Romans preferred history to poetry because their preferred heroes came from their past – mythical or fact it made no difference, but Greek literature became fashionable throughout the Roman Empire. The chief Roman virtues were: duty, patriotism, self-sacrifice, temperance, frugality, courage and self-control. These virtues were to be imitated in the home with the formal components of education such as reading and writing being minimal. The man of Rome was practical and knew the laws, he would know the traditions and lived them. Quintilian recognised that this required high moral standards and personal excellence of character and it is why he maintained a clear moral vision for education and sought to shape the character of his students. As he said in the *Institutes*: 'My aim, then, is the education of the perfect orator. The first essential for such a one is that he should be a good man, and consequently we demand of him not merely the possession of exceptional gifts of speech, but of all the excellences of character as well' and 'The orator must above all things devote his attention to the formation of moral character and must acquire a complete knowledge of all this is just and honourable'. Ultimately, the creation of the orator was the aim. Mothers played a role in the education of children, as did private tutors, and Homer's works were used. Seneca (5 BC–AD 65) thought that education must cultivate wisdom and virtue. He thought this to be particularly the case with the very young: 'The period of education calls for the greatest, and what will also prove to be the most profitable, attention; for it is easy to train the mind while it is still tender, but it is difficult matter to curb the vices that have grown up with us.' Seneca's ethical works, particularly *Espistulae morales*, were used by Christians throughout the Middle Ages.

Plutarch in his work *On the Education of Children* saw education as ethical and concerned with the formation of human character. Following Aristotle, he believed that good nature needs good nurture and without nurture there is no guarantee of good character. He said: 'We now reach a topic more important and vital than any yet treated – that of the right teachers for our children. The kind to be sought for those whose lives are irreproachable, whose characters are impugned, and whose skill and experience are of the best. The root or fountain-head of character as a man and a gentlemen lies in receiving the proper education.' In Rome non-school education was about conversations and the exchange of ideas in the public forum. The main educational agency was the home and Pliny in his *Letters* observed that: 'It was the ancient custom that we should learn from our elders, not only through the ear but also through the eye, those things that we should soon have to do and in our turn hand them down to our successors' (*Letters* VIII I, 4–6). How to conduct oneself in public was learnt from the father in the home. Aristotle discusses in his *Politics* whether the job of character formation is best done by the father or the community. We learn in the *Lives of Aristides and Cato* by Plutarch that Cato the Elder took the role of father-teacher seriously: 'he was his (son's) reading teacher, his law professor, his athletics coach. He taught his son not only to hurl the javelin, to fight in armour, and to ride a horse, but also to box, to endure both heat and cold, and to swim well.' Above all else, Roman education instilled a sense of pietas – devotion to duty and the elevation of character constituted the Roman ideal of perfection. Indeed, the moral qualities of character is sometimes given as a reason for the success of the Roman Empire. Cicero in *Officio* (2.5.18) argued that liberal education ideally facilitated the formation of character to develop the virtues which would discipline the substantive appetites and inspire goodness in the effective sentiments, while directing the intellect to truth and the will to right action. In this view knowledge breeds wisdom and can never be purely instrumental, but Seneca reminds us that a classical education cannot make a person virtuous – it can only prepare their minds to receive virtue. The goal is to encourage, not force, the student to live a life of virtue.

The Romans were strong believers in corporal punishment. One popular saying was: 'A man who has not been flogged is not trained.' The foundation of Roman education was, above all else, the home and family, from which children derived their character formation. Perhaps the most important role of the parents in their children's education was to instil in them a respect for tradition and a firm comprehension of pietas, or devotion to duty. For a boy, this meant devotion to the State, and for a girl, devotion to her husband and family. Character formation for the Romans consisted essentially of three things: imitation of the great men in history, loyalty to the traditions of their ancestors and reverence for their parents.

There is one final philosophy that built on the ideas of Plato and Aristotle that needs to be noted – Stoicism. It emerged around the 3rd century BC and developed notions about how to be virtuous which hugely influenced the emergence of Christianity (Colish, 1990). Stoicism concerned the idea of attaining inner control through the use of reason and the ability to discern the universal law and order that Stoics believed to be present in nature. The idea was to live a life in accordance with nature or reason which required self-discipline and self-control. The virtues were human in the sense they were not exclusively male and this opened up the possibility of female education and many Stoics opposed slavery. They believed the world was providentially ordered and that any suffering or pain in life was part of a cosmic plan for man to their ultimate good. Life was recognised as a trial, but attainment of the virtues was possible if you are indifferent to the material and external circumstances of life. Everything was to be rooted in nature, but you needed to overcome your emotions – to be free of the passions. Contemplation and inner calm were also emphasised and Epictetus, a leading Stoic, believed in a perfect contentment resulting from a willing conformity with nature – rather Buddhist overtones. To lead a good life, you needed to be wise and to live in harmony with reason. This philosophy very much influenced the Romans and the philosophy of virtue ethics. Christianity borrowed many of the ideas and terms from this philosophy. Even in Thomas More's *Utopia* we see virtue defined as 'life in accordance with nature' showing that Stoic ethical slogans were still popular in the 16th century.

The models of character formation that were predominant in this period could be described as conservative with instances of the practice of militaristic models and the virtue theories of Plato and Aristotle in circulation.

Chapter 3

Early medieval foundations

Jewish Origins

Christian character formation is indebted to both the Classical and the Hebrew traditions. The Hebrew part of this indebtedness is often ignored even though Western ideas of character have obvious Hebrew origins. While contemporary scholarship suggests that virtue ethics was not the prevailing system in ancient Israel, some foundational aspects of early Jewish ethics have undoubtedly had an enduring impact on the Christian tradition and Western civilisation more widely (Barton, 2014). This Jewish ethics arose in Jerusalem long before the more formalised Greek ethics of Athens, although the latter would later influence the Jewish tradition. The Hebrew Bible was not a philosophical text, but it provides broad patterns for character and conduct. It talks about human excellences that constitute the best life for human beings. The chief aims of Jewish education were both religious and moral. The young were to be trained in the 'fear of the Lord' which is 'the beginning of wisdom' and forming character was the good to be achieved (Psalm 111:10). Jewish tradition emphasised the centrality of training about the practical duties of life – to be taught in the family. This tradition spoke vocally about the need to attend to the needs of the poor, weak, aliens, orphans, widows – ethical behaviour was to be based on Biblical precepts.

This oral Biblical tradition had the aim of living a righteous life summed up in the Golden Rule – 'thou shalt love thy neighbour as thyself'. The Law of the Jews, found in the Bible, prescribed standards of conduct that covered almost every aspect of Jewish life. You could say it was a manual to live the good life, but there was probably less stress on the importance of virtue in favour of the notion of duty – more of an emphasis on the practical than the theoretical. The Jews and early Christians began to see virtue as an aid to doing one's duty, as opposed to appreciating virtue as valuable in itself. The ideal of human excellence was the ability to control human desires or temptations by obeying God's laws. As Christianity developed, many of these strict rules of the Jewish Law were disregarded.

The Synagogue school began around the 6th century BC to teach the Bible, but first by teaching reading and writing. The Synagogue school mainly taught adults, but children from the age of five were also instructed in godly living.

56 Foundations

These synagogues were available to all and the idea of Jewish schooling was not restricted to the elite (Aberback, 2009: 1), but schools were few and far between so it remained a largely oral tradition in an agricultural society. Schools and teachers did however increase in number after 70 AD (Aberback, 2009: 3). The Jews and Christians shared the common belief of modern research that the experience of infancy and early childhood have a lasting effect on the individual's behaviour and character. The Jews freely chose the Law as contained in the Hebrew Bible as a shared context or form of life which was devoted to justice and the good. Virtues and rules were therefore seen as working together in mutually reinforcing ways (Mittleman, 2007: 7).

Aristotle did address the function of human law as the basis for shaping character, as he taught that the political community (the State) had the authority to help shape the character of its citizens. For the Jews the good is found in the virtuous observance of the law of God – it is about living an ethical life. As Mittleman (2007: 7) says: 'The biblical literature has much to say about the ensemble of human excellences that constitute the best life for human beings.' The Jews created a theoretical-moral-political framework to live the good life which was formed by teaching in stories, poetry, law and wise sayings. Indeed, the Law was to be the schoolmaster. The continuous telling of stories is how a community of moral character is formed and Aristotle would have recognised this. Indeed, the Jews, like the Christians to come, found it difficult to understand how the pagan philosophers had achieved such insights without any apparent dependence on divine revelation.

The Law for the Hebrews provided what God expected by way of conduct and guidance on a righteous (virtuous) life. People were to be educated and taught through good example, discussions, parents answering questions from children, participation in festivals, and even the use of visual aids (*Deut* 6.20–21, 6.5, 6.67, 6.9, 8, 11.19, 11.20, 16.16, 31, 12.). Like the Greeks, the father and the family had the responsibility to educate. Like the Greeks, all citizens were also teachers and the moral character of the community is the context in which individual character is formed and lived. These combined in developing a normative form of life which gives an idea of communal life and an ideal of individual character. The laws became opportunities for the practice of virtues such as fidelity, gratitude and love, as well as the apparatus for the development of character. Mittleman (2007: 22) outlines how the Biblical texts *Job, Proverbs, Ecclesiastes*, and several *Psalms* focus on individual virtue, the development of appropriate habits and traits of character and the employment of successful action. People were called upon to imitate the qualities of God or the actions of God in their character and conduct. The *Proverbs* in particular had a goal of character formation through the family, which had the obligation under God to prepare children for the responsibility of living morally responsible lives. *Proverbs* also provided the means for parents to carry out this obligation; 'the employment of the rod, the use of wise reproof, the implementation of oral repetition, the art of discernment, and the skills of observing life' (Bland, 1998: 228).

Early medieval foundations 57

However, the Bible does not restrict appropriate moral virtues and correlative human flourishing to revelation alone. The Hebrews were a bearer of a theological moral tradition, but also of intense moral deliberation, discernment and moral action. While moral character norms arose out of obeying the Law, ethical living did not entirely amount to obedience to the prescriptions of the Bible. Jewish thinkers continued to debate and interpret the Law and constantly considered the right thing to do by providing different answers. They ceaselessly debated philosophical and theological questions such as whether goodness is constitutive in the idea of God. If A is a good action then is A an action commanded by God? Is what makes an action good the fact that is it commanded by God? Can we have moral knowledge without the Old Testament and does man have independent capacity for moral action and judgement? The Jews believed that they had a human capacity to seek wisdom and to learn from experience while recognising that the source of this was always God. Harris (2003: 37ff) provides a review of a range of Jewish scholars with differing views who debate these questions intensely and this tradition of enquiry was inherited by the Christian community. The formation of virtues within an individual was considered complementary to obedience to the commandments of the Law. While the popular Hebrew saying 'Train up a child in the way he should go and when he is old he will not depart from it' was known by all, it is embodied in a people who were self-conscious that they were created by God to decide how to live their lives. They had to give their lives which meant that they were to choose freely and decide on their character – so long as it was righteous.

There was a degree of polarity between Jerusalem and Athens or Hellenism and Hebraism. The Greeks and Jews were aware of each other's tradition and between 285 and 247 BC there was an attempt to make the Hebrew tradition intelligible to Greek culture. *The Letter of Aristeas* attempts to combine both Greek and Jewish ethical thinking in a kind of synthesis of Biblical and Hellenistic approaches. The Bible, just as in Theophrastus's treatise on 30 characters, recognised that people are flawed and provided exemplars of how Jews should think, feel and act as a model of exemplary character and conduct. The patriarchs in the Bible, just as the saints in later Christian writings or the heroes in Greek poems, were the archetypical character. The Jews really believed that all that was of genuine value in classical writings could be found in the Bible. Like the Christians to come, the Jews believed that all the wisdom of the Greek philosophers was implicitly contained in the Bible. The Jews in the Middle Ages were aware of the difference between a revelation-based analysis of the good and an analysis conducted by reason without recourse to revelation. Maimonides (1138–1204) gives a rational foundation for the ethical life of the Jew by emphasising that you can achieve a better character, but not a perfect character. He believed that a flawed character needs therapy because vice is a sickness (Mittleman, 2007: 109).

Christian culture

The Greek idea of *paideia* was the foundation of Christian culture, but as we have argued Christianity also engaged with Jewish literature in the period of primitive Christianity from the 1st to 4th centuries (Gamble, 1995: 24). The Jewish tradition interpreted by early Christians contained a good deal that accords with classical views on character and a good deal that does not. In other words, there is a large degree of overlap and therefore continuity of tradition with regard to character formation. The most important innovation or revolutionary idea of Christianity was the teaching that people were moral equals, irrespective of race or social position, and that they possessed freedom of conscience. This was revolutionary in the sense that Greek and Roman societies believed that the poor, by definition, could not be fully virtuous – only those who God favoured, the rich and successful, were capable of virtuous character. Consequently, Christianity's message that God loved the poor was shocking as was Christianity's attack on infanticide together with its idea of giving charitable aid to the poor.

Christianity's attitude to education and schooling was a continuation of the Jewish and Hellenic traditions, but it came to be largely dependent on the Roman legacy. Specifically, Christian education was to be given in the family and within the Church, not within schools. The Church did not establish schools and, as Marrou (1956: 319) notes, accepted Hellenistic humanism as 'natural' and self-evident. Indeed, Christians generally regarded the Greeks as having exhibited the highest moral character that human nature could assume without the light of the Christian gospels (see Turner, 1981: 12). If pagans could be morally wise and virtuous then Christians had to be more virtuous. However, at this point in time the Church was open to employing the best available ethics from whatever source, but as the years passed the Christian community began to define character by its aberrations, looking more at the darker side of human nature.

Starting with the early church fathers, Christian thinkers took differing views of the proper relationship between their moral system and that of the pagan philosophers of antiquity. On the one hand, St. Ambrose (c. 340–97), in *De officiis ministrorum* (On the duties of the ministry), was prepared to adapt the Stoic-inspired account of virtue set out in Cicero's (106–43 BC) *De officiis* (On duties) to the needs of Christians seeking eternal bliss in the afterlife. Porter (2013: 71) comments that Cicero's influence on Christian ethics cannot be overstated, but we also have Eusebius of Caesarea (260–340) who saw Greek philosophy as a preparation for the Gospels. On the other hand, St. Augustine (354–430), another doctor of the church, denied that Christians could learn anything from pagans either about virtue in the present life or happiness in the next, both of which were solely gifts of God's grace. Augustine saw Greek philosophy as decadent which he believed obscured God's law. Ambrose's conviction that the ancient framework of ethical theory could be extended and modified to accommodate Christianity found wide resonance in thinkers from the Iberian bishop St. Martin of Braga (c. 520–80), who wrote influential moral tracts closely based on the writings of the Roman Stoic Seneca (4 BC–65), to the Cistercian Abbot Ailred of Rievaulx (1109–1166), whose treatise *De spirituali amicitia* (On spiritual friendship) is modeled on Cicero's *De amicitia* (On friendship). As Gerwen (2005: 213) says, Christians agreed that 'morality depends on the training of character, and seeing and imitating concrete examples, such as Jesus Christ, the saints or the ordinary faithful'. Significantly, he claims that this did not depend on the role of reason alone, but tensions continued between pagan and emerging Christian ethics.

Some church fathers, such as the Greek speaking Archbishop Clement of Alexandria (150–215) were most favourable to classical education as they viewed all truth and goodness as one, regardless of the source. The early Christians debated whether their children should attend pagan schools, whether Christians could teach in them, and whether they should establish their own schools. They wrestled with the question whether Christian thinkers can simultaneously follow the teachings of, say, Aristotle and of Jesus Christ. Tertullian (155–240), however, had little sympathy with the efforts of some Christians to paint a positive picture of the connections between their faith and the ideas of the Greek philosophers. As he commented in *Prescriptions Against Heretics*: 'Away with all attempts to produce a mottled Christianity of Stoic, Platonic and dialectic composition.' Jerome (347–420) adopted a similar attitude and sought to avoid the use of pagan literature. It is interesting that the rabbinic tradition also had outspoken critics of the use of Greek and Roman literature, claiming it was extraneous to Jewish identity formation even if it contained wisdom worthy of emulation. Clement, by contrast, sought to train Christians in ethics and saw little differentiation between what any morally serious wise and pagan teacher of Alexandria in 200 AD would have taught his pupils. He believed that the Christian ought to be a good man first and that God used the existing pagan culture as a preparation for Christianity. In a sermon *To Young Men, On How They Might Derive Profit from Pagan Literature*, Basil the Great (329–79) takes a positive line in using classical literature in Christian contexts as he said: 'And since it is through virtue that we must enter upon this life of ours, and since much has been uttered in praise of virtue by poets, much by historians, and much more still by philosophers, we ought especially to apply ourselves to such literature.' Basil argued that the study of the classics trained the mind to comprehend and to prepare for the reception of the Christian scriptures (Stinger, 1977: 13ff).

The uncompromising position of Augustine was echoed by monastic moralists such as Abbot Rupert of Deutz (1076–1129), who rejected pagan philosophers out of hand on the grounds that they had no knowledge of spiritual or heavenly values. The monasteries adopted a practical approach to character formation, mainly using the virtues as remedies for vices. There was also an academic approach to virtue ethics that grew up in parallel to this practical or

60 Foundations

pastoral approach. The first medieval philosopher to put forward a serious challenge to Augustine's characterisation of virtues as gifts of divine grace was Peter Abelard (1079–1142). Abelard saw the virtues as human excellences that can be obtained without divine grace and he recognised that some of the pagans of antiquity possessed these virtues (Porter, 2005: 232). Drawing on Cicero and on Boethius's (c. 480–c. 524) commentary on Aristotle's (384–322 BC) *Categories*, he defined natural virtues as fixed dispositions that were acquired by the exercise of human powers and that could be transformed into Christian virtues by being directed towards God. Abelard was nevertheless acutely aware that while Seneca, the pagan philosopher he most admired, held that virtue must be sought for its own sake, Christians believed that virtue should be pursued in the hope of a greater reward: happiness in the future life. Peter Lombard (1100–1160) in contrast understood the virtues in Augustinian terms as expressions of Christian charity which presupposed grace. This idea of whether virtuous character could be obtained without God's grace continued through Scotus and Lombard, who appeared to maintain that virtue was possible without grace.

It was precisely this issue that made Aristotelian ethics, with its this-worldly orientation, particularly problematic for medieval Christians. Christians viewed Aristotle's focus on the value of special friends with suspicion since Christians were commanded to love all human beings equally as having been created in the image of God. In the *Nicomachean Ethics*, which began to be available in Latin translation at the end of the 12th century, Aristotle declared that humankind's supreme good was a life of flourishing that consisted of philosophical contemplation in the present life – a view that was clearly incompatible with the Christian belief that humanity's highest and ultimate goal was everlasting bliss in the afterlife. A solution to the problem was found in the mid-13th century by scholastic philosophers at the University of Paris. Building on a distinction originally made by the French theologian William of Auxerre (1150–1231), they maintained that the subject of Aristotle's treatise was imperfect happiness, a natural state attainable in the present life by human powers, while perfect happiness or beatitude, a supernatural state attainable in the next life through grace, was the subject of theological, not philosophical, inquiry.

The Christian attitude towards using pagan literature for character formation was complex and divided, but Christians at this time were the products of late classical antiquity and the virtues of character were entrenched in their discourse. The differences and similarities between pagan and Christian virtues became clearer as Christianity matured. The similarities included the idea that Jesus embodied the virtues and led an upstanding life. Christians were to be concerned with the good of others which meant the good of the community – very much an idea Aristotle shared. Aristotle saw everything in life as having a final aim, while Christians believed that everything has a divine purpose. The differences were that Christians did not believe the goal of life was happiness, but rather gaining eternal life in God. Revelation was the ultimate standard for conduct and character and they recognised that the pagan virtues,

Early medieval foundations 61

no matter how similar, did not require belief in God. However, perhaps the most important practical difference was the fact that Christians were commanded to love, to express love through virtue which meant you could only have virtuous character if you were able to love. The highest form of Christian love was *Agape* – a spiritual love. In contrast, the Greeks spoke of *philia*, the love of friendship which could be based on anything from hero worship to companionship.

Christians recognised that some pagans, who had no opportunity to recognise Christ, led virtuous lives; the Jews would have called them 'righteous gentiles'. They also were educated in a culture that was derived from pagan antiquity and one in which they admired the heroes of ancient Rome and Greece. The classical texts were considered by many as the best materials for teaching character and that they could not be much improved upon. While, as we have seen, Augustine (354–430) considered the pagan virtues not to be genuine virtues, this did not prevent the use of pagan literature to teach the virtues to Christians. In the end Christianity kept the classical forms, but substituted some of it for Christian content (see Gemeinhardt et al., 2016). Nevertheless, the debate about whether pagan virtues were truly virtue-forming continued through the Middle Ages and Reformation. The discussion of virtuous character became a key theme in Christian ethics during the medieval period. The year 529 AD is significant in that this was the year in which the Platonic Academy was closed by the Emperor Justinian and also the year in which St. Benedict founded Monte Cassino. It was also the year, that we could consider, marked the beginning of the Middle Ages.

This was a period of expansion for Christianity in multicultural and multilingual settings. During this period Christianity freely used the classical tradition of education and while it had an initial ambivalent attitude towards the pagan heritage, this gradually diminished as Christians used the schools that were available. Christians took what was necessary from pagan literature, but rejected anything that was contradictory to Christian teaching. There was little attempt to create a separate school system other than providing catechetical training for Christians of all ages. Pagan myths were treated with suspicion, but the classical education of Greek literature and character formation continued. However, during this period Christians also used and engaged actively with Jewish texts which demonstrated their concerns with the poor. They effectively combined both Jewish ethics and the moral teachings of the Greco-Roman world. It was only during the Patristic period, the 4th to 6th centuries, that a new Christian literature was forcibly created and it was only during the formation of Western Christendom, the 6th to 11th centuries, that Christian schools emerged in any serious way – mainly within the monasteries. Nevertheless, the best of secular culture was preserved and taught, including general pagan literature that had moral purposes acceptable to the Church. There remained a tension between viewing character formation as fundamentally religious or as fundamentally rational, a factor that continues to run deep in Western culture.

62 Foundations

Medieval schools were created to satisfy the needs of ecclesiastical recruitment, and these schools were largely in cities (Aries, 1962: 255). Christianity is a learned religion of the Bible, but the Byzantine culture that arose in the East was essentially Greek and Christian at the same time. Plato and Aristotle together with the Bible and the writings of the church fathers were mixed and taught together. Students needed some kind of literary education to read the Bible and Church documents. Choir and parish schools were found inside the Church parish and the instruction was mainly oral memory with taught psalms and plainsong. Charlemagne in 787 began to organise schools outside monasteries. As Archbishop of Canterbury, Dunstan, held a diocesan synod which in Canon 797 encouraged priests to educate the children in each parish (Perry, 1920: 33–8). Christianity built on the Roman foundations of education, but many of these parish initiatives, where they existed, seldom amounted to more than elementary catechetical instruction.

There had already been numerous failed attempts to establish schools, with the Council of Rome in 853 authorising that every parish should establish a school at the elementary level. The Third Lateran Council in 1179 required every Cathedral to employ a schoolmaster and the Fourth Lateran Council of 1215 extended this requirement to every major parish (Lawson and Silver, 1973: 15). However, it remained the case that what people learned normally came from the vernacular sermons of the priest. It needs to be remembered that schools did not disappear after the end of the Roman Empire. Students in these early schools had a huge moral influence over each other and there was no real moral responsibility exercised by the master as Aries (1962: 252) wrote: 'School was not yet regarded as unambiguously as a preparation for life.' The 1600s saw the new idea of the moral responsibility of the schoolmaster – to take an interest in the whole child, especially outside school.

Teaching materials to aid this learning process did not depend on texts to be read, as character building was part of the comprehensive moral instruction provided by the Church through Christian culture and which pervaded the whole of society. People saw moral messages everywhere – in carvings, paintings, stained glass, in churches and in preaching by clerics. They were told stories of the virtues of the saints or warned about the severe punishments awaiting them for not being virtuous. There were also positive reinforcements of stories and images of mercy – helping the poor, visiting the sick, being kind and so on. Priests had manuals to help them promote moral instruction as well as books on moral philosophy. Even the educated elite understood that service was infused with virtue, as seen in the knightly virtues. Chivalry emphasised physical prowess and loyalty and encouraged obedience to a rule, service to the Church, good faith, unselfishness and courtesy. It also adopted parts of Stoic philosophy and had a code of conduct bound to duty, honour and justice. It was a necessary condition for knighthood that the person was in good moral standing. However, it often also came with ostentation, contempt for inferiors and love of violence for some. In the 14th century, Chaucer uses each character

Early medieval foundations 63

to demonstrate a certain moral code unique to that person. Chaucer depicts a world in which right and wrong depend on a person's status or position in the social hierarchy. Particular virtues and vices are associated with specific classes of people – social inferiors and superiors.

Ordinary people would experience moral messages in the poetry of the time. as well as in games, and in the mystery plays performed in local towns. In teaching the skills of literacy, the instruction would have been infused with moral formation – even the method of learning the alphabet was intertwined with lessons in conduct. Christianity shaped the art, architecture, music, literature, culture and politics of the Western tradition. The Church set before the people images, statues and depictions of hundreds of Saints worthy of imitation were displayed in churches or mounted in public places. Each one of these saints in their diverse ways exemplified a character quality which was celebrated each year on the saint's day through a festival. These depictions could be found everywhere – in Bibles, prayer books, in homes and work places – and they encouraged the people to think about the moral messages conveyed in this Christian culture. It was a powerful language since it engaged the senses and the reason of the people with a clear didactic formative mission. By the early 14h century the Florentine artists created the Scrovegni Chapel in Padua consisting of fresco portraits allegorizing a different virtue or vice in fourteen niches. The Chapel included depictions of the classical virtues of prudence, fortitude, temperance and justice as well as the three theological virtues of faith, hope and love. The vices were represented by folly, inconstancy, envy, despair, anger, injustice, and infidelity. *The Imitation of Christ* by Thomas à Kempis was another powerful tool in Christian teaching character virtues (see Appendix E).

Christianity believed in the regeneration of society through the moral regeneration of converts. This was a process of instruction – a probationary period – before acceptance into the Church. It was often a two-year long process of instruction in morality and the various rituals of Christian worship. Catechetical schools were established to understand the faith. The Church did not found schools in the first four centuries (Orme, 2006: 18, 1973). The Church, as a physical entity, was the location of education. There was a living folk tradition that included heroic songs which were transmitted not by the teacher or scribe but by the minstrel. Monasteries had libraries, they collected books and produced scholars and by the 5th century they often provided inner schools for the training of monks and occasionally outer schools for lay people which taught the rules of conduct. These monasteries became the philosophical schools of Christianity. These schools led to the guild schools and grammar schools which by 1000 used the *Colloquy of Aelfric* (see Appendix D), a book about a moral conversation between a master, a young monk and various boys who represented the shepherds, ploughman, shoemakers, hunters, fishermen of the period – see Lawson and Silver, 1973: 9).

The curriculum of the Middle Ages was a direct inheritance of the classical tradition even though there was an interruption between the ancient and medieval school. The curriculum was essentially in two parts, first the *trivium* consisting of grammar, rhetoric and dialectics. Dialectics concerned the study of thinking and reason in order to argue well with valid information, while rhetoric was really the study of communication – meaning speaking well in order to be persuasive. Sayers (1947) believes that grammar, dialectic and rhetoric need to be recovered and are the lost tools of Scholasticism. The *quadravivium* consisted of geometry, arithmetic, astronomy, music and finally, theology. All this was simply the tools for learning and an essential prerequisite to character formation which Sayers believes we have lost. Jarrat (1926: 33) saw the medieval school curriculum as boys being taught how to speak, write, argue and sharpen their wit – accuracy of thought and word to make a good argument – a ready speaker. Bishops were active at this time in organising schooling for clerks (Aries, 1962: 139) and in England William of Wykeham, as Bishop of Winchester, founded St. Mary's College, Winchester in 1382 for the education of 70 poor scholars with the character inspiring motto 'Manners maketh man' – notice he did not choose 'Learning maketh man' or even 'Morals maketh man' since medieval thought did not distinguish clearly between morals and manners. These boys were to be trained for priesthood and the school resembled a monastery in many respects with an austere life for the boys. The school became the prototype of an education system – that of the English public school.

From the age of seven children shared the world with adults and certain things were required to be learnt in and out of medieval schools such as The Ten Commandments, the Creed and *Paternoster* and many manuals existed to teach them (see Watson, 1968: 29ff). Pierce the Ploughman's *Crede* (1394) was very popular and again used in and out of schools. Juan Luis Vives produced a school textbook for boys entitled Vive's *Dialogues*, covering advice on everything from getting up in the morning to eating, drinking and what to wear, concluding with principles of education which spoke about the good character of the young man (see Appendix F). In the absence of textbooks, the teaching tool was disputation. The evolution of the textbook essentially spread as a result of the invention of printing.

Scholasticism was the school of thought that prevailed in Western Europe throughout the Middle Ages and arose out of the monastic schools. Ideas and themes related to virtue theory played a significant role in the many debates at the time and with the re-discovery of Aristotle's work by the 13th century these debates intensified. Duns Scotus (1266–1308), William of Ockham (1288–1347) and Thomas Aquinas (1225–1274) refined and defended the versions that became dominant, but differed with each other. Duns Scotus for example did not think that infused grace was necessary for virtuous character. Aquinas was a Dominican philosopher and theologian and arguably the greatest teacher in the Middle Ages (see Peter Kreeft's (1993) excellent introduction to Aquinas's main works). Aquinas incorporated a significant part of Aristotle's moral and political theory in his great philosophic-theological synthesis. Aquinas agreed with Aristotle on the following: we can know what is good and

Early medieval foundations   65

right; the virtuous life is rationally grounded; reason enables us to attain what is good for us; the virtues are means between extremes; reason determines the mean and virtues are good habits/dispositions. He also agreed in the idea of seeking the final end or the highest good: the teleological view. For Aquinas this final end was God, as only God could be the highest good, and without God there is ultimately no moral law prescribing what we ought to do. However, Aquinas had to balance this against the fact that God created man with free will and without free will man cannot choose between right and wrong – a tension that needed to be resolved.

Aquinas first discusses the nature of dispositions in the sense that they are ordered to action. Then, in *Quaestions disputatae de veritate*, he speaks about how dispositions shape character. Essentially, they are seen by Aquinas as ways in which we have or determine ourselves (see Boland, 2007: 173). A good disposition is appropriate to the nature of a human being, while a bad disposition is inappropriate. Dispositions to act can be diminished by neglect and Aquinas says that a good disposition is a virtue. The virtues are therefore good operational dispositions of the human agent in the account given by Aquinas. Here the goal of education is to form the person by helping them to attain their full formation or their completeness as a person. This idea of forming the person coincides with both Greek and Jewish thought. Aquinas had very advanced ideas about the psychology and pedagogy of education and set out to investigate the nature of pedagogical activity in his treatise, *On the Teacher*. For example, he taught that learning is self-activity on the part of the student who, through reason, comes to a knowledge of the unknown. Teaching is the process which draws out of the pupil this natural reason – the student being a major agent in learning.

However, the teacher was worthy of some imitation by the student and the student should aspire to live up to his example until good character becomes realised in his own character. This in itself, independent of theology, has important implications for teaching character and citizenship for it means that all genuine learning is active, not passive. Learning involves the use of the mind, not just the memory and it is a process of discovery in which the pupils not teachers are the main agents. Teaching is seen as an aid to learning effectively and a variety of pedagogical methods need to be employed. For Aquinas, children need to develop habits and virtues which are settled dispositions or traits of character. Teachers are not to dictate answers, rather they should suggest possible directions for character development to the child through a process of reflection. Education is not about producing rigid character types with absolutely predictable patterns of behaviour. In this, amongst other things, Aquinas also follows Aristotle.

For Aquinas 'the advancement of the child to the state of specifically human excellence, that is to say, to the state of virtues' was the point of education. Aquinas found Aristotle a rich resource for his account of the virtues (see Porter, 1990). There were however, important differences. Aristotle was clear that the final end was human flourishing attainable through the possession of the virtues within political society. Aquinas believed that the possession of the virtues was important in developing a Christian life whose end was salvation in Jesus Christ. The Thomist tradition set the ancient virtues, into a new context: the teachings and person of Jesus Christ. Pure Aristotelian virtues were acquired through training and education and were viewed as a personal achievement. Aquinas on the other hand, believed that the acquisition of true virtues was not solely for us to achieve, but was dependent on God infusing us with them through the working of grace. Aquinas defines virtue as 'that which makes good he who has it and renders good his work'. Therefore, human flourishing for Aquinas is to live in accordance with reason.

Both Aristotle and Aquinas define man not only as 'a rational animal', but also as one that is social. Each person has consciousness, an awareness of being distinct and an individual self that relates to others and the world. Human society is the natural outgrowth of human nature and is constructed upon the family, community, town, city and state. The individual achieves happiness in life through living virtuously. This, for some, presupposes that the community provides sufficient material possessions to ensure good health and adequate leisure time. Every human being possesses an intellect and free will. The possession of knowledge of what is right is fundamental to Aquinas. Unless the morally correct position is known by the individual, how can he choose it? Morally good actions are controlled by the intellect and Aquinas did not reduce character to the moral virtues, but rather he emphasised the role of the intellectual virtues in any moral decision-making. Aquinas believed that the will should perform what the intellect judges to be right.

Failure in moral actions is either ignorance on the part of the intellect or weakness on the part of the will. Aquinas identifies two main problems in moral development, first, in ensuring that the intellect knows what is right, and second, getting the will to perform the action that is the subject of the morally correct choice once it has been identified. For Aquinas, human will, when gifted by God's grace, is (of its nature) inclined to act rightly or to do the true good, but we must be able to perceive and know what the good is in order to be attracted to do the good. In summary, character formation for Aquinas is therefore helping the intellect to know what is right and getting the will to do it. Students need to acquire certain virtues and be disposed to act on them on the basis of proper motives.

Aquinas not only accepts the virtues listed by Aristotle, but understands them in a new Christian context and adds to them. Indeed, Aquinas is credited with integrating the Aristotelian theory into a Christian framework. He speaks of some higher strata of virtues, not acquired by repetitive acts, but rather infused into a person by the free gift of the Creator. He calls them the 'theological virtues' and they are faith, hope and love. The Church can be the medium of these theological virtues through the Sacraments, through a life of prayer and worship, and through serving others in society. The moral character of a human being is determined by living the Christian faith. We receive grace and accept it as a gift, but it also demands that we freely co-operate with it. Virtue for Aquinas is an intentional willed good habit and that habitual practice brought incipient virtue to perfection. For as he said: 'From the multiplication of its acts, the habit grows' (ST Ia IIaa 52.3). He recognises the two-fold teleology in this plan – a modest 'human' happiness or flourishing that can be obtained through our own abilities and a more perfect end (union with God) that can be obtained only through God's grace (see Vogt, 2016: 183). Moral virtues are acquired through habituation and theological virtues are infused by God's grace.

Aquinas does not ignore the natural intellectual virtues and teaches that amongst these wise traits is the supreme virtue, but here he believes that wisdom attaches to the highest causes, the highest of these being God. Aquinas discusses virtues at great length and lists prudence and understanding as two other crucial virtues of the intellect. He teaches that all the moral virtues are exercised under the aegis of the intellectual virtues of prudence understood as 'right reason about things to be done'. For Aquinas moral virtues are habits enabling us to control the passions and desires that tend to lead us away from our true good. As habits are concerned with practice, these virtues must be guided by the principles of practical reason. Jarrat (1926: 33) notes that man seeks happiness which is driven by an impulse to seek happiness, but this ought to be combined with the three faculties: intellectual, moral and material – all three had to be satisfied before one could be happy.

Gillet (1914: 127) makes clear that Aquinas does not have in mind here only the intelligent person and he certainly does not advocate the pursuance of mechanical actions without reflection. He emphasises again and again that virtuous actions must be the product of liberty and deliberation. A person's character has eternal significance and a training in social skills alone is no education (Arthur, 2000: 33). Nevertheless, some degree of moral training is required which has been constantly emphasised by the Church as in the papal encyclical, *The Christian Education of Youth*, issued by Pope Pius XI in 1929 it is stated that 'the supernatural man who thinks, judges and acts constantly and consistently in accordance with right reason illumined by the supernatural light of the example a teaching of Christ; in other words, to use the current term, the true and finished man of character'. Bradshaw (2018: 105) summarises the pagan and Christian paths to virtuous character thus:

> Pagan ethics aims at integrating the individual into the larger cosmic order, whether through knowledge of the Good (Plato), performance of the human function (Aristotle), or living in accordance with reason (Stoicism). This focus on cosmic order gives pagan ethics a fundamentally static character. The pattern of the good life is largely fixed, however much the individual efforts needed to attain it may vary. Christian ethics seeks instead a relationship with a living God whose will for each individual has to be discovered through faith. That relationship requires the cleansing of the

heart, and so Christian ethics must go deeper than does pagan ethics, aiming to transform the depths of the heart that are accessible only through divine grace . . . it . . . gives Christian ethics a certain open-ended and unpredictable character.

In summary, Greek ideas of character prevailed throughout the medieval period. In the end Christians opted for a synthesis of Biblical faith and classical culture, while correcting the errors of the pagans in the light of Biblical revelation. The ethics of early Christianity consisted of a loose amalgam of Jewish, Platonism, Stoicism, and popular tradition, and it is this background which the early medieval period inherits. In the Latin context it is primarily the moral thought of Cicero and Seneca which undergoes Christian interpretation. However, Aristotelianism was the undisputed common currency of intellectual thought during the middle to later Middle Ages, but it was never all embracing or complete since there was a range of ideas under the banner of Aristotle. Christian, Jewish and Muslim thinkers – specifically Thomas Aquinas, Maimonides, and Averroes – embraced much of what Aristotle had taught in the *Ethics* and *Politics*. Western culture meant the culture of Christianity with deep Jewish roots. As Green (2009: 9) notes: 'For both clergy and laity, the acquisition of wisdom and eloquence was deemed inseparable from piety.' Character remained a key concern and Shultz (1995: 11) notes: 'In the Middle Ages nursing children were understood to imbibe the attributes of character and lineage along with their milk.' Goodman (1918: 111) provides an excellent summary as he writes:

> The adoption of Ancient Greek virtue ethics by medieval philosophers, Christian, Muslim, and Jewish, who wrote in Arabic, called for a synthesis of moral with religious ideas, setting human responsibility alongside divine agency in the framing of actions and the forming of character. Ancient ideas of the virtues were reshaped in the light of scripture and tradition, revealing both the flexibility and the robustness of virtue ethics, and casting new light on the dynamic interaction of the moral and intellectual virtues.

In 11th-century Florence a class of educated lay people emerged with a good knowledge of Latin and lay private teachers became more prominent from this time onwards (Thompson, 1963: 55). By the 14th and 16th centuries the control and influence of the Church over schooling in Europe began to weaken. The number and variety of schools increased from the 12th century with a demand for more literate employees in management and government service. Access to schools varied enormously depending on where you lived and how wealthy you were. There arose a debate on whether scholastic education was backward looking in methods, aims and curriculum (Black, 1991).

The predominant models of character formation in this period are theological, but conservative and virtue models continue in parallel.

Chapter 4

Early modern foundations

The educational traditions of the Middle Ages continued into the Renaissance. However, many historians have designated the Middle Ages as a negative period while the Renaissance, variously dated, is a good thing and the Reformation and Enlightenment very good things. The 'Dark Ages' was coined in the 14th century while the less pejorative Middle Ages was coined in the fifteenth, both by Italian humanists. Renaissance and Enlightenment are modern labels with the former introduced by Jacob Burckhardt in his *Civilization of the Renaissance in Italy* published in 1860. The word 'humanist' is a 19th-century label. The idea that there had been a thousand years of ignorance and superstition prior to the humanists of the 15th century rediscovering some classical learning is not credible, since many of the classics were already known and had been taught for centuries, as the previous chapter has shown. Burckhardt argued that the Middle Ages was a period of stagnation and superstition and assumes a sharp discontinuity between the Middle Ages and the Renaissance.

This has become the stereotypical view and one that makes the idea of character formation during the Middle Ages redundant, since it would not be possible if the people were ignorant, fearful and half-starved. The Middle Ages could not have been stagnant as it produced the first European universities – Bologna, Padua, Paris, Oxford, Cambridge, St. Andrews and Glasgow to name but a few; it built astonishing Cathedrals and monasteries; produced thinkers of the quality of Alfred the Great, Abelard, Dante, Chaucer, Roger Bacon, Marco Polo, William of Ockham, Duns Scotus, and Aquinas and even achieved great technological success with its own Industrial Revolution (Gimbel, 1992, Hannan, 2009). As Dupre (2008: 5) observes about the origins of Enlightenment ideas: 'there is a modern culture, a mode of thinking, feeling, and creating that stretches from the fifteenth through the twentieth century. But it arrived in successive waves, each one bringing its own principles, which, though continuous with those of the previous one, do not follow from them with logical necessity. Modernity is an ongoing creative process that even today has not reached completion.' Barnett (2003: 219) claims that the historical record has been distorted by some Enlightenment historians resulting in 'the perpetuation of myths about the origins of modernity', but Colish (1997) provides a more balanced account.

70 Foundations

It is the case that by the 16th century some intellectuals became conscious of a new age which called for a term to designate the previous age – the Middle Ages. A decisive break with what had gone before was envisioned. The Renaissance was indeed an attempt to look back and revive the best of the ancient civilisations of Greece and Rome and marked the long transition from medieval to modern attitudes. Education during the Italian Renaissance was carefully programmed to create students who were well-balanced and who embodied the values of their society. It was seen as a process of liberation, but remained elitist and male. As Siedentop (2014: 337) says, the humanists introduced a new emphasis on cultivating the self, 'on the refinement of taste and self-expression' and the individual was seen as a victim of social pressures with heroism seen as resistance to such pressures. Social institutions, including the Church, were presented as potential threats to the self. He calls it the pursuit of 'individuality' in the sense that the individual becomes the basic unit of society and not the family. Nevertheless, it was a Christian humanism of liberal education that was being pursued, but as Scholasticism began to wane so did the credibility of ethical accounts grounded in Christian theology. There was an increase in the lay control of schools, but many things remained constant from the Middle Ages through to the Renaissance and Reformation – discipline in the family and the school for example. Corporal punishment for poor behaviour by children and adults was standard in the West and changed little in British schools from Greek and Roman times to the 1980s. Disciplinary measures by parents and teachers were adopted in order to train specific characters because it was believed that this motivated people to do the right thing. Medieval schools taught the classics, but in the Renaissance schools taught these subjects with more intensity and the teachers understood them more. Even the status and pay of teachers changed remarkably little between the two periods.

An example of the continuation between the medieval and Renaissance periods can be seen in Leon Battista Alberti's (1404–74) work *On the Family* written during the 1430s. Alberti was considered a 'Renaissance man' because of his wide knowledge – it is also noteworthy that he was educated in one of the new humanist schools in Florence. In this four-book dialogue between members of the Alberti family, he discusses the education of children and the particular role of fathers in building virtuous character in their children – a concern that stretched back to well before Aristotle. Alberti uses Aristotelian categories to discuss character formation and Book One, 'Concerning the Duties of the Old toward the Young and the Young towards Their Elders and Concerning the Education of Children', begins with the words of the dying Loranzo Alberti in conversation with his boys Adovardo and Lionardo, (see Cochrane and Krishner, 1986: 81ff):

> *Loranzo* – 'Thus we conclude . . . that good habits will in time overcome and correct unreasonable appetite and every imperfection of the mind. It seems to me, then, that if a father notices his son sinking into laziness,

Early modern foundations 71

avarice, impetuousness, and the like, he ought to draw him back to virtue by having him work at and practise good and praiseworthy things. And if he sees that his son is already headed along the path that leads to virtue and commendable acts, he ought to support and strengthen him by instruction and by example. . . . Therefore fathers will be alert and foresighted in studying their sons' characters so that they can help them toward whatever is praiseworthy and turn them away from any dissolute manners or ugly affections'

Adovardo – 'I don't deny, Lionardo, that fathers who are as diligent as you say they ought to be can in good measure help their sons in acquiring good manners; nor do I deny that fathers can, with care and attention, correct their sons' defects and make them into good men. But I am afraid that the love most fathers bear their children all too often blinds them to the first signs of evil; when the evil itself at last becomes fully evident, then it's too late. Even you realise that it's pretty hard to uproot a vice that has become a confirmed habit.'

Lionardo – 'As everyone knows, the place to begin is with good letters (literature). Letters are indeed so important that without them one would be considered nothing but a rustic, no matter how much a gentlemen (he may be by birth). Let our family, then continue to take inspiration from the example of our ancestors, so that the young will be filled with the desire to acquire knowledge and refinement, and so that their fathers will take pleasure in seeing their sons become learned and wise.'

Lionardo goes on to describe what kind of activities in culture and even in the content of a school curriculum would lead to being thought 'learned and wise'. These included: learning good maxims, good morals, striving to be kind and considerate, and in order to do this you need to learn Latin and read Homer, Virgil, Cicero, and other good literature as well as participate in games, sport and appreciate music. Lionardo was simply repeating much that was already in medieval culture and schooling and which continued in many forms into the 20th century.

The direct reading of the classics, delivering moral messages, from the medieval period was clearly continued. Some of these new humanist educators emphasised both Christian and Classical sources to produce a broader education with the key guiding principles of persuasion, example and reason in teaching. As Garin (1957: 103) noted: 'The school created in fifteenth-century Italy was . . . an educator of man, capable of shaping a child's moral character so as not to be preconditioned but free, open to the future to every possible specialisation, but before all else humane and whole, with social links to all mankind and endowed with the prerequisites for the mastery of all teachings but in full self-control.' This was an assertion of critical consciousness and an awareness of self and others. It was about the conscious actions of human beings to self-improve themselves and it was about freedom to choose. Garin is very critical

72 Foundations

of the scholastic age, claiming that boys were taught contempt for the secular world and that education was wholly concerned with religious, theological and spiritual aims with teachers showing antipathy towards classical learning. In this he is challenged by the work of Grafton and Jardine (1986) who dispute that the education in the Middle Ages was barbarous and a sterile indoctrination. They point to the fact that it was an age in which technical and professional training increased, with doctors, lawyers and theologians being trained and that it also offered literacy in Latin as well as a training in logic (see Black, 1991: 317). Above all, they reject Garin's claim that character building was developed through the study of the new canon of texts of Renaissance education. In this interpretation Garin is rather idealistic in his claims if not entirely accurate.

Garin (1957) believed that the Renaissance was a revolutionary period for schooling because he argues that students engaged in activities that contributed to their humanity. Other scholars of the period such as Artz (1966) and Grendler (1989) believe that the Renaissance revolutionised the ideals and methods of education. Artz (1966: 88) however, goes too far in claiming that the Renaissance was a period of critical thinking and discovery learning in schools and that a 'lay morality' was created in which ethical conduct was seen as an end in itself. This would have been contrary to Church teaching and would not fit with Catholic humanist values of the period. There was certainly greater lay involvement in the provision of schooling and the *studia humanitatis* consisting of grammar, rhetoric, poetry, history and moral philosophy slowly changed the curriculum of medieval schooling, but the teaching of the Catholic faith actually became more systematic.

Giovanni Pico Della Mirandola (1463–94) was a product of this system of education and is often considered one of the great Renaissance humanists with a real sense of independence. His great work an *Oration on the Dignity of Man* in 1486 resulted in him having difficulties with the Church, but he remained a committed Catholic. As a philosopher he taught that man owes his moral character to himself, as Cassirer (1942: 325) says. He believed that man is his own arbitrary moulder of character – 'a sculpture who must bring forth and in a sense, chisel out his own form from the material with which nature has endowed him'. He did not reject the scholastic tradition, but rather defended it and was a greater admirer of Aristotle. He adopted a balanced view of humanistic thinking, rejecting the notion that any particular period in time could possibly represent the whole of mankind. The Renaissance did however begin the shift from viewing children as miniature adults to understanding them more as children in need of development.

Schooling derives from the idea of leisure time which meant that schooling was only suitable for those who were free and did not have to earn a living as children. It was expected that such men should be able to discuss moral philosophy, ethics, geometry, arithmetic, the movement of the stars, and much besides in polite society. In order for them to be prepared for this they ought to study the humanities meaning grammar, poems, orations, letters, plays, and biographies, historical texts, dialogues, and essays on moral philosophy – either in school or with their tutor at home. Much of this was to be taken from non-Christian sources. Pier Paolo Vergerio (1370–1444) wrote his *Character and Studies Befitting a Free-Born Youth* between 1402 and 1403 which focuses on teaching the virtues to form wisdom. He writes about how the young must be enabled to flourish in school. Vittorino da Feltre (1378–1446) was the example of this new Renaissance approach to education in his *On the Education of Boys and their Moral Culture* (1450). He founded a school at Mantua and experimented with various teaching methods, but character formation remained the chief goal of his school. He also upheld the Christian life as the purpose of education, but had no difficulty in appealing to the wisdom of the ancients. He laid great stress on strict moral training and emphasised the good influence of the teacher. Prior to this Petrus Paulus Vergerius had written a series of treatises on character and education (1404) and justified Liberal Studies in the following terms: 'We call these studies liberal which are worthy of a free man; those studies by which we attain and practise virtue and wisdom; that education which calls forth, trains, and develops those highest gifts of body and mind which enable man and which are rightly judged to rank next in dignity to virtue only.' (Curtis and Boultwood, 1965: 115).

Vergerius emphasised not dead heroes but living heroes for emulation:

> If, however, it is helpful to contemplate the outward form of a dead hero, how much more shall we gain from the example of living worth? For it is with character as with instruction: the 'living voice' is of far more avail than the written letter; the life we can observe, the character actually before us, affect us as no other influence can. Let, then, the examples of living men, known and respected for their worth, be held up for a boy's imitation. And, moreover, let those of us who are older not forget so to live that our actions may be a worthy model for the youth who look up to us for guidance and example.

This period initiated a slow transform in instruction in schools through a long series of progressive changes, including the rise of a scientific approach to moral questions. Life in these Italian city-states reproduced the same conditions under which the Greek *paideia* had originally developed. This involved preparing the young for a training for citizenship as well as building their character. The influence of these educational developments spread to England and Scotland, but most schools changed very little. However, we know that in 1631 over 12,000 copies of *Aesop's Fables* were printed for use in English schools, as were many other Greek texts. This was in addition to catechisms, primers, psalms, and other stories (Green, 2009: 40 ff).

The Quarrel of the Ancients and Moderns or The Battle of the Books emerged at this point in late 17th-century France – the ancients who thought education should be based on the canon of knowledge already extant while the

74 Foundations

moderns thought that the search for new knowledge was the future orientation. As Wotton in his *Reflections Upon Ancient and Modern Learning* published in 1694 (1694: 300) noted: 'All arguments or principles of philosophy must be in themselves intelligible, not because they are established by "celebrated philosophers".' Essentially, Wooton thought that new knowledge could be expected from the future through new methods of observation and experimentation, which meant that we should not rely on Homer, Socrates, Plato Aristotle or Christianity as we must be open to future learning. Past traditions are no longer essential, including the virtues that constituted character. All conclusions about human beings are to be avoided until experiments are conducted. He was proposing a new interdisciplinary approach.

The origins of the liberal arts, as the major focus and content of school education, are found in the Roman period which produced a coherent programme of study that was continued in the Middle Ages. Kimball (1986) discusses two different conceptions of liberal education; the liberal arts model based on a classical education which initiates the student into a cultural tradition, and the liberal free model which is exemplified by questioning, experimentation and critical thinking. Kimball (1986: 36, 119–23) outlines the aims of this liberal arts model or programme in describing seven characteristics that are generally advanced by Roman advocates and their medieval successors. First, to produce good citizen orators, a civic elite, who are literate, virtuous and competent leaders. Second, to identify the core virtues as moral standards for the formation of character and conduct. Third, to promote active commitment to these moral virtues. Fourth, to provide literary texts that embody these virtues as the school curriculum. Fifth, to elevate and prioritise those who live by these virtues in their personal and civic conduct. Sixth, to understand truth and the virtues as realities that can be known. Seventh, to pursue character formation via the virtues as a worthy pursuit or embraced for their own sake.

Kimball interprets this to mean that the school curriculum is infused explicitly and implicitly with these seven ideals, particularly in the literacy activities of reading, writing, speaking and listening. These ideals are seen within Western culture and are largely taken for granted as assumptions that structure our actions so that we are not aware of them or of the power of their effects on our actions. The Renaissance, he says, is best understood as a more intense revival of these liberal arts in order that students might act ethically and work for the good of society and the State. The Greek idea of liberal arts, pursued as an ideal conception of the human being, became dominant as an education that formed character to perform well in a variety of contexts. The Greeks invented this ideal as a purposeful means of training youth to pursue it as a means of character formation and they provided a justification for it (see Jaeger, 1945). It was an ideal that looked to the past for the source of texts to communicate good character to the next generation of students and therefore moulded human character in accordance with this ideal.

Any society institutionalises its fundamental values and principles through systems of education. The system of Renaissance education was so successful that it survived well into the 20th century. Up until the First World War, those who enjoyed elite education could know that they read the same books. It was believed that with the knowledge of greats – that is the ancient writers – you could be a proconsul of an empire, a captain of industry, or a general, or an admiral. You could do anything as long as you had the knowledge of classical antiquity and a good, correct Latin style behind you. The Renaissance upheld the dignity of the human being. It began the move towards academic freedom, emphasised liberal education, but still highlighted the virtues – moral and intellectual. It was believed that the classics provided a moral education – more secular, but against a solid Christian backdrop. Schooling remained for the rich and elite. Thomas More, in England, believed that it was societal institutions that corrupted people's character and he said that better institutions would lead to a better society. Moral philosophy in the medieval West derived from two main sources: Christianity and classical ethics. The attempt to reconcile these different traditions and develop a viable synthesis of the two continued to be a central concern of moral philosophy throughout the period.

Erasmus believed that the study of classical languages would strengthen religion and lead to a more intelligent view of faith. Indeed, that the study of the moral teachings of the ancient world would be a support to Christianity. In his influential manual *De Civilitate Morium Puerilium*, of 1530, which was translated into English as *A Lytell Booke of Good Manners for Children*, Erasmus speaks of the importance of well-being (flourishing) in the population at large and the connection between the study of behaviour and the worthiness of the inner life for civility of mind. Everyone had the capacity to learn, but there was a focus on the nobility. Martin Luther (1483–546) saw this as Pelagian, an early Christian heresy, in that it postulated inner goodness, and complete freedom of the will, and was not consistent with the theology of original sin. For Luther, divine commandments made up the true moral rules and these required no justification or rationale – they are God's commands. In *De Pueris (The Liberal Education of Children)*, Erasmus recognises parents and the home as the first educators and the foundation of building character. The home is the beginning of laying the foundations of the moral basis of life up until the age of seven, after which he encourages fathers to educate their sons. He placed emphasis on learning through play and allowed greater freedom for children to develop. This was entirely Aristotelian in outline – a move from scholasticism towards literary studies which came to be known as humanist. Human beings could be changed by education and the idea was to create good people and good citizens along the lines of classical Athens.

Education for Renaissance boys was of two sorts. There was classical education based on the Latin language for boys (not girls) who planned to go on to a university. There was also education through apprenticeships for boys who planned to pursue a trade. Literacy was emphasised, however, and a more instrumental turn occurred with the emergence of the Protestant Reformation – character education was to emphasise being thrifty – adopting good social manners – living a worthy life on earth to guarantee a life in heaven. Protestant virtues sought a complete refiguring of human character, but the idea that the notion of manners originated with the Renaissance, Thomas (2018: 22) says, 'is an optical illusion, created by the invention of printing, the replacement of Latin by the vernacular, and the readiness of Renaissance humanists to ignore or disparage their medieval predecessors'. However, the Catholic humanist emphasis was on the formation of character rather than solely on the acquisition of knowledge (Jarrat, 1926). It was the Renaissance that began the campaign to reform the Church and free it from superstition and ignorance as it did not look to revelation for inspiration, but to the Athens and Rome of the classical period. This is why the Reformation was a very different thing from the humanist thinkers. While the Renaissance thinkers emphasised the Greek tradition, the Reformation thinkers emphasised the Hebrew tradition and particularly the strict sense of morality and sin.

The importance of education was firmly established in the writings of the leaders of the Protestant Reformation – Martin Luther, John Calvin and John Knox. They emphasised that all should receive enough education to read the Bible. The Protestant churches were to share the responsibility of educating with parents and teachers to enable children to have good character. Students had to be prepared to be good citizens of Church and State, but above all the Protestant Reformation sought to reform the character of the young with a pedagogy consistent with Scripture which resulted in numerous catechisms appearing all over Europe. The establishment of schools was to be a priority as was working with the secular authorities to this end. It was Luther who called for the civil authorities, rather than the Church, to provide schooling (Naphy, 2007: 66) creating a kind of political Protestantism. This resulted in the rise of nationalism and patriotism in the Protestant State. In addition, Luther associated virtue theories too closely with popular notions of personal self-fulfilment and self-realisation which did not advance Christian ideas, as Pieper (1967: XI) observed: 'It is true that the classic origins of the doctrine of virtue later made Christian critics suspicious of it. They warily regarded it as too philosophical and not Scriptural enough. Thus, they preferred to talk about commandments and duties rather than about the virtues.' This line of thought was the main reason for a decline in virtue theory after the Reformation.

Luther denied human freedom, rejected tradition and believed that 'Almost the entire Aristotelian ethics is fundamentally evil and an enemy of grace' (cited in Russell, 2013: 133). In *An Open Letter to the Christian Nobility of the German Nation* (1520) he wrote that Aristotle, via medieval Scholasticism, should be discarded while claiming that Aristotle's *Ethics* is incomprehensible: 'his book on Ethics is the worst of all books' and Mitchell (2019: 26) notes: 'Luther's approach is revolutionary rather than evolutionary, an approach that comes to typify early modern thought'. Indeed, Luther broke with many traditions in

Christianity and advocated direct communication with God for all, abandoning the Church's guidance and laws. Dollinger wrote that children in schools were taught to despise past generations, even their own ancestors, as people in darkness and error (Dollinger, 1848). Protestants enforced a strict discipline in schools and in the public space which could be authoritarian and repressive in style. Obedience was expected from children and catechisms were the most common pedagogical device used to enforce a worldview on all. Basic rules of conduct rooted in scripture were recited and this was reinforced by primers, simple verses, poems, songs and stories. The catechetical method influenced the teaching in schools by emphasising learning by rote (see Androne, 2014).

Apprenticeships were probably more important than schools as virtues were also taught to more boys than attended schools. In England the State licensed teachers and schools to ensure doctrinal conformity with the new religion. Thomas Elyat's book on the *Governor* (1531) emphasised the importance of instruction in the virtues and he believed that those who become teachers must be morally fit and excellent. He advocated that the father should take over at the age of seven and that boys should be removed from the example and company of women. Roger Ascham in the *Schoolmaster*, published in 1570 after his death, advocates the study of moral philosophy in the school curriculum to develop the idea of human character – he clearly turns to Athens for inspiration. However, his book is Protestant in orientation and looks to English nationalism – it was the most influential education book in Tudor England. Virtue and wisdom were to be taught, but adapted to the needs of Protestant England.

Richard Mulcaster wrote two treatises on education, *Positions* (*Training Up of Children*) (1581) and *Elementarie* (1582) which were focused on education for character and for the service of the State. Much is said in the text about the moral qualifications of teachers, less about their intellectual qualifications. Much of it was devoted to prescribed knowledge, disciplining bodies and regulating minds. The Protestant understanding of virtues departs from Aristotle and Aquinas as they believed that character virtues have no bearing on the Christian soul and are therefore useless. Sin becomes more dominant for Protestant theology and God is outside and distant from any human community formed by a moral culture. The Bible became the chief reference for character formation in Protestant education. Luther dismissed the theology of Aquinas, particularly about reason and will as important elements in the forming of character. In England, the State regulated schooling like never before and intervened to ensure compulsory attendance at Church and the compulsory reading of the Bible in school, all in aid of creating religious uniformity. Schools assisted hugely in the transition of England from Catholicism to Protestantism. The Stationers' Company in London had authority from the Crown to publish set texts for schools which they controlled. In addition to Protestant catechisms and primers there were Cicero's *De Officiis*, Vergil and Ovid's poems, and a whole array of classical literature. The content of the non-religious curriculum

78 Foundations

remained largely moral in nature including Castellios' *Dialogues* and Culmann's *Pueriles Sententiae* (Green, 2009: 40–2).

The Catholic Church responded with the Counter-Reformation which was a period of Catholic resurgence that began as a response to the Protestant Reformation. The Jesuits adopted the methods of the humanists in their new teaching institutions of *Ratio Studiorum*. This *Ratio* was a set of rules specifically composed for teachers in secondary schools. Students were to be well supervised by teachers and the best methods of teaching available were to be employed. A definite syllabus was to be followed, feedback was to be given to each student, teachers were to be trained with skill in teaching and this was considered to be as important as scholarship, exams and tests and the best of Greek culture was used. This extremely successful movement became the main educational instrument of the Counter-Reformation.

Many historians believe that the 17th century sought to liberate minds from dogmas and encourage scepticism and critical thinking. These early Enlightenment thinkers had widely different views, however. English prose began to develop what was known as the 'Character', essentially a portrait of a type rather than an individual, often done with humour. The form is based on Theophrastus *Characters* which begins with a description of a vice and then describes the typical possessor of the said vice. It first began in 1608 with Joseph Hall, an Anglican Bishop and moralist, who published *Characters of Virtues and Vices* and this was used in schools (see Appendix G). Thomas Overbury published his *Characters or Witty Descriptions of the Properties of Sundry Persons* in 1614 and this was followed 1631 by Richard Braithwaite's *The Whimsies* – 24 characters that followed the alphabet, i.e. Almanac-maker, Ballad-monger, etc. without any reason given for this. This was followed in the 1660s, but not published until 1759, by Samuel Butler's *Characters*. All were concerned with moral character, but increasingly from Overbury's work onwards there was more focus on the common types of characters in England at the time and less seriousness about the ethical character dimensions of human nature (Roback, 1927: 31).

We know in 975 that the kinds of authors used in schools included: Homer, Juvenal, Horace, Boethius, Persius, Statius, Lucan, Terence, to name a few (Curtius, 1953: 49, Lewis, 1964, and see Appendix C). In each century the list of authors used in schools continued to grow and we also know that in the 12th century scholars translated a vast corpus of Greek learning into Latin and some of these authors found their way into schools (Charlton, 1965: 35). Thompson (1963: 55) challenges the widely held view that illiteracy was universal prior to the Italian Renaissance. The Middle Ages and the Renaissance were a continuation in this respect, building on previous developments, while the main differences were often about the quantity of Latin books, the rediscovery of Plato and the championing of Greek literature. The humanists were simply people who were interested in and favoured Greek and Roman literature and we know that many of these texts existed prior to the Renaissance. Thomas (2018: 19) has shown that the interpretations of some historians that good character formation was impossible in the Middle Ages because it was 'a time of unchecked impulses, when people lacked self-control and were given over to childlike oscillations of mood, accompanied by carelessness about the bodily functions and a disposition to spontaneous violence' is false. There was a long line of medieval injunctions for good behaviour in schools and in the general culture as can be seen in the teaching materials used (see appendices).

Renaissance Italy certainly had more teachers than in previous centuries, but as regards character formation there were more similarities than differences. First, the aims of character formation remained both religious and ethical, with the latter taught mainly through Greek and Roman literature which in both periods was thought to breed character. The humanists remained Catholic almost to a man and they also gave as much time and study to the church fathers as they did to classical antiquity (Bentley, 1983). There was a clear revival of patristic theology during the Renaissance (Stinger, 1977). Second, both periods educated the elite and were not concerned by the feelings and attitudes of the inarticulate masses. Indeed, for the middle classes learning increasingly became a signifier of social status and 'good character'. (Nejemy, 2004: 14). Third, the Greek and Roman texts used were similar in both periods as were much of the teaching methods. As regards texts even the critics of the medieval period say that the humanists 'supplemented' the texts, and did not completely replace them (see Grendler, 1989). In formal school teaching, memorisation and rote learning continued. Fourth, Aristotle's philosophy continued to be the most important philosophical tradition long after the 15th century. Aristotle was not ignored, but rather formed part of the continuity from the Middle Ages (Roick, 2017: 4), but some Renaissance humanists thought Aristotle's ideas were superstition and a 'relic of the dark, medieval past' (Rubenstein, 2003: 10). Above all, the Renaissance humanists lost none of the interest in forming character. Without the Middle Ages the Renaissance thinkers could not have committed the West to an ethos of rational enquiry and it may be well to remember the saying of the 12th-century Bernard of Chartres who famously said 'we are dwarfs mounted on the shoulders of giants' – it appears the new humanists had no such humility for their claims.

In sum, Renaissance practice of education was in many significant respects a continuation with its medieval predecessor. As Oakley (1992: 72) says, Scholasticism has been unfairly maligned while the Renaissance period has been correspondingly 'idealised and romanticised'. The Renaissance humanists certainly chose new labels to distance themselves from what had gone before, but the outcomes claimed by subsequent historians have been illusory. However, as Porter (2013: 89) notes, the Middle Ages was not a period of stagnation, but was rather a rich period for intellectual discussion of the variety of virtue theories: 'Virtue ethics is always located within a wider context of intellectual debates and practical concerns . . . we can expect to see diverse approaches to the virtues appearing, receding, and returning again.' Becker and Becker (2003: 59) demonstrate that late medieval philosophers, while recognising the existence of

80 Foundations

divinely revealed moral precepts and Church doctrine, maintained that some acts are morally right not because they have been commanded by God or the Church, but because they are in accordance with reason. One could say the same about character formation, which continued to be transmitted from generation to generation with all the group norms in values, beliefs, attitudes, traditions, conventions, habits, mentalities and so forth. The living historical community of the Italian Middle Ages and Renaissance possessed a core of these norms that was deeply engrained and had not been eroded by the passage of time and represented cultural continuity. Classical learning never ceased to influence the medieval period, but it intensified in the 15th century.

This intensity is perhaps best summed up in Raphael's great Renaissance painting commissioned by Pope Julius II in 1509 titled 'The School of Athens' with two major thinkers positioned at the centre of the painting indicating two different philosophical schools. On the left is the elderly Plato with his hand pointing up to signify that the real world is not the physical world, but only a mere shadow of a higher and truer reality. Plato represents the contemplation of ideas and his pointing to heaven is to denote that heaven is the seat of all ideas. Aristotle stands on the right pointing down and he holds in his left hand his *Ethics*. This signifies that Aristotle wishes to emphasise the earthboundness of the virtues, relationships, character and justice. It means that for Aristotle truth is to be found in gathering together empirical data received through our senses and subject to deliberation and reason. His philosophy denotes that the reality we see and experience on earth is the only reality.

Both these schools of philosophy had and continued to have enormous influence on the development of Christianity and on character formation. Kimball (1986: 119–23) reminds us that the history of liberal education is the story of the tense debate between orators and philosophers and we have already described the oratorical tradition as the liberal arts model. He states that different representations of liberal education, and hence of character formation, tend to gravitate to the arguments of philosophers or orators. Philosophers see orators as looking more towards finding persuasion techniques than to finding true arguments while orators see philosophers endlessly searching for the highest truth without ever reaching it. Kimball outlines the philosopher's position which includes: freedom from *a priori* standards, emphasis on intellect and reason, critical scepticism, tolerance, a tendency towards egalitarianism, the ethics of individualism and the pursuit of truth for its own sake. He claims that these seven ideals were manifested more intensely during the Enlightenment.

The Enlightenment period saw the traditional models of character formation continue, but there was more attention given to liberal ideas.

Key intellectual figures

A number of thinkers of this early modern period that led up to the Enlightenment period helped shape many of the features of modernity and understanding

Early modern foundations 81

of character. Many of those, briefly discussed here, were exponents of rationalism with its concern for man to take control over nature in order to alleviate the human condition. Francis Bacon (1561–1626) began this move to rationalism with his concern for individual duty to the public. He was concerned by the individual's control over his emotions in order to produce acceptable behaviour in the public space leading to an active moral life in society. Bacon was one of the founders of the modern scientific method and he rejected the idea that contemplation was the highest form of human life, preferring instead action and production. The Jesuit educated Rene Descartes (1596–1650) produced a model of the rational moral agent – an observer who would objectively examine the facts and then evaluate them. His idea of the person was one who is strong and virtuous and one who controls their passions. He was concerned with the control of the passions people displayed whom he believed needed rationality. This was a theoretical construct and is hugely influential, but fails to understand in turn that feelings will affect our reason. Baruch Spinoza (1632–77) was another key figure who prepared the way for the Enlightenment as he sought to demonstrate that there was only one reality, namely the material world and that all religious texts are no more than literature. He stressed freedom of expression and democracy while attacking superstition. Bacon, Descartes and Spinoza largely rejected Aristotle's ethical philosophy. The key figures that prepared the way or directly contributed to the Enlightenment are:

Thomas Hobbes (1588–1679) believed that scientific discovery could reduce the study of character to reason alone. He outlined in his book *Leviathan* (1651) that what is good can be reduced to three types of endeavour. First, appetites (attraction to); second, aversion; three, contempt (an attitude of indifference). For Hobbes the words good and evil had no moral connotations as they merely represented objects of human appetite and aversion. His theory was that our basic motivation is self-preservation and that fulfilling one's desires is the source of ethical behaviour. Even the Golden Rule is reduced to enlightened self-interest – I am good to you in order that you be good to me in return. Life is nasty, brutish and short for Hobbes, and he had an extremely low view of human beings – they are basically selfish, driven by fear of death and constantly in the hope of personal gain. Hobbes, while claiming to be Christian, dismisses the supernatural or theological virtues and sees no place for altruism or benevolence. The solution for Hobbes in keeping order was to put some individual or parliament in charge with absolute authority. Joseph Butler (1692–1752) provided a contrary response to Hobbes and in writing as a religious empiricist he refuted the claims of Hobbes, maintaining that man was less selfish and had an innate sense of right and wrong. He believed that from the observation of human nature one could suppose that this present life may be a probation leading to a future state and therefore it is likely that moral improvement may be the chief purpose of life on earth. He concludes that it is credible to believe that we should form 'men to live in the general practice of all virtue and piety' (Butler, 1961: 121).

82 Foundations

John Locke (1632–1704), like Hobbes, believed that mathematics could be used as a model to guide moral decision-making. Locke suggested a theory of *tabula rasa* which proposed that the human infant is comparable to a blank slate and that the infant's life experiences would be written onto the slate. The child's character would therefore be moulded by his or her life experiences. Nevertheless, Moseley (2007: 81) believes that the roots of Locke's idea of character are essentially Aristotelian in nature as he says: 'The premise of Lockean education is the securing of character before any positive instruction in the various disciplines.' Education for Locke is character formation and he accepted that it was acceptable to interfere morally in the life of children to help shape them. Locke was also extremely influential over progressive educationalists who sought to challenge the existing education provision. They believed that human nature was subject to improvement and in Locke's *Some Thoughts Concerning Education* (1693) he set out the aim of education as to change lives – to transform them, but his book was addressed to parents as well as teachers. Human nature he believed was malleable: 'education is not to be narrowly scholastic: it is not about being learned, but about learning for life, a training in character, habit and conduct' (Porter, 2000: 341). He believed that each individual was created with a unique character and noted: 'God has stamp'd certain Character upon Men's Minds, which like their Shapes, may perhaps be a little mended, but can hardly be totally alter'd, and transform'd into the contrary' (Locke, 1693: 66). He was against teaching fairy stories to the young and against beatings and threats made in the classroom by the teacher. He appeals to reason and winning over the will, not by breaking it, but by persuasion. He recognised that the environment in which education took place needed to be altered for different children. Education ought to proceed through praise and discipline to build character, as Moseley (2007: 117) notes: 'The young child is to be taught to be virtuous through filial and social applause and disapprobation, and is to be encouraged to sustain those virtues as they mature and when they can be severely tested.' To form virtuous character took time and effort, but Locke (1693: 30) believed it was worth it as he noted: 'Vertue is harder to be got, than Knowledge of the World.' However, Locke was only concerned with the education of gentlemen, people of good breeding, as he thought mental culture was not appropriate for men of low standing. He emphasised that character needed to be developed from the early stages and that ultimately a gentleman has to be a man of virtue who possessed prudence and good sense.

Jean-Jacques Rousseau (1712–78) speaks a great deal about virtue and even planned a work on character, but did not begin it (Elliot, 1913: 222). He believed that to recover our innate goodness and cultivate our conscience depends on us returning to nature and its simplicity. But conscience does not operate as he describes – some innate faculty tells us what is right or wrong – we hear a voice. There is no standard of moral evaluation of character here. He valued modelling to a point and the development of worthwhile habits. His

Early modern foundations   83

perspective was utopian and saw the child as pure, only their environment corrupted them. Character would be fine if we did away with negative influences in this environment. For Rousseau, individual freedom was key and he gave it greater emphasis than he did the collective. He never spoke of the outcomes from this perspective and simply believed that exposing the child to goodness would allow the innate goodness they possessed already to flourish.

Immanuel Kant (1724–1804) believed that people's circumstances, their nature, parents, human inclination, social roles and background made character development difficult, but not impossible. Despite being a devout Christian, he argued that moral law does not derive from God, but from ourselves. By the use of what he called 'pure practical reason' we can set forth a categorical imperative by which we generate maxims telling us what we ought and ought not to do – our duties – and our moral obligation to act accordingly. Consequently, what I ought to do is defined as what is my duty, while the moral status of my character is determined by my doing what I ought. By this Kant maintained that a role or principle for right living must be universal – for all people, in all plans and under all conditions. To be moral, an act must be done because of a good will and good will is to act solely on the basis of duty to follow the categorical imperative. This has come to be known as the deontological theory that judges some actions as ethical or unethical in themselves, regardless of the person's intentions and the situational circumstances. He separated moral action from the longing of human beings to achieve the good. He understood it in terms of duty alone and grounded morality in human reason alone (see Munzel, 1999, Rumsey, 1989).

Jeremy Bentham (1748–1832) was a radical liberal thinker of his day who had considerable influence on society and other thinkers such as John Stuart Mill through his moral theory of utilitarianism. This theory postulated the 'principle of utility' as the only valid standard of right and wrong. What he meant by this was that an action is right or wrong depending on whether it promoted or diminished the greatest happiness overall. The first requirement of this principle was that we ought to pursue our own happiness as the right thing to do. The second principle is to advance the happiness of others so long as it does not diminish our own happiness. Accordingly, the moral character of an individual should always act in a manner that maximises the overall sum of happiness in society. The idea of the 'good' was that which produces the greatest amount of pleasure and the minimum of pain. This theory has been subjected to constant critique and criticism outlying its many limitations and faults (see Parekh, 1993, Vol. 1).

John Stuart Mill (1806–73) wanted to write a great deal more about character, but according to Elliot (1913: 222) could make nothing of the subject, but commented that 'what is really inspiriting and ennobling in the doctrine

84 Foundations

of freewill, is the conviction that we have real power over the formation of our own character; that our will, by influencing some of our circumstances, can modify our future habits or capabilities of willing' (*Autobiography*). He is often associated with utilitarianism and he certainly saw character formation as a prerequisite to promote utility for others in the community. He believed in character formation as a means to improve society and that 'the only freedom which deserves the name is that of pursuing our own good in our own way'. He meant by this that we should ultimately determine the good through deliberation and discernment rather than being told what the good is by the politician or priest. His most famous message was the Harm Principle which is that every adult should be free to live as he or she pleases as long as no one else is harmed in the process. This is a serious challenge to any idea of government or schools imposing moral virtues on the people or students or attempting to shape character in the public space. Mill was concerned not just with government telling the people how to behave, but with what he called the 'tyranny of the majority' – the way social pressure worked to make us unfree. However, he did make a serious contribution to the conception of character formation, which is discussed in the chapter on Victorian Education.

Chapter 5

Scottish enlightenment foundations

In the previous chapter we offered descriptions of relevant aspects of the thought of earlier thinkers whose contributions are indispensable to understanding character formation in the 18th century. There is, however, a transitional figure who helped prepare the way for Scottish Enlightenment thinkers, particularly Hutcheson and Hume, by providing and defining the idea of 'moral sense'. Anthony Ashley Cooper, the third Earl of Shaftesbury (1671–1713) was an English philosopher who wrote *Characteristics of Men, Manners, Opinions, Times* (1711) which includes *An Enquiry Concerning Virtue or Merit*. Shaftesbury saw the purpose of philosophy as practical in nature, intended to create better people – it had a self-improving role. He used the language of character formation and many of the categories of Aristotelian thought, but he departed from strictly Aristotelian meaning in his ethical theories. He certainly introduced the ideas of 'sociability' and 'politeness' that became important to Scottish Enlightenment thinkers. He also introduced the idea of an innate moral sense in human nature that could, he claimed, be grounded in objective features of the world. He argued that religion can be separated from virtue and that character formation was about looking within oneself – a kind of self-dialogue that forms moral judgement through self-reflection (Klein, 1994). While he taught that, in order to learn how to live well, we ought to be attracted to virtue for its own sake and not simply out of self-interest, he denied that this was a social process. Virtues, he believed, also make a person happy. These ideas featured in the background to the Scottish Enlightenment and were built upon in the 18th century.

The Enlightenment was a cultural process that prioritised the sovereignty of reason and questioned traditional sources of authority. Historians speak of multiple Enlightenments of which the Scottish version is of particular note for understanding character formation. The contribution and prominence of 18th-century academics from Scottish universities in advancing moral philosophy and the understanding of character development is remarkable. This period was named the Scottish Enlightenment and arose within a rapidly changing society that was arguably the most literate in Europe (see Broadie, 1997: 10ff, Randell, 1978). There are of course many fields of study within the Scottish Enlightenment and we restrict ourselves to questions of character and conduct viewed

86 Foundations

through selected authors. It should also be noted that the study of this period remains fluid and is open to continuous re-interpretation. Serious interest in character formation began in 1725 with various philosophical treatises published by Francis Hutcheson on the virtues, followed in 1739 by the first volume of David Hume's *A Treatise of Human Nature* and then Adam Smith's *The Theory of Moral Sentiments* appearing in 1759 and 10 years later by Adam Ferguson's *History of Civil Society* in 1769. In between we have Thomas Reid's *Enquiry into the Human Mind* published in 1764 and in 1771 John Miller's *Observations on the Distinction of Rank*. They, and many others, sought to transform every branch of learning, but they never lost sight of their educational mission or their concern for the moral questions people face each day. The question for them was: how do human beings become moral beings? Specifically, in education two leading educational theorists of the Scottish Enlightenment ought to be mentioned: James Barclay who wrote a *Treatise in Education* in 1743 and David Fordyce who published *Dialogues Concerning Education* in 1745.

There were many 18th-century thinkers who advocated training in character and believed that the moral rather than intellectual aims of education were the most important. James Barclay, for instance, urged that teachers should only be selected for the role if they had strong characters, as he considered that the example they set was crucial. As he said: 'Example is allowed to be stronger than precept, and children especially are much readier to copy what they see than what they hear' (Hutchison, 1976). Barclay's ideas were strikingly modern, including his opposition to rote learning and the importance he placed on the consideration of the influence of a child's home on its educational progress. Another Scot, David Fordyce, spoke of developing the child's imagination in moral matters and wrote that 'dull, formal lectures on several virtues and vices' were of no use in the formation of good character. Francis Hutcheson, professor of moral philosophy at the University of Glasgow in 1747, advocated greater study of character. He sought to 'search accurately into the constitution of our nature to see what sort of creatures we are' (ibid.). What was needed, he argued, was an objective study of human nature, particularly motives and behaviour. John Locke also believed that character formation was more important than intellectual attainment, as did many others.

Adam Smith (1723–90) discusses specific virtues in *The Theory of Moral Sentiments* and in *The Wealth of Nations*. It is said that he spoke in the vocabulary of character (Griswold, 1999: 358) and that character for him entailed the virtues of self-command, benevolence, prudence and justice with self-command seen as an element in every virtue. His idea of prudence was not the same as Aristotle's, but character formation is a continuous theme in his books. Habits are emphasised and parents and family are identified as the first educators. He was opposed to boarding schools, but he has a notion of 'middling' moral virtues – not elite perfectionist ones (Griswold, 1999: 13). However, Smith selectively endorses Aristotle, and much of his ethical theory consists in discussion of specific virtues and the characters who embody them. His study of virtue could be said to represent an effort to demonstrate how 'corruption' can be ameliorated by 'virtue' (Hanley, 2009: 5). Smith's ethics was effectively a replacement of Aristotelian ethics and Christian morality with 'a new type of decision-making which may be termed instrumental reasoning or cost-benefit analysis' (Wooton, 2018: 5). Wooton (2018: 7) goes on to suggests that 'for Aristotle, prudence enables one to become virtuous: for Smith, it enables one to become successful'.

Smith develops an idea of circles of sympathy and care, beginning with the family which, he believes promotes love. It is this intense love that the family ought to provide in order for the child to develop a sense of self. The second circle is friendship among peers and the third is fidelity by discharging your duties in particular employment roles in society. He believed that we expand our moral selves by means of these various attachments which help us build our character. Accordingly, the older a child grows the more important outside influences are on their character. Like Aristotle, Smith would have agreed that it is difficult to replace or supply the foundations of the family if it is absent. Both would have agreed that the family is also not perfect. Religion, he felt, was not simply about suppressing selfish passions and emotions; Griswold (1999: 212) writes: 'One discerns in the background a critique of an excessively religious moral education that would treat certain emotions as though they were the enemy within.' Role modelling or moral exemplars were crucial to character building and he believed that good character formation teaches us to think and judge better. Above all, Smith believed that the formation of right character is greatly affected by society's institutions (Griswold, 1999: 273). Virtues were to be good for the community and for the person who possessed them, but Smith was largely hostile to the reduction of ethics to self-interest.

David Hume (1711–76) makes frequent reference to character throughout his works and Mahoney (2009) has written that it was a significant concept for Hume even though he used it ambiguously and failed to define it. Hume was not optimistic about significant changes in character development and this caused some of his followers to believe that he 'denies the possibility of character change' (Ainslie, 2007: 106). But this would be to overstate his position. Hume speaks of the progress of sentiments and the inculcation of morality and believed that character was the cause of actions and therefore that it had a practical function. He wanted to strengthen the moral sentiments of children so he was open to the possibility of character formation. Hume believed that certain impressions are habitually and formally inculcated into us by education. His morality was practical in nature and he is more interested in how we recognise and evaluate character than in how we are formed in virtuous character – a focus on evaluation over deliberation. Hume called the virtues 'qualities of mind' and believed that these reliably cause us to perform actions characteristic of the traits – a moral view that gives us a compelling and consistent reason to do the virtuous thing. He believed that someone could strengthen their moral sentiments into settled principles of action. For Hume, morality was a practical activity which naturally influences human actions. He wrote of 'the great force of custom and education, which mould the human mind from infancy, and form it into a fixed and established character'. Following Aristotle, he clearly believed that the process of socialisation demanded the inculcation of virtuous habits. However, he conceived human passion as the material of moral character since it is passion, he asserted, and not reason, that moves the moral agent to action. He had a broad understanding of the virtues as a kind of utility and classified them into four separate categories: (1) useful to self: i.e. wisdom, patience and judgement; (2) useful to others: i.e. gratitude, justice and truthfulness; (3) agreeable to self: i.e. good manners and wit; (4) agreeable to others (i.e. courage, dignity and humility). In order for character to form and be effective in social life you required a balance of these virtues.

Hume understood that stable character was formed by habituation and custom and could be observed in social interaction. Character formation was essential if ethical living was not to be evaded by luxury. He emphasised the importance of sociability and believed that it was acquired through social interactions. Character could not exist outside society as character could be observed, gained or lost by poor behaviour – it was treated as a kind of currency (Ahnert and Manning, 2011: 2). The debate about sociability moved beyond academia and into sermons, novels and conversations of the people, becoming a call to turn morality into a matter of conduct, where civil society helped produce character. It also meant that there was little need for divine providence in ethics and sociability. A secularisation of character had begun and Hume's idea of moral character looks very much like that of the English bourgeoisie he attempted to emulate (see Langford, 2000). However, Hume's main contribution to the idea and problematic nature of character formation is contained in his distinction between descriptive and prescriptive statements as found in his *Treatise on Human Understanding*. Descriptive statements involve assertions of what is or is not the case while prescriptive statements involve assertions of what ought or ought not to be done. Hume made the point – in which he is not entirely incorrect – that the former type of statement cannot provide us with adequate grounds for validly reaching a conclusion that is of the same nature as the latter type of statement. It means that many philosophers continue to hold the view that questions of moral character are entirely subjective and relative, reducing moral judgements to mere opinion. In summary, O'Brien (2018: 163) wrote: 'Hume's account of virtue is grounded in our sympathetic appreciation of the useful and aggreeable effects that various character traits have on ourselves and others.' There has been endless discussion of Hume's points of distinction between 'is' and 'ought' and one of the best at addressing this issue in a straightforward manner is Mortimer Adler's (1985) *Ten Philosophical Mistakes*.

Central to this new Enlightenment movement was the fundamental importance attached to reason together with the rejection of all authority that could not be justified by reason. The focus was on scientific thinking, observation and experimentation that was free and critical. Many Enlightenment thinkers were not content to accept appeals to Aristotle's authority or Christian beliefs, particularly in the realm of character and conduct. This inevitably led to widely differing views on character and conduct that were not constrained by traditional modes of thinking. An ethic of national improvement arose and a sense of basic solidarity which was understood as essential to human existence. This created a kind of social movement with a practical orientation, which meant that individual autonomy was less important than service to society. Character formation was seen through the eyes of 'sociability', of useful knowledge and practical skills. It was believed that character existed within society and was dependent on civic relations with others for its authentic formation. The conscious actions of human beings together could improve individuals and society. Understandings and interpretations of character formation were gleaned from common everyday practice and behaviour and consequently ranged widely in definition. Virtuous behaviour was judged by the degree to which it produced useful and happy citizens with good dispositions. How people make moral decisions was a key concern for them, but they tended to avoid making statements about what these moral judgements should be.

The leaders of the Scottish Enlightenment saw themselves as 'enlightened' when contrasted with those who held orthodox religious faith, but they retained belief in the authority of revelation in the Bible and Church. They remained part of the established Protestant Church and indeed some like Hutcheson, Reid and Ferguson were clergymen. It is important to understand this movement within the context of a Calvinist conception of moral identity. Almost every child in Scotland from the 17th century would have learned from the *Shorter Catechism* in Church and school, that 'the moral law is summarily comprehended in the ten commandments' (Stewart-Robertson, 1981). This catechism was commonly held to have formed the national character and the 'cast of the Scottish mind' (Anderson, 1995: 149). The Scottish Protestant Church held a concern for human morality and was part of a distinct religio-philosophical tradition of thought on matters of character and conduct (see Appendix H). The moderate wing of this Church was nevertheless entangled with this 'enlightened' new thinking and indeed upheld many of the tenets of the Scottish Enlightenment (Kidd, 2016, 339). The Church took a more secular turn in relation to questions of moral formation. There was a growing idea that the ethical was primarily practical and designed to improve the 'middling' citizens. As Ahnert (2015) observed there was an emergence of a less theological and more ethically orientated Protestantism: a move from doctrine to moral conduct that saw a belief in moral regeneration without the assistance of divine interventions. An ethics that was more ethical than biblical and that attempted to demystify religion by opening it up to rational scrutiny without necessarily being anti-religious.

While the vitality and intellectual horizons of these Scottish thinkers knew no bounds, collectively rejecting abstract metaphysics and utopian worldviews, they clearly remained part of the Scottish establishment engaging in society and

90 Foundations

the politics of the time. They, according to Jacob (2019), collectively opened up a new mental space in which to encounter the world on its own terms – effectively emphasising reason over religion. They inherited a Protestant anti-Catholicism which they attempted to rationalise while proclaiming the virtues of tolerance. Catholic practice and thought was not tolerated on the grounds that it was barbarous, superstitious and feudal. This bigotry was deeply engrained in Scottish culture and formed part of the Protestant mind-set. It led to a complete rejection of Catholic virtues such as celibacy, fasting, penance, mortification, sacrifice, self-denial, silence, solitude, and other so-called 'monkish virtues'. Hume, in his *Enquiry Concerning the Principles of Morals* thought them to be vices because they served no purpose, 'neither advance a man's fortune in the world, nor render him a more valuable member of society'. Adam Smith said exactly the same in his *Theory of Moral Sentiments* when he spoke of the 'futile mortifications of the monastery'. Hume and Smith were articulating an ethical vocabulary for a commercial society and yet Smith noted that 'the delicate sensibility required in civilised nations sometimes destroys the masculine firmness of the character', while Hume thought that 'modern politeness' could involve affectation, foppery, disguise and insincerity (cited in Thomas, 2018: 298 and 303), but it certainly meant good manners and refined conversation. It is interesting that Siedentop (2014: 350) notes that these Enlightened thinkers sought to minimise the moral and intellectual distance between the modern world and the ancient world, while maximising the moral and intellectual distance between modern Scotland and the Middle Ages. They understood the ancient world as secular, with citizens free from religious oppression. This conclusion is inconsistent with the historical record as antiquity was an age of deep superstition, strong religious belief, sexism, racism and elitism – the ancient world was not some shining ideal of social perfection. Siedentop (2014: 352) reminds us of the deeply religious nature of these times and of what he calls the 'moral enclosure' of classical Athens – 'in which the limits of personal identity were established by the limits of physical association and inherited, unequal social roles. This moral enclosure is illustrated by the Greek term describing anyone who sought to live outside such associations and such roles: such a person was called an idiot.'

The Augustinian understanding of the State limited its scope and powers, restricting its role to keeping order. The role of imparting morals or virtues in building the character of the people was previously considered the preserve of the Catholic Church – only the Church could inculcate goodness. The Reformation changed this by allying with the secular State in questions of public virtue. The Scottish Parliament, while the country was still Catholic in religion, had passed the first Education Act in the world in 1496 which made education compulsory for all first sons of Barons and substantial landowners from the age of eight or nine to study Latin, arts and the law – a liberal education. This Catholic culture was influenced by Italian Renaissance humanism and allowed these secular subjects in the existing grammar schools of Scotland. However, the Protestant Reformation produced the *First Book of Discipline* which decreed that every parish should establish a parish school and the Privy Council passed the Schools Establishment Act in 1616 to establish parish schools in Scotland. Subsequently the Scottish Parliament itself passed the Education Acts of 1633 and 1646 to enforce it with another 'Act for Setting Schools' in 1696. The goal was clearly to instil Protestant purity into the minds of young Scots and this constituted the background to all the prominent thinkers of the Scottish Enlightenment. The Calvinists, believing as they did in the supreme importance of Scripture, stressed the idea of literacy as essential to the truly enlightened life – the printed page itself was a source of divine grace.

The leaders of the Scottish Enlightenment were the establishment of their day, held political and civic authority and publicly professed their Protestant faith. Many of the key figures knew each other well, both professionally and socially and they established clubs and societies, mainly based in the university towns of Edinburgh, Glasgow and Aberdeen. These clubs were characterised by their cross-disciplinary focus and in Edinburgh, a private philosophical society, the Select Society, was established in 1754 to debate topical issues once a week and included members such as Hume and Smith. Debates on the moral character of the people and whether virtues and morality could be made consistent with commerce were held (see Jacob, 2019: 135–6). However, the Scottish Enlightenment had its own internal contradictions. A new way of thinking and approaching character formation arose that was more instrumental and related to social mobility than anything previously seen. Utilitarian ends as a way of getting on in the world and achieving social and financial success became a prominent concern, which is why there was much discussion about manners and politeness rather than simply virtue. Erasmus had previously seen good manners as a sign of inner virtue, but now appearances were becoming everything. There was rightly a focus on the effective exercise of the virtues since manners were once seen as the outward expression of moral character. Indeed, you could go as far to say that there was an avoidance of the traditional discourse on virtue in favour of personal development and manners. Manners came to be seen as a branch of morality and yet Joseph Addison adopted a restricted view when he wrote in 1711 that 'by manners, I do not mean morals, but behaviour and good breeding' (see Thomas, 2018: 15).

There were clearly tensions about what manners meant, but still, as Langford (2000: 8) says: 'Character expressed itself in what was called manners, a term of wider extent and more fruitful ambiguity than it is today.' Porter (2000: 54) summed up the Scottish Enlightenment views on this in saying: 'Our most fundamental character as Human Beings, they argued, even our moral character, is constantly evolving and developing, shaped by a variety of forces over which we as individuals have little or no control. We are ultimately creatures of our environment'. God was not excluded, but was perhaps pushed to the periphery with the new confidence in the belief that human beings could achieve their own good with that good being immanent and self-evident. There was

92 Foundations

certainly a self-referential tone in the writings of the Scottish Enlightenment thinkers and an emphasis on the intrinsic worth of the person. Protestantism assisted this move by viewing Christianity in a more secular fashion, focusing more on moralism, duty and self-interest. Human beings had the capacity and responsibility to re-shape the world through a disciplined life which helps create a disciplined society. Some, however, retained the Protestant idea that self-improvement requires God's intervention through grace and remained concerned that the new teachings might undermine the doctrine of salvation by grace through faith.

The Scottish Enlightenment was a period of civic optimism, liberal and progressive thinking and above all of self-improvement chiefly advocated through moral self-governance. Education was seen as a vehicle for both individual improvement and social cohesion. Conceptual changes arose around the concepts of character and virtue during this period as they acquired new meanings and understandings. The aim was to identify those desirable traits embedded by nature in all of humankind and consider what forces were conducive to their establishment and development. There were endless enquiries into how human beings become moral beings, but the Enlightenment leaders avoided writing about utopian aims in education. There was much talk about taste, manners, civility and politeness in the clubs and societies in Edinburgh. The virtues were seen through a more instrumental lens as being socially useful in producing citizens with a focus on the practical concerns of living in community. Utilitarian ends as a way of getting on in the world and achieving social success were emphasised. James Burgh's *Thoughts on Education* of 1747 gives something of this instrumental flavour, but Hugh Murray's *Enquiries Historical and Moral: Respecting the character of nations and the progress of society*, published in 1808, speaks about how society itself can improve the character of a people. Daniel Dewar (1812: 1) a few years later in 1812 argued that the leaders of the Scottish Enlightenment believed that using a scientific approach to studying character was the best way to build the character of people and make them happy. There was a real obsession about the national character of other countries, seen through numerous historical studies to discover whether other cultures produce particular types of individual character. These studies were inspired by Hume's essay 'On National Character' of 1748 from which modern racism emerged and led to attempts to demonstrate the superiority of one culture or race over another.

The Scottish Enlightenment leaders were well versed in Aristotelian ethics, but they saw virtues differently. As we have seen, Aristotle saw virtues as constitutive of a flourishing life which meant having a virtuous character and acting in accordance with it is what it is to flourish as a human being. Virtue, in this view, is its own reward. This constitutive view of the relationship between virtue and flourishing is defended by appeals to a conception of human nature according to which a virtuous character is the most perfect expression of that nature. Aristotle's idea of character virtues contains the notion of objective principles of moral goodness that are rooted in satisfying the needs of human nature. The activity of politics was to promote the perfection of citizens, but the Scottish Enlightenment thinkers believed this to be too utopian an ideal as it depended on controversial arguments about human nature and a teleological worldview that did not fit with enlightened liberal or scientific ideas. For the Scottish Enlightenment virtues were to be instrumental to a person's own flourishing and character. The leaders began to replace the idea that virtue was of itself inherently good for people with the promotion of the idea that virtue embodied an instrumental good. In character formation, the teaching of virtues was to be instrumentally justified by appeal to the effects on others' flourishing or 'improvement'. They were not content to accept appeals to Aristotelian authority and rejected some of Aristotle's assumptions about human nature and the contemplative life – they ignored ultimate concerns in favour of concrete problems and solutions. Industry and frugality were emphasised by the Scots, but Aristotle would not have counted them as virtues as they had instrumental qualities that you would perhaps look for in a craftsman (see Wooton, 2018: 7).

These enlightened Scots also believed that improvement required middle-class exemplars, as their principal concern remained the 'middling' classes in society. According to Porter (2000: 339), 'the model of an enlightened person was the educated adult, presumed affluent, independent – and male'. Many of them thought that they lived in a backward society which gave rise to an almost obsessive concern for 'improvement' of the individual and society. They also accepted the Church's control over education even when they considered the theological claims of the Church to be philosophically discredited. This contrasted sharply with the leaders of the French Enlightenment who were more secular and certainly more anti-clerical. Their aim was explicit: to create good people and good citizens without the intervention of religion. The Scottish Enlightenment was not entirely secular in orientation and certainly not overtly anti-religion, so it did not secularise character completely, but it initiated that process.

The Scots sought to turn the study of character into a science through 'progressive principles' which would 'refine and exult human nature' (Murray, 1808: 24 and 27). As Alexander Bain (1861) said of the leaders of the Scottish Enlightenment, 'our most fundamental character as human beings, they agreed, even our moral character, is constantly evolving and developing, shaped by a variety of forces over which we as individuals have little or no control. We are ultimately creatures of our environment.' While there were disagreements about what constituted character, in the main you could summarise the Scottish Enlightenment thought on character and the virtues as 'a set of qualities and moral values developed and displayed in social relationships, through idioms of politeness, by people imbued with finely tuned sentiments and the capacity for identification with others' (Mack, 1941: 125). Perhaps a more detailed explanation and summary might be the following:

1   A scientific study of human nature and character emphasising that science is an ethical enterprise with a close relationship between the moral and social self with ethical decisions taken in a social context.

94 Foundations

2   A more instrumental view of the social usefulness of virtues which comprised a view of character as self-improvement – human nature is improvable.

3   A move towards a secular view of character by separating character from theological virtues without rejecting a role for Christianity – this separation of reason from religion was key to the Enlightenment.

4   A more progressive and humane understanding of human nature that results in a view of education as being able to live well as cultivated, educated, and active citizens of society.

5   A dislike of utopian ideas of character such a Christianity's idea of the need for God's grace or the Aristotelian idea of human excellences – a rejection of teleology.

6   Solidarity was made the basis of human existence, with greater interest in national characters than individual character and hence a greater role for the State in promoting virtue.

7   The good became whatever one estimates will benefit the greatest number – a philosophy of utility.

The Scottish Enlightenment developed a broad view of character and virtues which was certainly more ethical than religious, even though Reid supported a Christian view of character. It was a view of ethics that could be taught and lived, with character defined as an individual's commitment to an achievable and utilitarian plan of life. It set the stage for a move from a prescriptive notion of character formation to one that was more descriptive, as Solomon (2018: 314) says: 'The Enlightenment Project was the attempt by moral philosophers to construct arguments for received moral rules and virtues based simply on the features of "man as he happens to be". Rules and virtues, intended in classical ethics to transform human agents, were reconceived after the loss of teleology as being derived from features of human agents as they are – and, thus, as losing their transformative power. What was supposed to be remedial became ... merely descriptive.' However, it also provided little in the way to adjudicate between rival ways of life as the virtues became largely a question of individual choice. Character formation had moved to self-fulfilment rather than the older idea of self-denial, and became more about self-assertion than self-examination. There was a belief that unencumbered by community and tradition one could engage in self-formation and self-improvement. It naturally led to the Liberal idea of self-perfection through education and the free exercise of choice. It also led to the idea that we can predict and control the future of humankind by accumulating and interpreting hard observable facts.

Towards the end of the 17th century, there was a pronounced shift in Protestant European apologetic from an emphasis on theological doctrine to moral conduct as the true measure of religious belief. It is the story of the emergence of a 'liberal', confessionally non-aligned and ethically oriented species of Protestant Christianity, sometimes known as 'slavish correction with the whip' (see

Lawson and Silver, 1973: 150). The Scottish Enlightenment is clearly associated with the rise of the social sciences and it rejected the contemplative ideal of Aristotle in favour of a stress on observation, prediction, control, measurement and mathematical modelling – all of which has been hugely influential in the modern world. These enlightened thinkers attempted to build a moral science of humanity as moral thought and feeling were to be understood through observable phenomena. They believed that no aspect of human life could resist the power of scientific scrutiny and in this they were in effect building on the 15th-century Renaissance thinkers. These 18th-century Scottish thinkers had their own critics, particularly in the form of the conservative thinker Edmund Burke (1729–97) who rejected the Enlightenment view that human beings are entirely rational entities. Burke believed that any attempt to create a system based upon the perfectibility of humankind is contrary to our innate character. He also refused to accept that technical experts were best placed to guide us in character formation and preferred instead the inherent wisdom in common-sense values or what he called the 'wisdom of unlettered men'.

McIntyre (1984: 55) concluded that this Enlightenment project failed because it was incoherent. He says: 'the eighteenth-century moral philosophers engaged in what was an inevitably unsuccessful project; for they did indeed attempt to find a rational basis for their moral beliefs in a particular under-standing of human nature, while inheriting a set of moral injunctions on the one hand and a conception of human nature on the other which had been expressly designed to be discrepant with each other.' The Scottish Enlighten-ment abandoned Aristotle's overarching idea of the human good in favour of a new moral character based on science and rationality. In the place of a trans-cendent God the Enlightenment focused on the world transformed by human reason guiding human action – a world characterised by progress and increasing rationality. In conclusion, it is worth considering further the important connec-tions between Protestantism in Scotland and the formation of character from a historical sociological perspective. The Scottish Enlightenment, according to Grey (2018: 57f) produced strong anti-Catholic, anti-Irish and racist currents in modern thought.

Max Webber (1904) conceptualised the Protestant ethic as a cultural force that exerted a general influence upon people's social behaviour and character development. Religion, according to Weber, influences who we become and the virtues it promotes endure across groups and across generations. He under-stood that religion influences a wide range of social conduct. The Protestant ethic was understood as a unique set of moral beliefs about the virtues of hard work focused on material success and entrepreneurial initiative and interpreted as God's reward. The Scottish cultural context during the Enlightenment period was influenced by Calvinism and the Enlightenment thinkers were educated in a culture infused with Calvinistic thought. This Calvinistic thought shaped the nation, its culture and education system, institutions and economic activity and the character of the people. The Calvinism of which we speak was comprised of a harsh ascetic discipline together with an extreme legalism and rationalised theory of action which produced unrealistically high standards for moral conduct. It also produced a culture of moralism, intolerance and an intense lust to judge and persecute others. The Scots were eager to enforce disciplinary measures for those who failed in these standards through laws and legislation as well as the penalties of Church censures, excommunication or social ostracism. This Bible-based character formation certainly influenced the Victorian period that we address below. The sociologist Overman (2011: 57) provides us with a way to understand the connections with character formation in his description of what he calls, after apologising to Thomas Aquinas, the 'Seven Cardinal Virtues of the Protestant Ethic': worldly asceticism, rationalisation, goal-directed behaviour, achieved status, individualism, work ethic and time ethics – none of these being classic virtues.

The first Protestant 'virtue' he calls 'worldly asceticism' which he describes as self-control, self-discipline and a fear of sensual pleasure. Only hard work meets the requirements for redemption in this Calvinist world view. The character so formed is one that represses bodily pleasures. Second, rationalisation refers to calculation, measurement and standardisation which were certainly themes in the Scottish Enlightenment. This so-called virtue was about control over the material world and Overman (2011: 63) believes that it 'led to a form of instrumentalism that would manifest itself on both the personal and organisational levels as goal-directed behaviour. The Protestants' quest to find salvation through rational conduct led to the subjugating of means over ends in ways that radically reshaped motives for social conduct.'

Third, goal-directed behaviour is about everything in life being done or motivated for some external goal – that you did not do anything for its own sake. For example, Webber (1904: 52) believed that 'honesty is useful because it assures credit; so are punctuality, industry, and frugality, and that is the reason why they are virtues'. Fourth, achieved status was attained among the elect of God through hard work and material success, which resulted in social elitism and exclusivity. Achieved status had the tendency to present the rich as justifiably wealthy and the poor as unworthy of better treatment. Fifth, individualism placed an emphasis on individual initiative, individual choice, individual responsibility, individual achievement and individual rights that obviously led to disagreements and schism. Sixth, the work ethic or lives devoted to work are seen as discipline and intrinsic reward, but these resulting virtues eclipsed other virtues in that charity and justice were made the servants of economic profit. Finally, there is time ethic, which relates to having the right kind of consciousness. The Scottish Calvinists and Enlightenment thinkers prided themselves on being right, but living well is often exhausted by being right. All of these socalled virtues led to a Spartan ideal of life together with a rationalisation of behaviour. It led to the beginning of the secularisation of the virtues as seen in the writings of the Scottish Enlightenment thinkers. The influence on character formation was undoubtedly significant, but it would take another book to explore Overman's interesting thesis, as it relates to character formation. However, Charles Dickens perhaps best captures this type of Calvinist character in his creation of Scrooge, who was not simply a hoarder, but rather his avarice is a result of his secularised Calvinist work ethic – that is devoid of charity and love.

The Scottish Enlightenment is not really a historical period, but a movement of thought whose influence still operates today. It turned away from many, but not all, of the Aristotelian conceptions of character formation by focusing more on the rights and duties of the individual as well as the usefulness of the virtues for practical living. It was characterised by a belief in the power of moral progress to improve character and human society through self-direction – the social utility of self-improvement and virtuous sociability being prioritised. Dugald Stewart (1753–1828), who was Professor of Moral Philosophy at the University of Edinburgh between 1785 and 1810, is often characterised as the last of the moral philosophers of the Scottish Enlightenment. Bow (2013: 207) credits him with producing a 'modern and practical system of moral education' the purpose of which Stewart says was 'to ascertain the general rules of a wise and virtuous conduct in life'. This was to be found in examining the principles of the human condition 'in the circumstances in which man is placed' (as quoted in Bow, 2013: 207). Stewart believed that those who developed the intellectual virtues possessed moral character as the ability to reason always co-existed with moral virtues which appears to go back to Plato (see Tannoch-Bland, 1997: 310). He saw character in the following statements: character does not seek public approval; good character is most authentic when a person is unaware that people approve of their character; and character that acts rightly is its own reward (Bow, 2013: 216). Aristotle would have endorsed these statements particularly when Stewart observed that 'the happiness of individuals depends very much on fixed principles [and] the characters of the greatest part of the men are formed by the influence of Education, Situation or Example' (Bow, 2013: 223). Education was clearly conceived as a means to ensure moral progress and improve the condition of mankind. There is no doubt that the idea of character received extensive and perhaps unprecedented treatment during the Scottish Enlightenment. Character as an ideal was a preoccupation of moral philosophers and Scot's generally as attention was shifted gradually away from religious questions towards secular ones.

The predominant models during this period included liberal-republican, conservative, virtue theory and theological, but there was a clear emergence of a more liberal approach with some distinct neo-liberal tendencies. Character which was once explained by religious principles was now explained by physical science or the emerging studies of the social sciences.

Section II

Practices

Chapter 6

The English public school and character formation

Public schools were first established to educate relatively poor boys in the classics, so the word 'public' meant available to the public. However, by the late 19th century the 'public' in English public school had come to mean private. English public schools also became intimately connected with the idea of character formation. This connection with the quality of character training reached almost mystical proportions and was certainly extravagantly praised (see Shrosbree, 1988: 8). As Gathorne-Hardy (1979: 85) noted, the English public school was seen: 'as a place to train character – a totally new concept so far – was what came to distinguish the English public school from all other Western school systems. It is what amazed and impressed foreigners – and amazes them still.' McCulloch (1991: 14) speaks of an English tradition of the classical and character curriculum that produced a sense of purpose and common attitude and which 'fostered a code of values'. These schools were essentially places to form the governing class and were transmitters of what was accepted as English culture. McCulloch (1991: 11), echoing Thomas Arnold, saw it as fostering a moral esprit de corps that was produced by a classical curriculum, training in character, communal living, and public service, but which was class-based and gender-specific. All of these key characteristics of school life could be traced back to the later Middle Ages.

As Trollope (1865) commented of his own education:

> There we learnt to be honest, true and brave. There we were trained to disregard the softness of luxury, and to love the hardihood and dangers of violent exercise. There we became men: and we became men after such a fashion that we are feared and loved, as may be, but always respectable – even though it is in spite of our ignorance. Who can define the nobility that has attached itself to Englishmen as the result of their public schools; or can say whence it comes, or in what it consists?

Trollope was of course speaking about character and it was a largely unconscious formation which emphasised 'manliness of character' and enabled them to do 'the right thing' in any situation through obedience, acceptance of role,

102 Practices

team spirit, loyalty (Richards, 1988: 13) and 'a manly straightforward character' (Darwin, 1929: 21). These schools attempted to mould their students into a recognisable type – the 'manly' man. They were principally focused on changing the character and the body of their students and it was through discipline and punishments that character was to be formed. However, the first half of the 19th century saw no emphasis on character formation in these schools and even Trollope found the experience extreme and considered committing suicide at Winchester as a boy (see Martin, 2018: 39). There was clearly a dark side to public schooling.

You could say that the public school in the early part of the 19th century reflected the English aristocracy's values whose world, according to Richards (1988: 9) was one of 'hard drinking, ruinous gambling, horse racing, blood sports and prize fighting'. Public schools in this period were effectively run by the students and according to Chandos (1984) their education consisted largely of street fighting, poaching and rioting. It was a harsh and undisciplined world that fathers willingly sent their sons to experience as they believed it prepared them for the wicked world that lay ahead for them. It produced survivors, characters of a type, but not virtuous character. These public schools were in a shocking state with caning and flogging being daily occurrences and there was a feeling that the aristocracy had become decadent. Allsop (1965) identified three themes that were common 'cruelty, conformity and homosexuality'. In an article written in the *Edinburgh Review* of 1810 Sydney Smith, himself a product and former Captain of the School at Winchester College, noted that the public-school system was marked by 'abuse, neglect and vice' and he concluded that it resulted in 'premature debauchery that only prevents men from being corrupted by the world by corrupting them before they enter the world' (see Chandos, 1984: 37). The *Edinburgh Review* launched a series of attacks on English public schools throughout the 19th century focusing on the financial corruption of the teachers, the poor teaching of the classics and the immorality experienced by the students. There was certainly a culture of extreme physical violence that included bullying and intimidation in these schools. The *Edinburgh Review* believed that the ancient languages were taught in the public schools as a badge of gentlemanly education rather than as useful subjects.

Sexual promiscuity was indeed widespread and John Addington Symonds (1840–93), a 13-year-old student at Harrow in the 1850s, wrote vividly in his autobiography that:

> One thing at Harrow very soon arrested my attention. It was the moral state of the school. Every boy of good looks had a female name and was recognised either as a public prostitute or as some bigger fellow's bitch. Bitch was the word in common usage to indicate a boy who yielded his person to another. The talk in the studies and dormitories was incredibly obscene. One could not avoid seeing acts of onanism, mutual masturbation and the sport of naked boys in bed together. There was no refinement, no

English public school and character formation 103

sentiment, no passion, nothing but animal lust in these occurrences. They filled me with disgust and loathing.

(Addington Symonds, 1984: 94)

He believed Harrow exercised a powerful influence over his formation and commented that 'the distinction in my character between an inner and real self and an outer and artificial self . . . emphasised itself during this period'. Chandos (1984: 30) quotes a number of contemporaries, such as Henry Fielding, who concluded that these schools were the nurseries of vice and immorality. Mack, (1941: 126) does not recognise this picture and seems to say it was held in check, but he writes of the latter half of the century: 'More widespread than pride in money, and indeed assuming the proportions of a real menace, was homosexuality . . . this vice began to sprout dangerously in the atmosphere of regimented manliness which prevailed in the late Victorian school.' It is interesting that the Rev. T. C. Fry, headmaster of Oundle in 1883, produced a list of rules to stop homosexual activity in the school (Martin, 2018: 56). In 1881 The Rev. J. M. Wilson gave a speech titled 'Morality and the Public School' (Renton, 2017: 220) which began the first public debate about sex education in schools.

Children's books were popular throughout Victorian Britain and were largely designed for self-improvement, meaning character formation. They variously emphasised virtues of a particular kind and were didactic in tone insinuating moral truths in each story. At the start of the century the approach to children's literature was dominated by the approach of Samuel Butler the novelist who saw a father's first duty as one of coercion: 'checking the first signs of self-will while the children were too young to offer serious resistance. If their wills were "well broken" in childhood . . . they would acquire habits of obedience which they would not venture to break through till they were over twenty-one years old' (cited in Turner, 1989: 7). He more accurately reflects his own strict evangelical upbringing by his father. However, with the growing interest in psychology and an increasing willingness to listen and be sympathetic to the child's point of view William Lecky the essayist wrote in 1969: 'there is a method of education which was never more prevalent than in the present day, which exhausts its efforts in making virtue attractive, in associating it with all the charms of imagination and of prosperity, and in thus insensibly drawing the desires in the wished-for direction' (Turner, 1989: 8). This led to story books that were less about moralising, but the use of Greek myths in schools was attacked by Nathaniel Hawthorne who described them as 'brimming with everything that is most abhorrent to our Christianised moral sense'. It was Charles Kingsley who gave the Greek myths a Christian meaning and understanding thereby saving them from disappearing from schools (Turner, 1989: 414).

F. W. Farrar wrote a series of popular novels about public school life in the mid-19th century which reveal that bullying, drinking, smoking, gambling, dishonesty and bad language were rife – he makes no reference to sexual vices of the time (see Jamison, 1968: 272). He saw boys as morally corrupt and possessing

104   Practices

an almost instinctive cruelty and he believed that schools were a difficult place to secure virtue. Farrar was a teacher, and later Headmaster of Marlborough, but set his moral standards impossibly high in his novels, which were full of moral exhortations. The *Edinburgh Review* was critical of Farrar's novels, claiming that Farrar made a false link between religious obligations and the routine life of the ordinary schoolboy. That he made saints of the boys in his novels in order to moralise about them (Jamison, 1968: 276). Lord Ashley (later the Earl of Shaftesbury) commented on Eton in 1844: 'I fear Eton . . . It makes admirable gentlemen and finished scholars – fits a man a man, beyond all competition, for the dining-room, the Club, St. James's Street, and all the mysteries of social elegance; but it does not make the man required for the coming generation. We must have nobler, deeper, and sterner stuff; less of refinement and more of truth; more of the inward, not so much of the outward, gentlemen' (cited in Tosh, 2002: 456). The claim is that it produced men who lived for appearances. The English public school was essentially about conduct and manners, status and appearance, reputation and social expectation. Like the leaders of the Scottish Enlightenment they prized the civilising effects of good company and placed a high value on the arts of conversation (see Tosh, 2002: 460). It was marked by social exclusiveness for the elite, and the *Edinburgh Review*'s (1858: 190) claim that these schools lacked real moral purpose was justified. The author of these critical articles in the *Edinburgh Review* was the controversialist Sir James Fitzjames Stephen, a former student of Eton who loathed his time there and continually attacked the idea of 'muscular Christianity'.

By the 1830s evangelicalism, with its serious mind-set, coupled with the expansion of the middle class, began to change the purpose of the public school with more emphasis on character training. This process began with Samuel Coleridge's *Aids to Reflection in the Formation of Character* of 1825. While a theological work, it considered ethics from a Christian perspective, seeing manliness as concerned with moral action and building strength of character to resist temptation. He was critical of both secularism and theological liberalism which he believed weakened character. Coleridge inspired the movement towards muscular Christianity which was eagerly embraced by Arnold. Manliness was largely understood as possessing character and virtue (Park, 1987), but Vance (1975: 115) suggests a number of other interpretations. Under the influence of an evangelical revival it became a common subject of discussion and manliness became the description of a person's moral character. In fact, it was initially seen as matching noble birth with virtuous action but was soon viewed as replacing noble birth with virtuous action.

Evangelicalism became a movement for sobriety and rectitude in public schools and in Victorian society more generally. The public schools provided poor teaching and had lost the idea that a classical education had the power to breed character. However, Thomas Arnold at Rugby and Samuel Butler at Shrewsbury placed greater emphasis on moral character and attempted to restore a sense of control and moral purpose to their respective schools.

Gradually elite schooling replaced noble birth as the mark of the ruling class. Society in 19th-century Britain was acutely class conscious and children were viewed as miniature adults to be inducted into the ways of social convention. Character was viewed as a class-based concept which contained within it a judgement regarding an individual's status as much as their good conduct. The growing middle classes realised that money alone would not secure them the coveted status of the 'character of a gentleman'. Increasingly they sent their sons to the rapidly expanding number of independent schools. There was a marked revival of interest in character formation for middle-class children in the 1820s which began first in the reformed public schools mentioned above (Rothblatt, 1976: 133–4). Teachers overtook wider societal experience to become the main facilitators for this shaping of character. It was considered important that pupils developed strong characters from which they could take a principled stand, usually in favour of the established virtues of society. Stefan Collini (1985) identifies these Victorian virtues as including: bravery, loyalty, diligence, application and manners.

Thomas Arnold, the Headmaster of Rugby, gave voice to middle-class aspirations by emphasising that the educational ideal should be the production of the 'noble character', the 'man of character' or more precisely the Christian manly spirit, better known as 'muscular Christianity'. 'Manliness' meant the interior man, the inner man which defined character. Tosh (2002: 460) defines it as the independent man, the man of courage and the moral quality of honesty – the inner self being more important than social expectation. Manly character had to be earned and was essentially a feature of the mind with education drawing boys into a state of moral and intellectual maturity by suppressing the tendencies to vice within them. It was inspired by a theology of sin. Bamford (1967: 41) saw 'The purpose and the ideal of education was the good, open and full life coupled with a manly spirit. Manliness here was the conquest of weakness – weakness in the moral rather than the physical sense – and although this may possibly show on the playing field it must certainly be apparent in work and character.' Seeley (1885: 862 ff) recognised that the public schools formed character by grafting what he called 'moral earnestness' onto the 'old English manliness', but he felt that they did not 'favour originality of character' and that British character had become 'blurred and indistinct'. Arnold's aim at Rugby was no less than the formation of the Christian character in the young through this evangelical initiative, as he said to the boys: 'you are here brought to godliness and good learning'. As David Newsome (1961: 33) notes, it was a movement to re-unite religion and morality. Arnold made 'earnestness' his guiding principle in training for character, but he believed that character formation would only come through intellectual development. He attempted to inspire the students with a sense of duty to public service which he considered more important than good form.

There is no doubting Arnold's religious fervour – he would frequently break down in tears in front of the whole school on hearing the story of the Passion.

He was obsessed by sin, particularly the urge to sin which he believed boys especially feel and he used corporal punishment in an attempt to eradicate it. Arnold in one of his sermons said: 'Public schools are the very seats and nurseries of vice. It may be unavoidable, or it may not; but the fact is indisputable. None can pass through a large school without being pretty intimately acquainted with vice and few, alas!, very few, without tasting of that poisoned bowl' (Renton, 2017: 217). Arnold listed six deadly sins of school life in his sermons: profligacy, lying, cruelty, disobedience, idleness and bond. The last vice concerns student companionship to do evil and he considered this to be the greatest enemy of his efforts at reform. His weekly sermon was dedicated to explaining how to live a righteous life. The use of harsh punishments, inflicting pain and suffering on the boys appeared to have some inherent moral virtue and was certainly accepted as an educational virtue. Arnold reformed Rugby in the 1830s along explicitly moral lines and related the idea of manliness to character, but he still accepted the common Victorian idea that character needs to be tested and strengthened through a degree of adversity. The boys had to struggle and do battle to overcome temptation. His idea was to train the mind and character, but his successors as headmasters of the main public schools focused more on character and the body as they believed sport was a valuable means of character formation. The public school as a place for the explicit training of character was what came to distinguish the English public school from all other Western school systems. By the later part of the 19th century team games, which had been entirely at the initiative of the boys, were incorporated into the school curriculum (Holt, 2008: 121).

Thomas Hughes (1957 edition: 65), in *Tom Brown's School Days*, describes how after dropping Tom off at Rugby, his father reflects on his hopes for the outcomes of Tom's education: 'if he'll only turn out brave, helpful, truth-telling Englishman, and a gentleman, and a Christian, that's all I want.' The novel follows how Tom defeats the bully, Flashman, later the subject of a number of books by George McDonald Fraser, and gradually demonstrates the strength of character that wins him true friendship among his peers. Hughes (1957: 52) notes: 'The object of all schools is not to ram Latin and Greek into boys, but to make them good English boys, good future citizens.' Many Victorian novels provided a common and influential frame of morality that effectively set ideals and standards for the conduct and socialisation of boys. In this approach learning was secondary, acting and living primary, and it was through acting and living by the educational philosophy, i.e. character virtues of Rugby School, that the boys would become the miniature model of national society with their virtues shared throughout respectable society. Hughes believed that cricket and football were indispensable for character formation and praised the character forming values of team games (Armitage, 1952: 90). In contrast, Arnold idealised the potential for the manly hero to be developed rather than the athletic champion as he thought games played an auxiliary role in developing the strengths of character.

The idea that one's social environment helps shape character was the basis of Robert Owen's *Essays on the Formation of Character* of 1813. It is not surprising therefore that architecture was employed to form character with new buildings in the public schools 'intended to control behaviour and shape ideas, to exert influence and express identity' (Whyte, 2003: 604). Most schools turned to the mock medieval Gothic as the preferred style of building and to the monastic associations of the quadrangle and cloister with the school chapel built large in a prominent position. A headmaster declared that these buildings 'have the power to mould character' (Whyte, 2003: 604). For Edward Thring, headmaster of Uppingham in 1888, architecture had the power to shape behaviour as he said: 'The mere force of fine surroundings would make the low views and meanness connected with lessons and learning drop off' (Whyte, 2003: 618). It was believed that school buildings could, if designed well, combat disobedience, bad behaviour and vice and there is some truth in this even for school buildings today.

Supporters of Arnold were strong adherents of character formation. As well as instituting stern disciplinary regimes in their schools, they encouraged reading of selected great authors to discern the essential core of 'common' values. The Rev. G. G. Bradley, Headmaster of Marlborough College in evidence to the Taunton Commission (1868), which considered the endowed secondary schools (*Schools Enquiry Commission*, 1868: 420), wrote: 'I would give unusual weight to the teaching of English language, literature, and history, to attempt to humanise and refine a boy's mind by trying to familiarise him with English poetry, and to inspire him with the best authors whom I could place before him.' The teaching of the classics infiltrated their minds even if there was no practical application. They enhanced their social status. F. W. Farrar's *Essays on a Liberal Education* (1868) concluded that the classics did not result in good character and was generally critical of their use for character formation purposes. Mack (1941) argues that the moral took precedence over the intellectual. Literature was judged on its didactic power, its moral usefulness. The Clarendon Commission (1864: 56 ff), which reported on the nine principal public schools, found that among other virtues it was partially 'their love of healthy sport and exercise' that helped 'in moulding the character of the "English gentleman"'. There was a strong belief that games developed manliness and inspired, *inter alia*, the virtues of fairness, brotherhood, endurance, honour, self-restraint, loyalty, courtesy, moral and physical courage and co-operation. Games in the private schools were thus constituted as a course in ethics, and Mangan (1981: 9) reminds us that public school games became 'the wheel round which the moral values turned'. Edward Warre, sports master at Eton and later Headmaster, justified sports as an antidote to vice as he said he kept the boys busy and out of the way of temptation (see Vance, 1975: 122). H. H. Almond, the headmaster of Loretto School in Edinburgh, listed the aims of his school in 1862 as comprising: 'First – Character. Second – Physique. Third – Intelligence. Fourth – Manners. Fifth – Information (see Turner, 2015: 103). By information

108 Practices

he meant knowledge. Health was also central to character building – keeping fit through games playing, but the primary goal of sports was character development. As Park (1987: 17) says, great men possessed exceptional character and were vital to society because they showed the way. Games-playing became a cult – much in common with the Spartan and Athenian ideas of the purposes of sport (Dishon, 2017). Mangan (1998: 18) saw the virtues of games as inculcating robustness, perseverance and stoicism as the main instrument of training a boy's character. Kurt Hahn (1957) believed that character ought to be associated with 'physical rectitude' and 'moral probity' and he adopted many of Arnold's ideas to this end. Sport and team games, it was believed, helped to develop moral character (Haley, 1978) and for Mangan (1981) games-playing in public schools was accompanied by an endless stream of poems, rhymes and songs that were rife with the language and metaphor of self-sacrifice and character development. Mangan (1981: 9) believed that public schools had become obsessed with sports and that there was an excessive commitment to physical activity in order to form the character of those who would serve the Empire:

> Hark the Empire calls, and what we answer give?
> How to prove us worthy of the splendid trust?
> Lo! We serve the Empire by the lives we live;
> True in all our dealings, honesty, brave and just.
> Training mind and body for the Empire's need.

Mangan and Walvin (1987: 3) say that the idea and commitment to 'muscular Christianity' had become so exaggerated in the schools that 'muscle' was more important than Christianity, making the attainment of Christian character elusive.

The public schools also socialised young men into the habit of good manners. In this view character was a form of social and moral capital and the function of the school was to provide the right environment in which the 'right' people could, at an early stage, get to know one another. The upright stance of the Victorian gentleman seemed to provide the external confirmation of an acquired well-formed character. It often amounted to little more than the visible sign of conformity to a set of public virtues, revealing nothing of any inner moral qualities. In this sense manners were a façade for character, which is well captured by Jane Austen in her *Pride and Prejudice* when she wrote: 'There is certainly some great mismanagement in the education of these two young mem. One has got all the goodness, and the other all the appearance of it.' For many, character was not an ideal, but a display of the required manners solely to those they considered their elders and betters. This was an education designed predominantly for the social elite and for men – it was gained through a person's upbringing, education and experiences. Sheldon Rothblatt (1976: 135 and 102) reminds us that it was in the 1860s that character formation made a forceful appearance in Oxford and Cambridge Universities, but it often resulted in conduct by undergraduates and dons alike that was 'self-consciously painful'. This class-bound society was changing rapidly and it remained impossible to develop workable notions of character for all. As Darwin (1929: 21) notes: 'many a lad who leaves an English public school disgracefully ignorant of the rudiments of useful knowledge, who can speak no language but his own, . . . and who has devoted a great part of his time and nearly all his thought to athletic sport, yet brings away with him something beyond price, a manly straightforward character, a scorn of lying and meanness, habits of obedience and command, and fearless courage.' They were not expected to be clever, but rather to know when to put on the right clothes at the right time. The connection between character and athletics goes back to the ancient Greeks, but the Victorians were also interested in health and the connection with modern science – a mixture of traditional and modern. Mind and will played a decisive part in the formation of character, but were largely seen as an individual's responsibility.

It is important to remember that British society was relatively homogeneous in religious outlook at this time. There was a common set of values derived from Scripture and Protestantism. Morality was not a controversial issue for most school teachers since the generalised Protestantism which pervaded culture was implicitly accepted by teachers and by those who wrote the school textbooks of the period (Arthur, 2001: 61f). The strong moralistic strain in Protestantism strengthened the general assumption that moral instruction was synonymous with religious instruction and if this was not always the case, then religion could certainly be relied upon to aid moral instruction. Protestantism in late nineteenth- and early 20th-century Britain consisted of a spectrum with strict evangelicals who battled the forces of evil at one end and liberal Protestants for whom religion was more cultural than theological at the other. Character formation for the parties at both of these extremes was clearly very different. It was also a time when the heroes of society were religious based exemplars such as Dr. Livingstone and General Gordon. Even when a Victorian abandoned religious belief, this did not necessarily mean a lowering of ethical standards. Instead, agnostics pursued the moral life as a good in itself. For them, the motivation was neither eternal reward nor punishment. Their enthusiasm for instilling moral character in the masses was often greater than that displayed by some evangelicals. In many ways they continued to live on the moral capital of their Christian inheritance. There was a move to downplay the religious elements and increase the character formation elements of the public schools as time passed. And by the 1880s schools stood more for academic attainment (Richards, 1988: 13).

The evangelical campaign against the perceived immorality of independent schools from the 1830s onwards was successful. Bradley (1976) says 'The evangelical, characterised by an intense seriousness of purpose, immense industry, enthusiastic missionary spirit, censorious high-mindedness and puritanical abstention from worldly pleasures, mounted a full-scale and successful assault on every level and aspect of society, promoting religion, education, duty, and hard work, . . . they created a cult of respectability, and conformity . . . the result was the pacification and purification of society.' The growing middle class wanted a morally sound education for their sons and the writings of those engaged in public school reform recommended more intimate and individualistic schemes of character formation (see Holt (2008: 119). These schools provided a common core of behaviour and way of thinking and elite schooling became just as important as noble birth. Middle-class evangelicals produced a new conception of the gentleman which stressed mental and moral character qualities. It is important to realise that in 1861 there were only 2,708 boys attending private schools out of a total population of over three million. The nobility of the country had focused on their social appearance, their conspicuous consumption and idleness as opposed to any inner virtues.

Public schools used powerful moral principles in forming the character of their students imposed by demanding headmasters, which is why many historians of the Victorian period place the concept of character at the centre of their analysis (see Collini, 1991, Mangan, 1981, 1998). However, it is of note that a number of historians of Victorian public schools fail to address the question of character formation. Turner, (2015: 105) while acknowledging its importance, gives only perfunctory attention to the concept while Bamford (1967: 59) says that 'Although one cannot ignore the character aspect, there were several other more tangible factors' which he lists as links with Oxbridge, leadership and public schools as places of excellence. Chandos (1984) also largely ignores the character dimensions of these schools. Recent and more popular historical studies of public schools also ignore the character dimension in any explicit way (see Martin, 2018, Renton, 2017). Yet Collini (1985: 40) reminds us that it was a period obsessed with the language of character as 'part of a wider reaction against the alleged vices and indulgencies of the . . . aristocracy'. The predominant models in operation in these schools became largely theological and conservative.

Chapter 7

Victorian character formation

Victorians looked to the past for inspiration to improve their character and there was nostalgia for an idealised chivalry of the medieval period. Character became the language of the age, as Collini (1985: 52) notes: 'the idea of character enjoyed a prominence in the political thought of the Victorian period that it had certainly not known before and it has, arguably, not experienced since.' Howe (1975) provides a good summary of the ambitions of the Victorian preoccupation with character:

> The intended product of Victorian didacticism was a person who would no longer need reminding of his duties, who would have internalised a powerful sense of obligation and could then safely be left to his own volitions. . . . A society composed of such persons, the Victorians hoped, could get along with a minimum of government; thus, the Victorian political ideal of liberalism was linked to moral seriousness on a private level. The Victorians also expected that the individual self-assertion of such persons, hard-working and conscientious, would be the most effective way to promote the general material welfare. The Victorians themselves called the quality they sought to create 'character'. This was not a set of rote responses but an intangible strength of purpose, combining self-reliance, self-discipline, and responsibility.

Respectability was a function of character and, according to Himmelfarb (1995: 32–3), the working class understood what it meant to possess this respectability: 'for men it meant having a job, however lowly, and not being habitually drunk; for women, managing a clean, orderly and thrifty household; for children, being obedient at home and school, doing chores and contributing, if possible, to the family income.' It was this idea of respectability of character that ensured Victorian stability and cohesion in society. There was a growing middle-class scepticism about the superiority of ideas of inherited or inborn character. The potential for acquired character grew out of this scepticism.

There was also immense fascination with Greek culture during Victorian Britain (Turner, 1981: 1) as well as a revival of medieval gothic influences on

112 Practices

architecture, art and literature. This interest 'occurred within the literate classes already familiar with the ancient world as a source of prescriptive values and of illustrative moral and political illusions' (Turner, 1981: 4). Livingstone (1917) and Ogilvie (1964) defended a politically conservative view of the types of character needed by society and provided many different reasons for the teaching of the classics, the Latin language and Greek philosophy in schools for the socially elite. The classics were still considered to be the best curriculum materials to train students in wisdom, but Ogilvie (1964: 115) noted that 'Victorian England was in tune with Plato and the education which she evolved under the influence of Plato's vision was an education to serve her purposes. It inculcated loyalty, courage, responsibility and truthfulness: four virtues indispensable to the new governing class of a great empire.' He went on to say: 'It was not the good or the kind or the meek who were venerated, but the courageous and the handsome and the patriotic: for it was they who secured England's position in the world' (Ogilvie, 1964: 134–5). The kind of character formation represented by this view equated virtue with manliness, taught morals by teaching manners, emphasised physical bravery and sought to build the character of the English gentleman through aesthetic appeals to 'good form.' It is a form of character marked by social status and elitism and was clearly in opposition to all forms of liberalism. It was marked by inequality, class distinctions and the expectation of success, and was very much the kind of character that was common in antiquity, but of course not intended for the masses.

However, Spring (1813: 12–13) believed it was not good enough simply to have an 'unimpeached character' in the view of the world – you had to believe in Christian doctrine as well, otherwise character meant little. This was the Protestant view of character. Many Victorians believed in the union of the good and the true – better knowledge would make better people and morals could potentially be divorced from the religion. Catholicism had made good character an asset to salvation. Aquinas had said that humans are naturally inclined towards their rational end or good – thus there is ground for a natural morality available to the knowledge of rational persons – and that this is given by God – Protestants rejected this idea. The Protestant view was that fulfilling moral requirements leads not to salvation, but to the presumption of righteousness before God. For Protestants the tendency has always been to emphasise the relationship of the individual to God while for Catholicism the tendency has been to emphasise the individual's relationship to God as a member of a community. Notions of character for Protestants were to be interpreted in terms of duty. There was also the widespread belief that lowly character was wholly the responsibility of the individual, particularly of the poor, as Kay-Shuttleworth remarked: 'It is melancholy to perceive how many of the evils suffered by the poor flow from their own ignorance and moral errors' (cited in Johnson, 1970: 102).

During the Victorian period character formation for the poor replaced all other educational priorities in schools with the idea that it was better to be good than intellectually able in common circulation. Inculcation of appropriate manners and morals was the chief aim of this character formation. There was a national consensus concerning the content of moral character, and teachers had considerable authority in schools to impose this rather repressive Protestant cultural formation which was all-pervasive. The teaching of the virtues was considered superior to intellectual education and children only became good through character building. Public school stories and novels were held up to working-class children as the optimal way to experience their youth (Holt, 2008: 3). These rather static virtues of the time represented the goals of cultural conformity and included thrift, self-help, self-control, submission, frugality, industry, deference and reverence, together with obedience. In schools, prescriptive codes of virtues were rigorously enforced and the habits of order, passivity, punctuality and regularity expected. The State also enforced these secular virtues as seen in the Revised Code for Scotland in 1879 with the section on discipline that required schools 'to bring up the children in habits of punctuality, of good manners and language, of cleanliness and neatness, and also to impress upon the children the importance of cheerful obedience to duty, of consideration and respect for others, and of honour and truthfulness in word and act' (cited in Anderson, 1995: 197).

The late Victorian era saw the rise of three ideas running parallel to each other: first, growing acceptance of the State as a prime organiser of domestic public policy; second, the development of theories of human evolution which brought doubts about Biblical passages, and third, developments in society that shifted the conception of citizenship, the origins and meaning of Englishness as well as the duties and rights of the English people. These powerful forces interacted with each other influencing the State's growing support for the new school system. Schooling which emphasised economic efficiency, commercial and technological progress and a curriculum also centred on the development of patriotism, secular civic ideals and knowledge about the nation and empire. Within this social and political mix ethical societies arose for better moral training of the young by seeking a clearer delineation of the boundaries of right and wrong, which gave a fresh focus to character building. All theories and new knowledge were welcomed by these ethical societies so long as they could reinforce the distinction between right and wrong. These societies aimed to extend the range of moral co-operation through uniting people of diverse views and beliefs in the quest of studying practical problems of social, political and individual ethics.

Growing liberalism and progressive ideas helped establish the climate that encouraged the growth of secular views of society and Christianity, particularly witnessed in the empiricism of David Hume. This legacy was reinforced by the social transformations of industrialisation and urbanisation in 19th-century England. The expansion of the middle class was another transformation of the period, which came with a corresponding concern to reconcile these social transformations with sustaining public order. The Judaeo–Christian tradition dominated schooling, which was strongly associated with the development of Christian-based moral virtues. Many within the middle classes acquired both a generalised sensitivity about human suffering as well as real fears for the future social order. This fear was largely invented by the late Victorians, for while the population increased from 19 million to 33 million, the number of serious crimes declined. Alongside these anxieties, however, middle-class opinion also experienced a desire to provide relief for those in situations of extreme poverty, but they rarely questioned the system that sustained this inequality which saw progress coexist with social and economic inequality. Their answer to this contradiction was 'Victorian moralism' or what Barnett (2011) called a 'revolution in moral sentiments' resulting in a sense of compassion for the poor. At the end of the 19th century English middle-class society also witnessed an enhanced concern for moral instruction which formed part of their paternalistic view: they believed they had a duty of moral guidance over the lower classes. The new naturalism in the literature of the period was also marked by a dread of moral decay and its consequences. This is perhaps reflected in the novels of Emile Zola which suggested the idea that genetics determine one's character, also in the 'National Efficiency' movement which sought to improve the physical and mental health of the lower classes. The Headmaster of Harrow, J. E. C. Welldon, proclaimed that there was a need to 'cultivate a certain hardness of character' while Holt (2008) illustrates how boys' school stories reflected this stance.

The radical, philosophical and political thoughts of Thomas Hill Green (1836–82), were hugely influential in late Victorian England. He believed that education should develop character, but he shared Hegel's pursuit of transforming religious consciousness into a conceptual and metaphysical theory. Green merged the philosophical, religious and ethical life and he opposed sectarianism, considering that it was wholly unnecessary for people to accept the full theological and doctrinal understanding of Christianity. Green's effort sought to provide a firm intellectual basis for religion which would be undogmatic and sympathetic to practical social action. He emphasised the shared goals and values of the community and believed that the common good should be promoted by the State through basic educational provision for all. Schooling, for Green, ought to be provided by the State since without it children could not develop their character and therefore pursue morally good ends. The Church of England also saw the role of the State as not simply educating citizens in democratic processes, but in terms of moral character. Green himself was educated at home until the age of 14 by his Church of England minister father. Green's view influenced Mrs. Humphrey Ward's heterodoxy and particularly her bestselling and popular novel, *Robert Elsmere* (1988), which depicts an earnest Oxford clergyman's loss of faith in conventional Christianity and his adoption of a liberalism that stressed social action among the poor.

Victorian education had conscious moral purposes, particularly in the economic and religious domain. The production of characters suited to the needs of work was one of the principal goals of 19th-century elementary schools for the poor. Children in these schools were taught the 'habits of industry' (Barnard, 1961: 6) for they were destined for either the factories or domestic service. Character training formed the core of their schooling and included a form of moral development firmly based on the Ten Commandments and stories from the Bible. Moral conduct was taught in the context of religious doctrine and Sunday Schools, in the absence of an elementary school, taught the basic skills of literacy whilst extolling the virtues of Christian living. The teacher's role in these schools was to inculcate specific social roles typified by a pattern of behaviour in children. Children accepted without question the moral training provided and expected to be punished for bad habits. The emphasis was on obedience and duty to all forms of authority in society and absolute conformity to predetermined social roles for the child. The virtues connected with economic success were central and work itself which was seen as an almost sacred virtue with the virtues of ambition, dependability, hard work, patience, orderliness, cleanliness, punctuality, initiative and ingenuity. It was thought that if only people lived these virtues the stronger and better society would become. The Victorian concern for the 'education' of the poor is best understood as a concern for authority over them. The middle class held an entrenched prejudice against the character of manual workers, who were not viewed as respectable. The teachers themselves were often not well educated and were selected for their ability to exhibit virtues in and outside school. The overwhelming majority were women. They held a restricted outlook on educational matters, which resulted in crude and mechanistic methods of teaching. Moreover, the catechetical approach to teaching religion influenced their approach to education in general.

A circular letter from School HMIs in 1849 (quoted in Hunt, 1999) specified that teachers of the poor were to 'improve their (pupils') habits and manners, to promote a sense of order and decorum, a respectful obedience to their parents, teachers and superiors, to cultivate an intelligent disposition to fulfil the duties of their station in life, and to enable them to see how their interests and happiness are inseparable from the wellbeing of other classes in society'. In 1862 Samuel Smiles published his *Self-Help: With Illustrations of Character and Conduct*, which sold 20,000 copies in its first year and which reached sales of 250,000 by the end of the century. Whilst we cannot underplay the influence of Scottish Calvinism on Smiles' thought, the underlying philosophy of the book promoted a kind of secular ethic. Smiles appears to have adopted a kind of Aristotelian approach to character formation (1862: 331) for as he says: 'Knowledge must be allied to goodness and wisdom, and embodied in upright character, else it is nought . . . the acquisition of knowledge may, it is true, protect a man against the meaner felonies of life; but not in any degree against its selfish vices, unless fortified by sound principles and habits.' Smiles preached a gospel of self-improvement through diligence, thrift and good character and in his sequel, entitled *Character*, published in 1871, he attempted to divorce the idea of a 'gentleman' from its upper-class connotations so that the virtues he recommended could count as constitutive of the moral worthy person no matter what their class. Anyone could build a respectable character, but he also promoted the idea that found wide acceptance in Victorian society that character flaws were entirely the responsibility of the individual. According to Smiles (1871: 1–6), character was 'formed by a variety of small circumstances, more or less under the regulation and control of the individual'. Every action, thought and feeling contributed to its formation: 'man is not the creature, so much as he is the creator, of circumstances . . . energy of will – self-originating force – is the soul of every great character.' By locating the virtues of moral character in individual deeds and habits, rather than in social descent, Smiles legitimised the social rise of Britain's industrial and commercial leaders, while holding out the promise of improvement to many. Revealed in the 'transactions and commonplaces of daily duties', a good character could be acquired by anyone. He advocated the establishment of a national education system in order to teach his virtues of character. It should be noted that his book *Character* was published in the same year as Darwin's *Origin of Species* and John Stuart Mills' *Liberty*, but his *Character* outsold both.

Quentin Bell (1968: 28) sums up this whole secular movement: 'Thus, in Victorian England, we find that the apostles of progress, having swept their churches clean of sacraments, altars, priests and pulpits, leaving nothing save a bare structure of ethical assertions, returned to curtained, cushioned, upholstered homes in which every sort of buried sexual superstition, traditionalist tyranny and emotional cant served as covering for dirty unswept corners and nameless secular filth.' Initiatives to promote Christian character education continued with the establishment of the Young Men's Christian Association (YMCA) in London in 1844 with the explicitly stated aim: 'the winning of young men to Jesus Christ, and the building in them of Christian character.' Many of the lectures given at the YMCA were nationalistic and evangelical rants which dwelt on the inferiority of the Catholic characters in Europe as compared to those in England (see Bardsley, 1861). Alexander Bain published the first psychology of character in 1861 and character was prominent among the progressive thinkers who perceived it to be a major force for social, cultural and material improvement. This approach was largely prescriptive and related to moral outcomes and can be seen in Rufus Clark's *Lectures on the Formation of Character* which was a popular US guide.

As the religious basis for morality began to decline, for some the latter became the surrogate of the former; there developed a heightened awareness of ensuring that moral standards in society and in individuals were upheld. Gertrude Himmelfarb (1995: 27) reviews a number of prominent Victorians who, whilst abandoning a revealed religion, nevertheless gave their full support to the task of transmitting 'duty' and moral behaviour to the young. This was the secular ethic, which profoundly influenced the progress of character education in schools. Secular character training became an alternative to the moral lessons derived from Bible teaching and those who used the term 'character training' were often the progressives in education. They used this language to avoid conflict with religioun-based moral education, but it remained an ethic firmly based on puritan foundations. Until 1870, the Church of England and other Protestant denominations dominated the provision of schooling, but their constant disagreements pushed the supervision of education increasingly into the hands of the government. The Education Act of 1870 in England did not establish free State education for all, it merely supplemented the provision of schools already provided for by the Christian denominations. Because of the deep divisions within Protestantism the religious teaching in these new schools could not be based on any one denominational creed – instead a morality, free from any denominational influence was taught. This led to the separation of morality from religion despite the retention of compulsory Christian worship and religious instruction in State schools. Many Anglican schools converted to State school status as it was felt that the general moral ethos in them was compatible with Anglican ideas. The secularisation of State and many Church schools grew throughout the early part of the 20th century, encouraged by the campaigns of the National Secular Society, founded in 1867, for secular and compulsory education for all.

The perceived need for some form of character formation in schools was clearly evident from the alarm displayed by many eminent Victorians when they discovered the state of the social and moral conditions of the poor in the industrial cities. Alarming social statistics began to be produced. These spurred on some to emphasise 'self-help' policies whilst others sought to improve social conditions. Educational progressives like Charlotte Mason organised systems of character training through the Parents National Education Union founded in 1892. Arthur Acland (1980: 206), Chairman of the Co-Operative Society and a Fellow of Christ Church College, Oxford, gave a series of lectures in 1883 to groups of workers advocating improved training for teachers so that they could develop critical thinking in their charges rather than continuing to teach by rote. He believed that the examples of the great men in English history would help develop the character of both the young and old alike and make them better Englishmen. He divorced Christianity from this character training and retained this view even when appointed Vice-President of the Committee of Council on Education in Gladstone's last administration.

The Victorian period was certainly a high point in character education, or perhaps more accurately, in the use of the language of character. The Victorians meant many things by character, and many of these meanings did not apply to schooling. They were much more concerned with the idea of the will – the power of the will to do the right thing, for it was generally assumed that people did know the difference between right and wrong and it was only weakness of will that caused them to do wrong. The theory of character formation they promoted led to much ambiguity and contradiction in behaviour. Robert Owen's experiment in the social reconstruction of character through integrating character with society was an example of a utopian theory of character

118 Practices

formation. Much more general was the view that character formation equalled a socialisation in good manners and in a particular form of social conduct – it was an attempt to alter the values of the poor to make their behaviour more congruent with the respectable middle class. Whilst there was a recognition that human nature could be directly shaped by education, the notion of character was also embodied in laws, institutions and social expectations and was shaped by the community.

Owen's central precept was that an individual's character was formed exclusively by their environment as he said: 'we can materially command those circumstances which influence character' (Armitage, 1952: 316). Owen believed that an individual's happiness was dependent on the community in which they lived, the roots of which could be found in the Scottish Enlightenment. He believed that the early years were crucial as character is 'correctly or incorrectly formed before he attains his second year' (Howlett, 2013: 218). He held an ambitious and radical conception of character formation seen in his *A New View of Society: Essays on the Formation of Character* (1813: 20–3) which states: 'Every day will make it more and more evident that the character of a man is, without a single exception, always formed for him; that it may be, and is, chiefly created by his predecessors; that they give him, or may give him, his ideas and habits, which are the powers that govern and direct his conduct. Man therefore, never did, nor is it possible he ever can, form his own character.' Owen held a determinist theory of character and thought that character formation could be calculated with mathematical precision. For him, character was the product of external forces, which meant in reality that those who governed society showed the working class how they should conduct themselves. Owen was a progressive and radical, and like many others of this persuasion he strongly believed in direct character formation, but he also sought State involvement in forming the character of the working class. Schools as places to train character was not a totally new concept, but as we have seen in the previous chapter it came to distinguish the English private school – with character associated with manliness (Freeman, 1907: 11). In the end, Owen was concerned with the formation of social character and placed less emphasis on the intellectual and moral virtues.

Character formation was a mixture of traditional beliefs and various distillations of modern science – schools were designed to discipline bodies and regulate minds together with the formation of conduct and beliefs. A leading evangelical educator Hannah More declared: 'Beings bring into the world a corrupt nature, an evil disposition, which it should be the great end of education to rectify.' Disobedience and academic error were considered the work of Satan and needed to be eradicated through corporal punishment. This resulted in beatings at home, in school and in the workplace, a practice underpinned by a theology of sin. Education for More was essentially 'to train up the lower classes in habits of industry and piety' (Lawson and Silver, 1973: 233). However, the most important influence of evangelicalism was the fact that its virtues were interchangeable with the virtues of the merchant and this character formation was equated with social improvement. Aries (1962) has noted that before the modern period the very idea of childhood did not exist, but as mass education expanded, so too did the concern for character formation.

Successive societies from the 18th century onwards which aimed to suppress immorality were established, beginning with the Society for the Reformation of Manners in 1690. This was followed by the Proclamation Society for the Discouragement of Vice in 1787, and in 1802 William Wilberforce founded the Society for the Suppression of Vice which eventually merged with the National Vigilance Association in 1885. All these evangelical organisations represented middle-class people advocating thrift for the working class and insisted on the purity and sobriety in individual character. The chief goal of this middle-class moral movement was to prosecute (mainly working class) people for illicit and immoral acts. These included swearing, reading obscene books, blasphemous publications, brothels and prostitution (Quinlan, 1941). However, in 1869 Bernard and Helen Bosanquet founded and led the Charity Organization Society. This organisation, also concerned about moral deterioration in society, was established to advance character formation. Its explicit aim was to improve the character of the charity's recipients – the deserving poor (Johnson, 1970: 119). It was considered the responsibility of the better-off to protect and form the character of the poor. The charity was concerned with the distinction between the deserving poor and the underserving poor, but it had a narrow interpretation of the deserving poor, which excluded the sick and old. Poverty and disease were less important than developing strengths of character and those who joined the Society believed in self-help and wanted to restrict any State involvement by way of aid to the poor. Voluntary effort, they believed, was the only way to restore the character of the individual. Poverty and personal failure were directly related to character weakness, with no thought given to the contribution of socio-economic structures. In its Reports the organisation sought to eliminate 'from society those animals who represented themselves to be men, but who really were nothing more than animals groveling in the earth and mire, living on the bread of idleness, and a festering sore in society' (cited in Humphreys, 1992: 2). It followed from this negative view of humanity that if the poor were to be helped develop their character in order to be worthy of assistance they needed to develop: 'self-denial, discipline, responsibility, hard work, thrift, temperance, and foresight' (Humphreys, 1992: 1).

These economic virtues of character were particularly emphasised by Helen Bosanquet in her book *The Strength of the People: A Study in Social Economics* (1902) in which she makes clear that character determines circumstances rather than vice versa. Character could make you rich or poor, a view largely accepted by the most authoritative economist of the day, Alfred Marshall, Professor of Political Economy in the University of Cambridge. Marshall, according to Collini (1985: 30) had 'displayed a pervasive concern with the shaping and the efficacy of character under modern industrial conditions, and he had always insisted that it was a central part of the economist's professional task to identify

120 Practices

those forces which will help to build up a strong and righteous character' (Collini, 1985: 30). Even Socialists justified their economic proposals on the grounds that it would produce 'a higher type of character' and believed that the end purpose of the State 'is, in fact, the development of character'.

There were materialist and idealist notions of character formation prevalent within Victorian culture which gave rise to a tension between the free-will of the individual and social determinism (see Anderson, 1993: 30). The materialists included the progressives and positivists such as Robert Owen who were concerned with character as externally determined. They wanted to apply scientific method to character formation and believed in the malleability of character which made the reform of character possible. Against this view were the idealists who saw character as self-created through reflection. They opposed the idea of character as instrumentally determined, which they believed simply replicated the worst excesses of the mechanised society produced by the Industrial Revolution.

We return to John Stuart Mill who attempted to adopt a middle way, but did this largely in the language of the materialists in his work *System of Logic* of 1843. In Book VI Chapter V entitled 'Of Ethology, or the Science of the Formation of Character', Mill attempts to create a new branch of science which he calls Ethology. He outlines a series of propositions and laws which state that 'our characters follow from our organisation, our education, and our circumstances' (Roberts, 2002: 316). Character could be formed either by external forces or by individuals themselves: 'We are exactly as capable of making our own character, if you will, as others are of making it for us . . . the work is not so irrevocably done as to be incapable of being altered' (see Reeves, 2007: 169). He wanted a science that was capable of delineating the process by which a character is formed and believed that it must draw on the findings of psychology. His attempt was not entirely successful and he never developed the science of character or what he called 'Ethology', but he does try to balance the materialist and idealist conceptions of character formation by saying that while circumstances influence character, character in turn influences circumstances. Therefore, it appeared that you could 'form' character as well as allow for free moral agency. However, he felt that our inner desire to shape character was dependent on external circumstances – he did not answer the question of where the desire to change our character comes from. It cannot be that it was entirely from the circumstance we found ourselves in. He certainly held that you could modify your character by will power and that the virtues and habits of character were cultivated only through freedom of the mind (see Anderson, 1993: 28–34). Mill believed that 'our actions follow from our characters' and that character can only be shaped indirectly, but he held that the formation of character was higher than all other ends in education. Mill wrote that people 'are under a moral obligation to seek the improvement of our moral character' and that only through people of good character could society improve. In *On Liberty* he wrote: 'it really is of importance, not only what men do, but also what manner of men they are that do it' (Reeves, 2007: 170). He wanted people to live virtuous lives, but he consistently emphasised their right to choose such lives freely and warned against majority opinion and State coercion that narrowed the liberties of a person to 'prevent the formation, of any individuality not in harmony with its ways, and compel all characters to fashion themselves upon the models of its own'. Mill rejected Owen's idea of character formation, but his idea of character was at odds with the more conservative view in his day which generally emphasised the formation of a passive character that was conventional and conformist in nature. This conservative type of character Mill thought prized uncritical thinking and unquestioning obedience to existing authority and which was more reflexive than reflective. Mill contrasted this conservative idea of character with his priorities that in order to form character the person must be free, reflective, engaged and unconstrained by fear.

This concern for ethical instruction had been given further impetus with the establishment of the Union of Ethical Societies in 1895, a movement that aimed to 'disentangle moral ideals from religious doctrines, metaphysical systems and ethical theories'. Only two years later the Union, together with other 'progressive bodies' such as the National Secular Society and the Independent Labour Party, founded the Moral Instruction League (MIL). The language of Thomas Green's philosophy of education was not distinct from that of the Moral Instruction League. Ideas of inheritance and biological predestination were evident in the debates in the 1890s. A pamphlet, entitled *Our Future Citizens*, published by the MIL in 1900 set forth its aims 'to substitute systematic non-theological Moral Instruction for the present religious teaching in all State Schools' and 'to make character the chief aim of school life'. The Independent Labour Party was dominated by Nonconformist Christian socialists who joined with secularists to found the MIL and their aim was to promote 'non-sectarian' character education which is how they understood 'secular'. This is why the Independent Labour Party became the first British political party to campaign for compulsory free secular education despite the religious views of many of its members, including its leader, Keir Hardie. The socialist critique of education began with an attack on the religious moralising in the period, but it included a commitment to 'the development of Personal Character'. Socialists argued for a change in people's character as a panacea for social ills. Robbins (1959: 172–8) noted that it represented 'ethical idealism as a substitute for supernatural religion'.

In 1903, the MIL published its elementary school syllabus on moral instruction, a document that was more pragmatic than radical. This restated traditional Judaeo-Christian moral virtues in relativistic terms and quite without theological foundations. The School Board Regulations of 1904 and the Code of 1906 both contained elements of the MIL's aims including that 'the purpose of the public elementary school is to form and strengthen the character and develop intelligence, of the children entrusted to it'. It should also be noted that the MIL was only one of a number of organisations and events that were established at the time to improve the character of the working class. Others included the Empire Day, the Duty and Discipline Movements, as well as the Navy League. The MIL did not advocate a particular philosophical system to justify its approach, but rather focused on the 'function of morality' (see Wright, 2017, 2018).

The November 1907 meeting of the MIL led to the establishment of the Eugenics Education Society (EES) with some of the same people as members. The MIL values were largely shared by members of the EES, but the EES held that low moral character was something predominantly inherited and one solution was to sterilise the morally inferior and restrict marriage for the poor. The logic was clear: *biological inferiority = social inferiority = inferior moral character*. EES members therefore followed the teachings of Francis Galton who believed that character was hereditary. However, the EES had learnt from the MIL that it ought not to alienate Christians if it was to influence education policy. Similarly, in 1907, the Secular Education League was established on the basis of a concern for the moral education of the working class and not surprisingly some prominent members of MIL joined it (see Arthur, 2019).

By the early 1900s Professor John Muirhead at the University of Birmingham had already begun to lecture to trainee teachers on the importance of character and virtues and had encouraged other university and college training courses to do the same. Three Scottish professors of philosophy, John Mackenzie, President of MIL (Cardiff University), John Muirhead, Vice President of MIL (Birmingham University), and John McCunn (Liverpool University) produced texts of intellectual note on what a secular moral education might look like. McCunn published the highly praised *The Making of Character*, which was re-printed nine times between 1900 and 1931. The MIL approach to moral character was clearly both practical and largely secular in nature; it sought to provide advice to schools on non-denominational secular moral instruction. Moreover, the advice was based on a non-religious worldview. The organisation eventually limited its concerns for the educational promotion of character to education for citizenship. The middle-class members and supporters of the MIL saw themselves as the moral guardians of society and they 'idolised morality, giving it that supreme importance which they were increasingly unable to accord to God'.

The late 19th and early 20th centuries were certainly significant developmental stages towards conceiving character formation, or more accurately, in the development of the language of character in England. This was a time at which character education encompassed a broad range of ideas, beliefs and practices, not all of them compatible or reconcilable (Roberts, 2004). Tensions abounded in the usage and the language was significantly class-inflected and, for many, character building was simply training in the manners expected towards those considered their elders and betters. This is expressed in the hundreds of books that appeared in the 1880s through to the 1900s on character with titles such as Wells' *How to Read Character* (1892), to *The Secret of Character Building* by De Motte in 1893. This was replicated in the USA with *The Building of*

Victorian character formation   123

Character by Miller in 1894 (see Appendix I and J). It is worth here considering briefly American Victorian character initiatives through the work and legacy of William Homes McGuffey (1800–1873).

The McGuffey family immigrated to America in 1774 from Scotland and brought with them a strong passion for both Christianity and education. William was the second of 11 children, born in America in 1800 and he grew up on a farm, but by the age of 14 he had become a roving teacher and in 1826 graduated in classics from Washington College, a Scottish Presbyterian foundation. By 1836 William wrote the first of a series of Readers for American elementary schools to teach reading. However, these books were not simply intended to teach a child how to read, but provided them with a wider purpose of how to see the world and how to live. The Readers contained stories from the Bible, larger than life stories of heroes, poems, essays, speeches by great men, all with an eye to the formation of character. As Vail (1911: 11) wrote: 'without conscious effort they received moral instruction and incentives towards right living.' The Readers had very strong Scottish Calvinist religious overtones and promoted the Protestant virtues of frugality, hard work, cleanliness, honesty, dedication, patriotism and obedience. Between 1844 and 1920 they sold over 120 million copies and were only exceeded in print by the Bible (Anderson, 1956: 53). They are the most famous reading textbooks in the history of American education and are still in print today selling thousands each year predominantly for home schooling and some private schools. It is interesting that the 1879 editions, a few years after the author's death, were heavily edited to remove many of the overtly religious overtones, but the intention remained that they could strengthen character, and help in the pursuit of goodness and truth in those who learnt from them. McGuffey eventually became Professor of Moral Philosophy at the University of Virginia, but remained a practitioner and educator of character. Vail (1911: 3), in writing a history of the series, makes a comment that sums up McGuffey's goals: 'Knowledge gives power, which may be exerted for good or for evil. Character gives direction to power. Power is the engine which may force the steamer through the water, character is the helm which renders the power serviceable for good.'

In examination papers for the certificate in education that trainee teachers would have been expected to pass in Cambridge, Manchester and London the following questions were set (Roberts, 2004: 177): Give an analysis of the nature of character. In what does character consist? How would you cultivate it? Character has been described as 'a completely fashioned will'. What does this mean? A study of character formation was required for classroom practice. It also shows that character was a critical topic of discussion in education at the time, and was a dominant part of the culture of Victorian Britain. Haley (1978) shows how the games-playing 'cult' swept Victorian Britain, particularly among the poor, and the athlete was seen as the new hero – proclaimed to be the man who was an 'aristocrat of character' not an aristocrat of birth. It was thought that by strengthening the body one could also strengthen the will of the poor.

The use of the language of character and virtues was used to justify the possession of empire. Character was considered to be the key to British success in the world through energy, industry, thrift, perseverance and honesty (Cain, 2007). This was influenced by the Scottish Enlightenment ideas that commerce and civil society were the twin pillars that secured character formation. The Empire was seen as the training ground for character formation and in a lecture as Chancellor of Oxford University Lord Curzon (1907: 56) in 1907 spoke specifically about character being 'moulded . . . in the furnace of responsibility and in the anvil of self-reliance'. He called the University of Oxford 'the nursery of character'. By the First World War character formation had become associated with co-operation, teamwork, loyalty – more related to citizenship – the good citizen. Character became more corporate in orientation – about fitting into a group.

The 19th century saw a great explosion of periodicals for working-class children with stories of adventure some of which sought to improve the character of the poor. Cheap fiction for working-class children began in the 1830s and combined moral instruction with entertainment, but by the 1860s the emphasis was largely on entertainment as could be seen in the *Boy Detective*, a successful 72-part serial. The 1860s saw the emergence of the 'penny dreadful' with the focus on adventure. This was later countered by the widely read *Boy's Own Paper* (1879) with its more didactic moral stories while preserving the entertainment elements (Musgrave, 1985: 114). As has been noted in this text there has been a long tradition of using literature to reform the moral sensibilities of people and that this tradition of humanist conservatives going back to Erasmus and More saw man as a moral actor. Prominent literary critics of this tradition in England such as Milton, Pope, Johnson, Reynolds, Burke, Coleridge, Arnold and Newman believed that 'literature held significance more as an ethical than as an aesthetic enterprise, and the moral or normative use of the past as a guide to the human condition in the present predominated over other possible uses of historical experience' (Turner, 1981: 15). Together they were very critical of materialism, scientific reductionism and individualism when it came to character formation.

The models of character formation predominant in this period included the theological and conservative with the emergence of liberal and even radical models.

Chapter 8

20th-century influences on character formation

In the *Introduction to the Education Code* of 1904 and 1905 (and subsequent Codes), it was stated that: 'The purpose of the public elementary school is to form and strengthen the character and to develop the intelligence of the children entrusted to it.' The Code had a clear moral tone about it and advocated that children should learn about the heroes of England's past through the medium of storytelling by the teacher. Sir Robert Morant, who compiled the Code for the Ministry, also produced in 1905 a *Handbook of Suggestions for Consideration of Teachers and others concerned in the work of the Public Elementary Schools.* This Handbook has a section on the formation of character in which teachers are encouraged to try and improve manners in pupils along with punctuality, neatness, cleanliness, truthfulness, respect for others and a 'cheerful obedience to duty'. The 1927 (20) version of the Code states: 'direct moral training can most easily be given when a clear appeal to reason is possible. . . . But the teaching of morals must often be dogmatic rather than reasoned. Against dishonesty and other faults which undermine character, children must be definitely and seriously warned.' The language and the notion of character here is more Greek than Christian in origin and the kind of Christianity that was encouraged in schools was more ethical than religious. The approach is one of duty, particularly to the Greek virtues of prudence, justice, temperance and fortitude. At the time, the Moral Instruction League had some influence on government policy, but perhaps only because there was a degree of convergence between liberal Protestant thought and some of its thinking. Most politicians concerned with administering schooling were devout Christians who despised those who promoted a secular morality.

A number of Christians produced books which linked character training with the Christian religion such as those by Watkinson in 1904 and Lord in 1926. After all, the majority of schools in this period were still operated by the churches. The Sunday School Movement was also eager to instil virtuous character in pupils, but Dorothy Entwistle (Arthur, 2003: 19) indicates that even in this Christian approach there was a surprisingly secular outlook. The virtues promoted by the Sunday School Movement, such as 'good temper', 'self-sacrifice', 'helping others', etc., could have been accepted by the Moral Instruction

126 Practices

League as common human values. The Roman Catholic Church placed great store by the character of the teacher in the classroom and sought teachers 'who combine a love of and sympathy with children' (Wenham, 1892: 198). Teachers were encouraged to mix with children in the playground to influence them through example – showing them the virtues of a good Christian life.

In response to the activities of the Moral Instruction League a number of books were written for parents and teachers. Ernest Hull (1911: 117), an English Jesuit, wrote *The Formation of Character* in 1910 to help guide the young to form a character based on *principles*. He provided the following definition: 'Character is life dominated by principles, as distinguished from life dominated by mere impulses from within and mere circumstances from without.' The Roman Catholic Church also had the work of the French Dominican, Martin Gillet (1914) which was translated in the same year and entitled *The Education of Character* – it gave a good response to emerging secular alternatives. The Catholic tradition of Thomism has always accepted that basic morality was available to all men without the necessity of religion. In Catholic schools morality was still firmly rooted in notions of faith. The Anglican and Nonconformist Churches increasingly focused much of their attention on extra-curricular activities in forming character and they established or allied themselves with the Boys Brigade in 1883, Boy Scouts in 1908 and Girl Guides in 1910. The Scouts movement was really a way of providing the same character training for the poor as the privileged gained in their independent schools and was seen as character training in the service of the nation by correcting moral, physical and military weaknesses in the poor (Rosenthal, 1986). There was a feeling that religion intruded into the study of character with metaphysical conceptions of what progressives considered should be a purely scientific study (Elliot, 1913: 222). They wanted to banish all religious associations with character and make it a completely secular study.

There was great interest in character formation in the early 1900s. Michael Sadler (1908: v) conducted a major international enquiry into moral instruction to ascertain whether or not British schools could learn how to strengthen the character of the young. This was a major study on the influence of education upon character that has never since been repeated. It is interesting that the study found that many British teachers were uneasy with moral education in schools and disliked the moral syllabuses on offer, whilst at the same time agreeing that character building was part of their role. Little appears to have changed. The 1910 Board of Education Circular 753 (para. 36) envisages its own literary canon: a body of great literary works to which pupils need to be introduced. It made clear that pupils 'should be taught to understand, not to criticise or judge' the great works. Moral education continued to be taught in schools in a fairly conventional and non-critical way.

After the 1920s there were fewer books specifically addressing character training in the school – training in character was often incorporated into ideas and discussion about citizenship. Nevertheless, the *Report of the Consultative*

Committee on the Primary School (1926: 93) recognised that: 'The schools … have broadened their aims until it might be said that they have to teach children how to live' and E. A. Mountford provided a textbook on teaching the virtues for school teachers in 1933 entitled *The Education of Character*. The Board of Education's Handbook for 1937 continued to make explicit that: 'The purpose of the Public Elementary School is to form and strengthen character.' The handbook emphasised that the corporate life of the school should avoid anything that undermines character formation and listed the habits of industry, self-control, duty, respect for others, good manners, fair play and loyalty as the kind of virtues that should be cultivated.

In the same year the Church of England held a conference in Oxford on education and condemned the promotion of individualism within education circles, especially the concept of what it called 'free personality' in which children were being encouraged to do as they pleased. The Conference warned about the role and development of the State in areas like character formation with Fred Clarke (1938: 2) claiming that the increasing role of the State in schooling would eventually be 'committed to a particular philosophy of life and seeking to organise the whole of life in accordance with a particular doctrine of the end of man's existence, and in an all-embracing community life which claims to be at once the source and the end of all human activity; a State, that is to say, which aims at being also a Church'. In the same year the Spens Report on Secondary Education spoke of education as 'fostering the free growth of individuality'. The Education Act 1944 saw the duty of schools as being 'to contribute towards … moral development in the community', it did not ask schools to wholly provide it. Four years later the Ministry of Education's Advisory Council for Education produced a report entitled *School and Life* (1947: 97 ff) that expressed concern about the danger of a moral vacuum and strongly advised schools to provide some kind of moral code for their pupils. The report, whilst recognising that schools should help build 'strong characters', noted that for many people the division between right and wrong was no longer a strictly moral one thus causing 'increased moral perplexity and confusion' in society and schools.

In 1949 the Ministry of Education published a paper entitled *Citizens Growing Up: At Home, At School and After* in which it is stated that 'good citizens must first be good men'. The document has a section on character which briefly details why and how it must be improved and there is an appeal to 'public virtues' and an exhortation to develop an improved moral tone in schools. The Ministry's (1949: 11) yearbook also advocated the introduction of 'social activities' in schools in order to develop character. The Scottish Education Department produced *Young Citizens at School* the year after which was the result of a government-organised conference of teachers, that addressed the issue of training character in schools. The document concluded that: 'Direct moral teaching, in the sense of precept dealing with virtues in the abstract, evidently found little place in the thought of the great body of teachers. But stress was laid on the focus of example on the formation of good habits' (1950: 13). After 1950 it is difficult to find any references to character in government education publications until 2001. It also becomes rare to see Protestant accounts of character formation for pupils in State schools – one of the last being W. H. Backhouse's *Religion and Adolescent Character* in 1947. In 1951 the editors of *The Yearbook of Education* at the Institute of Education in London produced a *Yearbook* that sought to examine 'the ways in which . . . the school contributes to the formation of moral character, sentiments, attitudes, ideals and ethical standards' (see Lauwerys and Hans, 1951). In one of the edited papers, T. H. Pear (1951: 313) claimed that it was still generally assumed by most English teachers that they were involved in the training of their pupils' characters. Pear proceeded then to attack the kind of character training extant in English private schools as narrow and class-based.

The idea of character training in schools did not die off completely within the English context as it was still promoted by people such as Sir Richard Livingstone (1941: 5) who was Head of an Oxford College. In a lecture at Doncaster Grammar School in 1954 he explained that we must form good habits in children together with appropriate virtues, in order to build character. He did not believe that teachers or teacher educators gave sufficient attention to character formation and he produced his own litany of alarm. He believed that character should be associated with 'national ideals and . . . national virtues'. Independent and Church schools continued to give attention to character formation. John Dancey (1963: 90), writing on public schools, emphasised the continued interest of private schools in character formation. The development of self-confidence, capacity for leadership, loyalty, and social skills were all part of the rhetoric of a private education. Boarding schools, of course, have unique opportunities to help build character, above all, through the fact that pupils live in the school separated from their parents. This provides a setting in which greater influence can be exerted on the formation of the pupil's character. Sport was still seen as an excellent tool for character training, but a private education by itself provided no guarantee of a good or well- formed character. Church schools also emphasised character formation and Grech's book on *Educating Christians*, published in 1960 and concerning the formation of the Christian character, was used by many teachers in Catholic schools. Professor Alan McClelland, the then newly appointed professor of education at the University of Hull, gave his inaugural lecture on the subject of general character education in 1979. There was obviously still some interest in discussing character formation within mainstream education.

Character education also has a long association with activities outside the school. The Outward-Bound movement, which Kenneth Roberts et al. (1974: 12) called the 'character training movement', avoided using the term 'character training' because of its connotations with fascist youth organisations. However, character formation was an explicit aim of these courses such as the Duke of Edinburgh Awards, which were extremely popular among Britain's youth between the 1950s and the 1970s. These out-of-school field courses were run by voluntary bodies and involved hill-walking, rock-climbing, sailing, lectures and discussions. The idea was to build character through living together and taking responsibility for one's actions. The emphasis is on community service and duty to one's neighbour. It was character education by doing – through experiences in common. Opportunities for these types of character-building activities declined after the 1970s in response to a decline in demand, but they were and still are key elements in any attempt at character building.

The movement for character education appeared to mirror the times in which it appeared. Whilst the majority of schools in 1900 were still Church schools, there was a movement away from Christianity as the basis for character education in schools. The amount of writing about character in the British context had declined by the 1920s and 1930s: there were a number of reasons for this. During these decades character training became associated with the youth policies and practices of totalitarian regimes in the Soviet Union, in fascist Italy and finally in Nazi Germany. For some, the term character training had become tainted by association, however loose, with organisations like the Hitler Youth Movement. In spite of this, virtually every school in Britain was responding in some implicit way to the educational goal of developing character.

It is debatable whether the negative findings of The Character Education Enquiry conducted by Hugh Hartshorne and Mark May (1928–39) in America adversely affected the very strong character movement in the USA or had any influence in Britain. Hugh Hartshorne was a Protestant minister and actually taught courses on character education at Yale University. He outlined his objectives for the research in the December 1924 edition of *Religious Education*. The goals were threefold: (1) collect examples of how to measure character, (2) test some of these measures with statistical procedures, and (3) devise a set of tests to serve as tools for future research and experimentation. He used 8,150 public school students and 2,715 private school students in the study aged between eight and 16. This enquiry denied that there was anything that could be called character traits, which it defined as the persistent dispositions to act according to moral principle in a variety of situations. The research methodology employed was limited and we should treat the conclusions with a degree of circumspection (see Kamteker, 2004: 465–6). They took the profile of a morally mature person as their model and asked a series of questions of young people on stealing, cheating and lying. The conclusions were, first; that there is no correlation between character training and actual behaviour; and second, that moral behaviour is not consistent in one person from one situation to another. Third, that there is no relationship between what people say about morality and the way that they act, and finally that cheating is distributed, in other words they claim that we all cheat a little. This could have dealt a major blow to traditional character education since it was a research claim that character education was not effectively producing behaviour that conformed to the principles being taught by the modelling, lecturing and use of rewards and punishments.

130   Practices

The report did recommend more experiential learning for building character rather than attempting to teach discrete virtues. However, the report was not widely distributed and James Leming (1993: 35) indicates that books continued to appear, at least in America, on character education.

Ethical relativism also had an influence on the character education movement and most definitely on Hartshorne and May. They shared with many of their contemporaries certain presuppositions about human behaviour that made their methods and their conclusions likely to be confirmed. Johnson believes that they thought in crudely naturalistic terms (1987: 67) and he explains:

> Any particular behaviour was thought to be learned in specific situations, as it produced results satisfying to the individual, and it would be repeated only in response to situations sufficiently alike to call for that behaviour. Learning thus becomes essentially atomistic, situation-specific, and little if at all related to any general form of reasoning. Hence it will do no good to teach moral principles – if there are any, . . . or to hope that such principles, if taught, will produce any general form of recurring behaviour we could call general conduct or character.

Whilst British education was certainly influenced by developments in the USA it is extremely doubtful that this American research is the reason for the decline in publishing about character education in Britain. The provision of moral education continued on the British school curriculum in a fairly conventional way throughout the 1940s and 1950s with very little in the way of intellectual discussion or analysis of what actually went on.

Perhaps the most important educational theorist writing in the 20th century was John Dewey (1859–1952). He wrote about character formation largely from a psychological orientation and in *Democracy and Education* (1944: 346) wrote: 'It is a commonplace of educational theory that the establishing of character is a comprehensive aim of school instruction and discipline.' The following year in *Problems of Men* he believed that discussions of the meaning, nature and content of character 'are integral portions of any adequate ethical theory' (1946: 236). Character education for Dewey was a part of democratic education and he wrote (1934: 186) that character is composed broadly of 'all the desires, purposes, and habits that influence conduct . . . The mind of an individual, his ideas and beliefs, are part of character'. Good character was formed by social interaction and through membership of a group and he writes (1934: 187): 'every influence that modifies the disposition and habits, the desires and thoughts of a child is part of the development of character.'

Dewey did not believe that character formation was restricted to a school and indeed thought that character formation was going on all the time and not confined to special locations or events. While he thought of all education in terms of its moral or character formation (see Salls, 2007: 53–8) Dewey was also a major critic of character education practices in schools and argued that the imposition of behaviours and attitudes on children cannot achieve the goal of character education since the child's inner life will run contrary to this imposed discipline. Dewey had a broad definition of character and was especially critical of what he saw as narrowly conceived and ineffective character education programmes. His target was the teaching methods employed at the time and an example might have been the child-rearing publication of the University Society of America entitled 'Step by Step Character Leads to Success' of 1929. This was an advert to help guide mothers with the upbringing of their children. It depicted a child crawling at the bottom of a staircase with different character traits on each step in the following order: obedience, cheerfulness, self-control, generosity, orderliness, courage, self-reliance, respect for others, honesty, initiative and finally at the top, leadership. The guidance is straightforward and uncomplicated and ignores the findings of cognitive psychology. Dewey was certainly a progressive and liberal voice and a very influential educational reformer. He recommended that greater attention should be paid to the child's experiences and interests – something that was also affirmed during the Italian Renaissance. His educational philosophy has been subsequently seen as a pernicious influence on character formation in schools and he has been accused of undermining efforts to build the character of students. Many defenders of Dewey have stepped forward to claim that he believed in character education in schools (Pietig, 1977, White, 2014). It is also the case that many of his followers misinterpreted what he said, and in his lifetime, Dewey was often alarmed at the excesses of his followers.

By the 1950s and 1960s cognitive psychology became a discipline and placed great emphasis on Lawrence Kolhberg's theories, helping to make them popular in education. The success of Jean Piaget, Lawrence Kohlberg and Eric Erikson was due to their themes of development which indicated progress. These themes satisfied the demands of culture at the time and were compatible with the liberal tradition of critical thinking with its presumption in favour of moral relativism. British culture and society had become more pluralistic and therefore schooling became more sensitive to the increasing heterogeneity of children in many schools. These cognitive approaches to moral education – character education – were also more compatible with the liberal traditions of critical thinking rather than a didactic virtues-based approach: with no substantive content for character education, it was believed by many in education to be less susceptible to criticism from ethnic and religious groups in society. Many of those who still explicitly talked about character had to continue the use of 'moral education' to describe their character goals.

There is a wide variety of theories by Dewey, Piaget, Erikson, Kohlberg, and Peters concerning how character is formed, but none of these are comprehensive theories (Arthur, 2003: 59 ff). For example, in the 1980s Lawrence Kohlberg (1927–87) became a major figure in the study of making moral decisions or moral reasoning – we could say he looked at one aspect of character formation. His interest began with his doctoral studies at the University of

Chicago where he produced a PhD dissertation titled 'The Development of Moral Thinking and Choices in years 10–16' (Kohlberg, 1964). This was a focus on the thought processes in the child and not in the actual moral decisions they made. He was not convinced that character traits even existed and was clearly influenced by the character studies in the late 1920s of Hartshorne and May (see Kohlberg, 1968) whose conclusions he accepted, calling education for virtuous character little more than an arbitrary 'bag of virtues'. Kohlberg agreed with Piaget's (1932) theory of moral development and used his storytelling technique to develop stories involving moral dilemmas. In each story he provided a number of questions so that the child could choose between just and not so just answers. These questions were adapted for different age ranges, but in his research, he used 75 American boys and the stories were artificial, largely unrelated to the lives of these boys. However, he claimed to identify three distinct levels of moral reasoning with two sub-stages at each level. The first level he called Pre-Conventional Morality in which the moral code of children under the age of nine is shaped by significant adults. The second level he called Conventional Morality and most people could be found in this level displaying the norms of the group to which the person belonged – it was essentially about conforming to moral rules. The third level, Post-Conventional Morality includes the capacity to make decisions for yourself and he thought only 10–15 per cent of the population reached this level (Kohlberg, 1984).

Each level represented a very different mode of moral thinking. Kohlberg dismissed the virtues as unimportant to his theory and furthermore he did not recognise the central role of habit in the formation of character traits. He effectively downplayed socialisation in character formation and emphasised the individual as the one who judges what is morally right or wrong. In regard to character formation it was clear that this research emphasised that educators need to be sensitive to the developmental levels of children and create educational activities and programmes that match a child's reasoning skills. Aristotle was clearly conscious of this, as were many educators that came after him. Kohlberg's developmental model effectively turns the individual into a kind of rational, skilled judge who depended on the ability to reason at a high level. Those less educated or less able to reason in his scheme were viewed as less morally sound in their judgements and actions. The many criticisms of Kohlberg's model conclude that he failed to find a universal, invariant sequence of stages in the development of moral judgement. The tensions between habit inculcation and the development of autonomous reasoning continue. Both Kohlberg and Piaget before him focused on reasoning and deliberation as essential qualities of any Aristotelian character formation approach, but Kohlberg believed that traditional forms of character education were arbitrary.

Carol Gilligan (1982) challenged Kohlberg's scheme and rejected his two key claims. First, that the stages of moral development are universal, and second, that justice is the highest aim of morality. Kohlberg's samples were boys and Gilligan found that the focus of girls was on preserving human connections regardless of the principles at stake and it was these human connections that constituted the 'different voice' that women brought to moral deliberation. Rather than operating with what Kohlberg termed abstract and universal principles, Gilligan found that women base their actions on the needs of those with whom they are connected. Nel Noddings (1984) in turn provided a philosophical grounding for the ethic of care by emphasising that the 'good' is not to be found in abstract ideas of justice, but in caring relationships which originate in the relationship between mother and child. The emphasis here is on moral interdependence as Noddings (1984: 6) puts it: 'How good *I* can be is partly a function of how *you* – the other – receive and respond to me. Whatever virtue I exercise is completed, fulfilled in you.'

In the 1960s there was increasing discussion about the development of character and the *British Journal of Psychology of Education* held a number of symposia on the theme in the early 1960s (see Peters, 1960). The Newsom Report (1963) (*Half Our Future*, 1963: 52–9) devoted a chapter of its discussion to moral and spiritual education, but saw a restricted role for schools: 'Theirs is a limited, though a vital role and they are neither the community nor the church. Society must not look to schools to solve its moral problems, but it expects and gets from them an important contribution towards their solution.' Even the Plowden Report (1969) (*Children and their Primary Schools*, 1969: 572), which gave such emphasis to child-centred learning, was still able to recommend that pupils 'should be brought to know and love God and to practise in the school community the virtues appropriate to their age and environment'. Here we have a firm assertion of the promotion of virtue and the link between religion and morality. Still, child-centred learning and the promotion of stage theories of development appeared to remove some degree of responsibility from teachers for the education of their pupils. The new disciplines of educational psychology and sociology seemed to indicate that many elements in education and schooling was essentially pre-determined and that ideas such as character education were of limited value to teachers.

The important work in the USA of Peck and Havighurst (1960) on character education helped to revive explicit thinking in the area, even though they concluded that each generation tended to perpetuate its strengths and weaknesses of character and that character formation in the early years was relatively unmodifiable. The 1960s and 1970s were concerned with values clarification and procedural neutrality in the classroom and there was a widespread presumption in favour of moral relativism. The idea behind values clarification was that each student gain clarity regarding his or her values. It included seven steps with three processes that included: students choosing freely from alternative values; prizing these values by a willingness to affirm them in public; and acting upon the choice of values. The teacher role was to design strategies to help the student decide, and whatever decisions the student arrived at were to be accepted by the teacher and class. Through this process it was claimed students would identify their own personal and meaningful values and beliefs, thus making them better critical thinkers and more socially aware. Authentic character formation also aims to develop a person who can reason, discuss and evaluate issues, but values clarification failed to engage with relevant content or language in order for this to happen. This hyper-critical approach combined with dubious curriculum content limited the critical engagement. The whole process of value clarification approaches was largely utopian despite its popularity with teachers and it raised issues with student privacy, but ultimately the method was superficial, increased ethical relativism and had a therapeutic base. It was the reaction against this relativistic thought and culture that has seen the re-emergence of more traditional character education approaches. In Britain, people like John White (1990) have explicitly called for the return of character education in schools despite the fact there had been little in the way of empirical research or major evaluation of character education programmes in the USA or Britain.

There is a long history of ill-conceived, ineffective and failed efforts at character education in Britain. The kinds of character that teachers and educational thinkers espoused and the training methods they used also varied enormously. Liberal Protestantism sought the reduction of religion to morality in the 19th century and the early part of the 20th century; in this mission it was more effective than the small number of vocal secularists in Victorian society. Basil Mitchell (1980: 161) aptly comments: 'This is why the Victorian Age, although possessing much that we are in process of losing, cannot be cited as a paradigm of Christian morality. The Victorians idolised morality, giving it that supreme importance which they were increasingly unable to accord God. Hence the morality they believed in and practised was in constant danger of becoming legalistic and joyless.' The progressives at the beginning of the 20th century were reacting against educational practices such as rote learning and the enforcement in schools of patterns of traditional formal behaviour. However, they did not provide many viable alternatives to the various pedagogical methods used for teaching character education at the time.

The rhetoric of character was abandoned in 1960s in favour of 'self-discovery' and 'personal growth'. Character had given way to a more inward concept of 'personality'. Character development suggests that core character qualities are innate to the individual and just need to be drawn out rather than put in. The 1960s certainly marked a turning point in British character education efforts. Psychology became the dominant discipline in moral and character education and few philosophical, sociological, and theological accounts were advanced. Progressive theories in education increasingly put an emphasis on individual rights and child-centred learning. The focus was on the needs of the child. Moral education had to be inclusive and uncontroversial. Some, like Gilbert Ryle (1975), wrote about the possibility of teaching virtues in the mid-1970s, but this was rare. By the 1980s and 1990s we see a growing interest in the virtues and their re-discovery for character education and this was accompanied by trenchant criticism from some, such as Nash (1997) who quipped:

'the character education genre smacks of ultra-conservative special pleading.' The government's Green and White Papers in education of 2000 re-discovered education with character, but are really a furtherance of pre-1950s government thinking on character education, which explicitly attempted to promote certain specified virtues through providing opportunities for 'social activities' in schools. There are striking similarities between government policy on character in 1949 with that of 2001 which will be examined in the next chapter.

Section III

Policies and issues

Chapter 9

Contemporary policies and themes

This chapter examines three contrasting contemporary approaches to character formation policy in different contexts. In each case the issues, ideas, underlying ideology and language is different. First, positive education theory and practice in the USA; second, the emergence of a government-inspired character education policy in the UK; and third, an exploration of State character formation policies outside of the Western tradition. The first corresponds largely to the psychological model, the second to the neo-liberal model with elements of the conservative model and the third to a combination of the hegemonic and conservative models. The chapter also reviews some of the issues associated with character formation and discusses whether character formation constitutes indoctrination; how it relates to religion and liberal education, and what advocates of character education generally mean by the term within school programmes. It is important to realise in this chapter that there has never been a static understanding of the meaning of character formation.

Positive education

Character education in the USA today is polarised politically, but it was Democratic President Bill Clinton on 4 February 1997 in his State of the Union Address to Congress who proclaimed, 'I challenge all our schools to teach character education'. To underscore the seriousness of this challenge he established a series of White House Conferences on character building. What he meant in this advocacy of character education was not explained, but he found the rhetoric of character attractive and there appeared to be considerable political support for strengthening character education in schools from other politicians on both the left and right divide. Clinton's appeal had limited success, with many States protecting their educational policies from any hint of federal interference. This was a time when self-help therapies based on popular psychology books encouraged people to seek personal empowerment through positive thinking in the belief that everything could be improved instantly and effortlessly. These best-selling books, and later therapy apps, told a story of how we could control, manage and improve our behaviour and emotions – how we could

140   Policies and issues

think and act more positively, which would lead to a flourishing life. They had their advocates and techniques that included mindfulness and meditation and the market was huge for these kind of books, such as Caroline Miller's *Creating Your Best Life*. These self-guided improvement texts promised happiness, but the so-called science behind them was unproven, oversimplified and open to endless interpretations. Against this background we ask how character and positive psychology/education are connected.

Positive psychology is reputed to have been founded by Marty Seligman as a new branch of psychology in his Presidential Address at the 1998 American Psychological Association Annual Conference, a speech in which he does not mention character. The message was – we must focus on what is going right with people and not on the negatives. Essentially positive psychology claims that your external circumstances make very little difference to your happiness and that happiness and flourishing in life are dependent on your intentional activities. Therefore, it followed that to think positively will have positive consequences irrespective of your socio-economic, cultural or educational state. This appears to resemble the self-improvement movement that the Scottish Enlightenment thinkers began and which so marked the Victorian age. The sweeping claims made by Seligman have received sustained and persistent criticism, not least that they lack an underlying theory, fail to define terms, advance unjustified generalisations, identify causal relations where none exist, overstate research findings; it also created a fraternity uncritically following every word of the movement and citing and publishing each other's work (see Miller, 2008). There is certainly a culture of scientism that pervades positive psychology with an emphasis on attempting to quantify happiness, but Hunter and Nedeliskey (2018) effectively debunk much of this. Nevertheless, positive education emerged as a spin-off of positive psychology in the early 2000s and at the level of rhetoric incorporated 'character' and 'virtue' terms as one of its stated goals.

Peterson and Seligman (2004) had previously produced a handbook on character strengths which led to the development of the Values in Action (VIA) Classification of Character Strengths and Virtues framework and survey. Twenty-four character strengths are clustered under six core virtues which the authors claim are represented across most of the world's cultures. The survey part of this framework is an assessment tool designed to help you identify your character strengths that contribute to personal flourishing. However, no attention is paid to possible conflict between the different character strengths in real-life situations (see Kristjansson, 2012). This subsequently led to five elements that Seligman recommended that schools pursue for increased flourishing: (P) positive, (E) emotions, (R) relationships, (M) meaning and (A) achievement. This PERMA teaching approach treats the character strengths as skills that can be taught and improved, and it is claimed that it helps students feel good about themselves and to function better. Many of the experimental interventions that involved young people took place without reference to real-life situations or consideration of culture. Some of Australia's most exclusive private schools have

Contemporary policies and themes   141

led the way with PERMA, but it is difficult to see what is new or original in positive education. The character and virtue rhetoric is thin at best, and Kristjansson (2012) charts how the whole idea of positive education existed prior to positive psychology. The International Positive Education Network (IPEN), established in 2014, claims that we must blend academic learning with character, but there is nothing new in this claim, as this text has shown. IPEN's ideas of character and virtues remain underdeveloped. As a result, a largely instrumentalist conception of character strengths is prioritised as a means to achieve the goals of academic achievement and 'success' in school.

This is illustrated concretely if we consider the KIPP (Knowledge is Power Programme) adoption of positive psychology's character strengths as part of its 'academics and character' approach to running schools. KIPP was founded in 1994 and is the largest of the charter school management organisations currently running over 224 schools in the USA. Charter schools are public schools and have a degree of independence over what educational philosophy they adopt and KIPP influences a number of these charter schools, but it is a minority influence as there are over 6,000 charter schools in the USA with many adopting different character programmes and philosophies. Charter schools are best compared to the UK's free schools and were established to close the achievement gap and increase college completion rates for largely socially disadvantaged students. Charter schools, particularly KIPP schools, are often associated with prolonged school days, teaching aligned to standardised tests and strict discipline policies. In academic terms they appear to have been successful, although there is much debate about the reasons why. KIPP schools were concerned with character from the beginning, but this concern has become an explicit philosophy or perhaps 'science' as a focus on character strengths is used as a scientific basis for predicting a child's long-term success in life.

Seven character strengths are prioritised in KIPP schools for an engaged, happy and successful life. These are: zest, grit, optimism, self-control, gratitude, social intelligence and curiosity. All these character strengths are to be cultivated through four complementary components: modelling, explicating, encouraging and monitoring. KIPP schools emphasise clear language, high expectations, the positive role of character exemplars, and positive mind-set growth. However, the first thing that is noted is that KIPP schools avoid any talk of virtues and attempt to speak about character in value-neutral terms. There is a complete lack of moral principles and an avoidance of moral judgements. Dishon and Goodman (2017) in an examination of the character approach in KIPP schools found that they are focused on control systems with rules to manage prescribed forms of conduct resulting in high levels of compliancy to imposed behavioural roles. They outline a number of tensions in KIPP's use of character and conclude that KIPP schools have adopted the instrumentalist approach to character education that positive educators recommend, because it supports the desirable behavioural habits they wish to instil. They argue that while KIPP schools are couched in the language of 'character' their approach is incompatible with authentic character formation since it narrows the meaning of education, is amoral and careerist in intent, and reduces it to a form of compliance.

Dishon and Goodman (2017: 198) conclude that KIPP promotes the behaviours needed to succeed in school with a 'strictly utilitarian rationale for building character' which is better understood as a form of training and therefore 'labelling such effort as the development of character is imprecise at best, and is a disservice to research and practice on character and moral education'. Even the choice of a KIPP school on the part of the parents is guided by instrumental goals as they have confidence first and foremost in the quality of the school and the explicit link between academic qualifications to be gained and enhanced employment opportunities. Promoters of positive education have been able to persuade many school decision-makers that their thinking is valuable and they have captured media attention to guide debates and discussions towards their own interests and concerns. However, moral considerations transcend the realm of psychological analysis. Yet the human sciences continue to believe that every aspect of human life is subject to scientific scrutiny – as Schwartz (1987: 3) says: 'While moral philosophy attempted to teach people how they should live, what they should value, what roles they should play in the community, social science teaches people how they do live, what they do value, what roles they do play in their communities.' Many branches of psychology have attempted to find ways to talk about character that are intended to be tradition and value-free, which have origins in their scientific aspirations towards objectivity. It is not a project that is either complete or entirely successful.

UK policy on character education

The Labour Government of 1997 set out to articulate new goals for schooling and in its first White Paper, *Excellence in Schools* (1997: 10) it stated that families and schools should take responsibility so that children 'appreciate and understand a moral code on which civilised society is based'. In the National Curriculum Statement of Values, Aims and Purposes (1999: 10ff) it identified certain virtues that ought to underpin the school curriculum. Education according to this Statement should reaffirm 'our commitment to the virtues of truth, justice, honesty, trust and a sense of duty'. The school curriculum should aim to 'develop principles for distinguishing between right and wrong' and pass on 'enduring values'. A Green Paper was published in 2001 titled *Schools: Building on Success* (2001) which spoke about 'education with character' as a policy aim and this was reinforced in the White Paper of the same year called *Schools: Achieving Success* (2001). We see here the explicit mention of virtues and character in government policy development, but these terms are not defined anywhere in the statements made (Arthur, 2005). The government recognised that schools may not be the ideal learning environments for building character and virtues, advocating experiential learning through extra-curricular activities. Hunter (2001: 225) questions whether character education can be promoted

Contemporary policies and themes | 143

by a government policy since such policy values 'have, by their very nature, lost the quality of sacredness, their commanding character, and thus their power to inspire and shame'. He argues that the social life in which character formation makes sense has all but disintegrated and that schools are naturally reluctant to be involved in explicit character formation. Labour was attempting to rediscover character formation for schools, but without a sound conception of what character or virtue truly meant or of their implications for education. Labour lost office in 2010, but Shadow Secretaries of State Stephen Twigg (2011–13) and his successor Tristram Hunt (2013–15) made numerous speeches promoting the idea of character education, particularly character, creativity and resilience. They even recommended, without much by way of evidence, that State schools should learn from the private sector how to implement character education.

The riots of August 2011 in England resulted in the Riots, Communities and Victims Panel which produced a report in 2012 recommending what it called a new approach – 'building character'. The report made clear 'we propose that there should be a new requirement for schools to develop and publish their policies on building character'. By 2014 there was a new Secretary of State for Education, Nicky Morgan (2017), who began to advocate explicitly for character education in schools (Arthur, 2018: 142). She wrote *Taught Not Caught: Education for 21st Century Character* soon after leaving office, which promoted her ideas of character formation in schools. There was increasing mention of character building and development in debates within Parliament, and the DfE had a newly formed Character Unit to advance the character education agenda. There was certainly a higher profile for character initiatives and there was cross-party support, but once again there was a lack of clarity about what it meant for schools. By 2015 both the Conservative and Labour manifestos made reference to building the character of young people in schools, and character building in schools has been a continuing theme at their political conferences. Labour sought to use character education goals in a pragmatic and instrumental way which linked raising pupil attainment in tests, meeting the needs of the new economy and promoting democratic participation in public life. The Conservative Party was also much less influenced by these goals.

The appointment of Damian Hinds as Secretary of State for Education in 2017 further advanced the idea of character education as he reinvigorated the Character Unit at the DfE with new staff. In almost every speech he made there was a reference to character, which was not surprising as he had previously chaired the All Parliamentary Committee on Social Mobility from 2011 which advocated character education in schools. In 2014 he published the *Character and Resilience Manifesto* that defines character as the capacity for teamwork, commitment, resilience as well as for health and general well-being. In 2017 the Department for Education published 'Developing Character Skills in Schools' which was a commissioned piece of research that explicitly understood character to mean support for academic attainment, preparation for employment and making a contribution to British society – identical aims to the previous government, which suggests that the political consensus on character education was maintained. However, this paper also left the door open to other interpretations when the report noted that a 'multidisciplinary field of theory and research is emerging around how best to conceptualise character education' and referenced the Jubilee Centre for Character and Virtues. At the Conservative Party Conference in October 2018 Hinds said: 'Character is something you will never see on a certificate of education, but you know it when you see it.' He had previously said that character was more important than academic qualifications. He made a major speech on character on 7 February 2019 in which he repeated much of what had previously been said, but significantly he employed the use of the word 'virtues' to describe honesty, humility, courage, and kindness as central to developing character. This new language indicates a borrowing, however slight, from the virtue ethics model. Hinds also re-launched the National Character Awards for Schools and established an Advisory Committee on Character to report on how character education should be promoted in schools, demonstrating clearly the government's continuing and sustained interest in promoting character education in schools.

Hinds recognises that character formation has an intrinsic value, but he often presents it as an instrumental benefit that can be quantified, which therefore corresponds to the neo-liberal model of character. Too often character is spoken about as if its justification is to increase economic competitiveness. There is a modern objection that State support for character education could be construed as undue preference on behalf of certain virtues. This is a part of the idea of liberal neutrality argued for by Ronald Dworkin in his work *A Matter of Principle*. Dworkin states that 'government must be neutral on what might be called the question of the good life' (1985: 191). This theory 'supposes that political decisions must be, so far as is possible, independent of any particular conception of the good life, or of what gives value to life. Since the citizens of a society differ in their conceptions, the government does not treat them as equals if it prefers one conception to another' (1985: 191). According to this view, a government would seem to violate liberal neutrality if it supported the character formation when some citizens in a society might not hold this as part of their conception of a good life.

The OFSTED Education Inspection Framework included the following statement:

> The 2019 Consultation was the first time that character was ever mentioned in an inspection document and it became a key factor in the personal development section. Inspectors will make a judgement on the personal development of learners by evaluating the extent to which the curriculum and the provider's wider work support learners to develop their character – including their resilience, confidence and independence – and help them know how to keep physically and mentally healthy. This judgement focuses on the dimensions of the personal development of pupils that our education

Contemporary policies and themes   145

system has agreed, either by consensus or statute, are the most significant: 'developing pupils' character, the set of positive personal traits, dispositions and virtues that inform their motivation and guide their conduct so that they reflect wisely, learn eagerly, behave with integrity and cooperate consistently well with others. This gives pupils the qualities they need to flourish in our society.

The OFSTED proposed definition of character is: 'A set of positive personal traits, dispositions and virtues that informs their motivation and guides their conduct so that they reflect wisely, learn eagerly, behave with integrity and cooperate consistently well with others. This gives pupils the qualities they need to flourish in our society.' This definition, with its use of 'virtues' and 'flourishing', is another indicator of how virtue language is being adopted by State inspection agencies.

Grade descriptors for personal development are first, Outstanding (1) – The way the school goes about developing pupils' character is exemplary and is worthy of being shared with others and second, Good (2) – The curriculum and the school's wider work support pupils to develop character. The Early Years Inspection Handbook under the Personal Development criteria states: 'The curriculum promotes and supports children's emotional security and development of their character. Children are gaining a good understanding of what makes them unique' (2019: 37). The Further Education and Skills Inspection Handbook under Personal Development (2019: 48) states:

> Providers can take effective action to extend learners' experiences, but the impact may not be seen for many years. Inspectors will not make judgements about the impact of the personal development of learners. Their judgements about learners' personal development are concerned with the opportunities that learners get to help them develop their character, confidence and resilience. These include opportunities and support to keep themselves healthy, both physically and mentally. Inspectors will consider the support learners get to develop their plans for their next steps, including to employment.

It further states: 'The curriculum and the provider's wider work support learners to develop their character – including their resilience, confidence and independence and, where relevant, help them know how to keep physically and mentally healthy' (2019: 50). In the Education Inspection Framework Overview of research it is stated: 'However, intentionally investing in character education using a whole-school approach, modelling desired behaviours at both school and teacher level, integrating character development with a strong curriculum rather than doing this as a standalone separate activity, developing pupils' intrinsic motivation, shared core values and positive relationships have been posited as key ways in which schools can develop pupils' character' (2019: 30). The

146   Policies and issues

Consultation, in regard to character development, received overwhelming support from schools and the Framework was published officially on 14 May 2019 with the same content and definitions of character development detailed above.

International dimensions of character policy

It is interesting to look at character formation from outside the Western tradition in societies that have been little influenced by the thoughts of Aristotle. This is especially enlightening when we consider the policy dimensions of character education from the point of view of governments. The English Secretary of State for Education, Nicky Morgan, announced in December 2014 that she intended to secure England's place as a global leader by expanding the nation's provision and evidence base for character education. She travelled to Japan to discuss and to discover what the Ministry of Education was thinking about in making provision for character education. Character education policy is usually a reflection of the prevalent values of a particular political context or jurisdiction. National cultural traditions are also a major determinant and influence on education systems and therefore these State systems are localised and culturally relative. Morgan's interest revolved around the questions: Why should national governments legislate for and promote virtue in their school systems? Why is it assumed that there ought to be a role for governments to improve the moral character of people? What would such interventions look like? These questions invite normative justification for any State intervention in the school curriculum. In Asia there is a diverse range of philosophical and religious approaches underpinning educational thinking, including Confucianism, Taoism, Buddhism, Maoism and Christianity. In England and in the West more generally the focus is almost exclusively on Western philosophical traditions as described in this text. It is worth therefore looking at some of the policy implications of character education initiatives in these countries (see Arthur, 2016).

Character education in Asian schools is experiencing a remarkable revival and re-emphasis. The purpose of education, as expressed through government legislation and regulations, in China, Vietnam, Taiwan, Singapore, South Korea and Japan has traditionally been explicitly linked to the building of character. Each of these governments has shown new and sometimes intense interest in looking at how to refresh and operationalise character education in schools and have either introduced new goals for character education or are currently planning a new curriculum. Parental and societal concern about the behaviour of students is a factor fuelling the move to revitalise character education. On a broader level, what is happening is perhaps symptomatic of the vacuum of meaning engendered by consumerism and materialism. There is much agreement on broad aims for character education in many Asian societies, but considerable variation in the political operation of character education, resulting in divergence of content, practices, teaching approaches and assessment within these different jurisdictions. As in England, these Asian societies are largely marked by competitive, data-driven standardised public-school examinations, and many believe that such systems have had a detrimental effect on attempts at character building in students. The renewed focus on character education is intended to counterbalance the perceived materialistic and selfish tendencies generated by an exclusive focus on academic success in which a student's worth is judged solely by their academic attainment as measured in public examinations.

The current 2006 Fundamental Law on Japanese Education, which is still seen in Japan as controversial and contested, refers to character in three places. First, in the introduction, it speaks of the purpose of education as the 'perfection of character'. Second, in paragraph three, it says that schools and teachers must 'polish the character' of their students. Third, in paragraph 11, it says that moral education is 'the foundation of character' in schools. While the importance of character is already recognised, the revision of the National Curriculum in Japan is reviewing how to ensure that character education is implemented in every school. Moral education is already compulsory in Japanese schools, but its practice and quality vary. The Ministry of Education believes that there has been a failure to determine what moral education ought to be in the classroom. To this end there is a unit in the Ministry preparing new content for moral education for introduction in 2019. Japan has decided to follow Singapore, China and South Korea in introducing a specific timetabled place in the school curriculum for moral and character education. It could be argued that character building activities in Japan lead to high degrees of social conformity at odds with independence and autonomy in school students – the kind of character education promoted is quasi-collectivist in style and relies on the cultural homogeneity of society.

While there is some Confucian thought invoked in Japanese character education there are also Buddhist, Shinto and even Christian influences (Luamer, 2009: 172). The most important Confucian influence is the emphasis on interpersonal relations and the promotion of humility. The purpose of voluntary after-school clubs in Japan (*Bukatsudo*) is to help socialise Japanese youth as 'part of the group' (see Cave, 2004: 384) by emphasising participation, habit, repetition, routine, ritual, order, shared responsibility and discipline. Such clubs are run by teachers and involve sport, art and music, but generally discourage competition between students in favour of self-improvement, good manners and getting on with others. These clubs, originally inspired by the English public school of the 19th century, emphasise cheering others on so that everyone contributes to success. Such clubs are often compulsory, begin at the end of the school day and last for two hours up to six times a week. Some have suggested that these are vestiges of a previous 'militarised character training', others that they are about engendering obligations to the community and the promotion of the common good.

In Korea, a government report entitled 'The agenda of education reform for the establishment of New Educational System' published in 2009 by the Ministry of Education spoke about the need for the development of 'sound moral character' and the 'development of virtues involved in positive human relationships', as well as of preparing young people to make good ethical decisions in their lives. The three specific stated goals of character education are: understanding oneself, caring for and respecting others, and cultivating the ability to cooperate with others. Filial piety, a Confucian ideal, is emphasised and involves learning how to demonstrate respect for parents, grandparents and elders in the community. Co-operation and sharing are important, as well as developing a sense of balance and order. The intention is to empower students to make responsible decisions that are ethical and socially acceptable. Previously, students took the purpose of ethics or moral education classes to be simply about memorising information. The South Korean government passed the 'Character Education Promotion Act' in January 2015, but until then there had been no consensus about the meaning of character education. The Act offers an official definition of character (building) education. Korean schools (from kindergartens to high schools) are required to teach students how to develop 'humane character and capabilities'. The definition of character education refers to teaching students how to 'develop the mentality and attitude necessary for living with others, and in nature. [and] . . . key values include etiquette, filial duty, generosity, cooperation, communication and responsibility'.

Character education is compulsory in Singapore schools and needs to be understood as occurring within an evolving political and social framework that highlights social integration and consensus. Character, civic and moral education now play a major role in schools, emphasising honesty, commitment to excellence, teamwork, discipline, loyalty, humility, national pride and the promotion of the common good as part of the character and citizenship education provided in every school (Tan and Chin, 2004 OMIT REFERENCE). The needs of family and community are considered more important than the needs of individuals; collectivism and a paternalistic approach is prioritised. Taiwan has also preserved traditional Chinese values and has stressed the moral dimensions of education, but has been more controversially divided between conservative and progressive camps. There are no formal timetabled lessons in moral education in schools, which has been criticised by more conservative voices. Conservative voices in Taiwan want the transmission of virtues to take place in schools, while progressives appear more concerned with the process of decision-making for social justice. However, character education is expected to be taught through all subjects, through the school ethos and in extra-curricular activities.

The Chinese Communist Party uses moral education in schools to promote patriotism and socialism. The Confucian idea of character development is to cultivate virtuous behaviour in society with teachers modelling the virtues. Character education is therefore directly related to building up society, and China shares many of the classroom practices of Japanese schools, including an emphasis on extra-curricular activities. Confucian ethics is accepted as a secular moral philosophy by the Chinese government. The State therefore exploits popular support for Confucian ideas for its own social purposes (Zhao, 1998). In Vietnam, character education forms part of moral education and is provided from pre-school to tertiary levels of education. It has a strong national education policy grounded in Vietnamese law and emphasises the promotion of manners and right conduct. Character education in Vietnam also reflects socialist ideology. Primary schools focus on character building while secondary schools give more emphasis to building the good citizen.

Many Asian states are quasi-paternalistic about character education, regarding it as justifiable to interfere in the lives of students because they will in the end be better off as a result. There is a tendency towards a nationalist based character education which demands loyalty to the ideology of the State. The goals of character education in England are not as clear as those officially stipulated in these Asian countries, and as a result, Asian governments normally dictate clear and ambitious goals that serve to reinforce character education, supporting it with resources and training programmes to ensure effective implementation. There is very little that can be detected as Aristotelian in these character initiatives other than the obvious overlaps seen in Confucian and Aristotelian thought.

Significant contemporary character themes

Historically, the rhetoric of character has been employed to advance ill-conceived policy goals and practices of character formation. The three policy examples discussed have in common a tendency to see character formation solely in terms of behaviour outcomes to be taught in a behaviourist fashion. This approach has produced a great deal of erroneous content and teaching methods throughout history. Despite this, each generation returns to advocating character formation in our schools and families, somehow recognising in the background the importance of the inner virtues which we need to build character as well as the right actions required for that purpose. Aristotle's influence on ideas of character formation remains profound even when it is not made explicit, remaining, as it often does, subterranean. We are indebted to Aristotle for helping us how to think through our ideas about character formation. In this book we have looked at the factors that cause or prevent character formation; surveyed numerous definitions of character, examined the best and worst ways of developing character and looked at how politics and culture play a role in setting standards of social conduct and social convention. We recognise that there has been criticism of character formation when it has simply been used as a means to maintain the status quo or even promoting a harsh Protestant work ethic.

Nevertheless, there has been a growing renaissance of virtue and character and a return of virtue theory since Anscombe's 1958 paper. Support for character formation is strong and growing around the world as it appeals to diverse audiences who link it to a sense of moral decline, a loss of economic

150 Policies and issues

competitiveness, and a loss of common culture. This movement is wide and diverse and the claims made for character building in schools and colleges are huge: prepares students for the workforce; improves academic attainment; fosters active citizenship; creates safer schools; teaches universal values. Character education has been endorsed by many governments, which has caused critics to question it in the following terms: it focuses too much on the individual; it perpetuates the status quo, it teaches uniformity and leaves political, economic and cultural initiatives unquestioned. Character formation can sometimes also take a negative view of human nature. Character is not simple either in theory or practice and it is often so embedded in common sense as to be taken for granted and not open to question.

Terry McLaughlin and Mark Halstead (1999: 136) take issue with contemporary approaches to character education. They claim that character educators generally begin with detailing the social ills of society and then offer character education as a remedy. Character educators also, they claim, leave the explanation of difficult moral concepts until later in the pupil's development. They then criticise these views by outlining that character education is narrowly concerned with certain virtues, that it is restricted, limited, and focuses on traditional methods of teaching. Also, that there is a limited rationale given for the aims and purposes of character education by those who propose it in schools and further that there is a restricted emphasis on the use of critical faculties in pupils. They observe that (1999: 139) the character education movement 'lacks a common theoretical perspective and core of practice'. It is perhaps why McIntyre (1984: 2) notes the progressive confusion and disintegration of the moral vocabulary in the West over the last five hundred years. There exists, he says, a state of grave disorder and we have lost our comprehension. However, out of this confusion McIntyre hopes that a new version of the virtuous life will emerge. He suggests that it will only come from those who plan a social life in which virtue has genuine meaning. He compares the present moment to the decline of the Roman Empire when men and women turned aside from the task of shoring up the Roman imperium, but instead tried to plan new forms of common life, forms in which the virtues could be lived, sustained and formed (1984: 245). He believes that we today are in a similar moment and foresees a green twig growing from the dead stump of our present culture.

There have always been throughout history tensions between the education of the individual and education for the *Polis*, and there have also been tensions between education and training. Teaching is a deliberate act to induce learning in another person – it therefore cannot be a neutral activity. Indoctrination is a pejorative term in modern educational discourse as something objectionable or an abuse of teaching, but it is open to wide misuse in its great variety of meanings. It made an aggressive appearance in the 1960s as an attack on traditional educational content and teaching methods by liberal advocates of openness and freedom in school education. Anything that was not considered to be critical or independent was considered to be indoctrination, including attempts at character formation. Critics of character education in schools, such as Kohn (1997: 429) continue to assert: 'Let me get straight to the point. What goes by the name of character education nowadays is, for the most part, a collection of exhortations and intrinsic inducements designed to make children work harder and do what they are told. Even when other values are promoted – caring and fairness, say – the preferred method of instruction is tantamount to indoctrination.' Education from this liberal or progressive perspective was considered to be not about transmission or information, but rather about values clarification, discussion and engagement with a belief that education could be neutral. Consequently, it was easy to label anything you disliked as potentially indoctrinatory or even that character education is ineffective and a waste of time.

Real indoctrination stops the development of rationality and restricts authentic autonomy, but is exceptionally difficult to achieve. It could be defined as an attempt deliberately to implant into the experiences of an individual any belief or set of beliefs, to the exclusion of others, in such a way as to prevent these beliefs being adequately evaluated and questioned by the individual concerned. Is it possible that by the mere fact of living within some particular socio-cultural historical context this would of itself prevent such an evaluation? Indoctrination makes the decisions for the student and in the context of character formation, tends, as liberal educators would claim, to moralise by asserting moral injunctions. However, this would not count as character formation which depends on the ability to think, analyse and understand – you cannot develop virtuous character while being indoctrinated. Consciousness and free will are essential requirements of a neo-Aristotelian notion of character since our actions must be self-conscious and intentionally chosen or caused by our own free volition – we need to think, judge, and choose before we act.

In the *Republic* (343a–345b) Plato discusses the Sophistic uses of 'persuasion' in order to change someone's mind, not through argument, but through obfuscating their understanding of truth by dissimulation. He calls this process an injustice particularly if it is combined with force. Pieper (1967: 22–31) comments on this: 'people are subtly intimated into acquiescing in their own coercion and simultaneously into believing that this acquiescence is entirely reasonable because they are persuaded that what they are coerced into doing is the very thing they want to do, in any case.' This focus on teaching methods is key to understanding indoctrination since a teacher who deliberately engaged in any of the following activities in the classroom would not be engaging in authentic character formation: lying, misrepresentation of facts, distortion of evidence, use of corporal punishment and excessive coercion, over-generalisation, inadequate explanation, isolating students from contrary influences, and so forth. It may even involve the improper use of the teacher's charm and charisma as in the case of *The Prime of Miss Jean Brodie*, particularly if they push for uncritical acceptance of ideas and beliefs and ignore or disregard contrary evidence. However, Callan (1997: 202) reminds us that: 'A moral education

152 Policies and issues

cleansed of everything that might give offence is not a coherent philosophy.' Augustine captures it better when he said:

> For do teachers profess that it is their thoughts which are perceived and grasped by the students, and not the sciences themselves which they convey through thinking? For who is so stupidly curious as to send his son to school that he may learn what the teacher thinks? . . . Those who are pupils consider within themselves whether what has been explained has been said truly; looking of course to that interior truth, according to the measure of which each of us is able. Thus, they learn, and when the interior truth makes known to them that true things have been said, they applaud.
>
> (*De Magistro*, 389 AD)

Ryan and Bohlin (1999: 15) perfectly capture the absurdity of not deliberately teaching a child to act virtuously in re-calling the record of the conversation between Samuel Taylor Coleridge and John Thelwall on 27 July 1830: 'Thelwell thought it very unfair to influence a child's mind by inculcating any opinions before it should have come to years of discretion, and be able to choose for itself. I showed him my garden, and told him it was my botanical garden. "How so" said he, "it is covered with weeds". "Oh," I replied, "that is only because it has not yet come to its age of discretion and choice. The weeds, you see, have taken the liberty to grow, and I thought it unfair of me to prejudice the soil towards roses and strawberries'. There appears to be an irrational fear of indoctrination in modern progressive educational circles. The fact is that character formation that fosters sound intellectual judgement enables students to transcend the boundaries of what they have strictly inherited. They ought to be skilled and able to reinterpret what they have learnt and use it as a base for future development.

As Carr (2005) explains, there are justifications of substantial values that are likely to be acceptable regardless of cultural differences, but the liberal opposition to the coercion of individuals into any 'comprehensive theory of the good' remains unresolved in contemporary educational theory. Bloom (1987) was concerned that young people display an excessive openness to everything without any notion of right and wrong against which to judge their own and other's cultures. They learned, he claims, to doubt beliefs, before they themselves believed anything. For McIntyre (1984: 28) every society has its stock of characters, 'the moral representatives of their culture and they are so because of the way in which moral and metaphysical ideas and theories assume through them an embodied existence in the social world. Characters are the masks worn by moral philosophies.' A person does not simply fulfil a social role but a very specific individual personality merged with the role, which means others in society are able to recognise the character portrayed by the person – to interpret the actions and behaviour of the person of those of that particular character: inspiring goodness by remembrance and imitation of good examples. For

McIntyre the goals of education are also the goals of character formation and the educational process places the student in the leading position as one who assumes an increasingly dominant role in their education, eventually becoming life-long learners. It is not, as we have seen, simply about imparting information, but rather about learning to live well and to lead lives of direction and purpose coupled with sound judgement.

There is a more radical form of liberal education which frees people from adherence to their unexamined opinions. Since we generally look at the world through opinions and views that we normally inherit from parents and society we can simply endorse those views without examination or reflection – liberal education is rather more about questioning. Character is the ability to make the best decisions when a decision is required. However, education and formation are normative concepts that indicate some standard that ought to be attained. Livingstone (1941: 68–9) uses the ancient Greek idea of a liberal education to define its aims as concerned with bodies, minds and characters each capable of excellence. The body for fitness and health, the mind to know and understand and the excellences of character lies in the great virtues. Richard Gamble (1995: XVII–XVIII) writes: 'This invitation goes out to all teachers, parents, and students who seek ways to defend liberal learning from the onslaught of careerism, utilitarianism, and numbing technique . . . who seek to reconnect themselves with an ancient yet living tradition.' He goes on: 'and embraces an enduring community of learning that values liberal education for its own sake; desires to educate for wisdom and virtue, not power and vanity; finds tiresome the present age's preoccupation with utility, speed, novelty, convenience, efficiency, and specialisation; refuses to justify education as a means of wealth, power, fame or self-assertion.'

The cultural tradition of the West has been Hellenic rather than Biblical, providing us with an ethical view of character. However, it could be argued that Western tradition only makes sense historically if a religious view of the world is presupposed. For many centuries the Bible was the only book that mattered and therefore an adequate discussion of character, as this text has already shown, must acknowledge the fundamental relevance of the Judeo-Christian tradition. The wisdom and the moral instruction in the Old and New Testament was the sole template to measure one's life for countless millions and provided both justification and motivation to act on certain virtues that form a complex of ensuring habits normally described as a person's character. Alfred the Great once commented in his foreword to Pope Gregory the Great's *Pastoralia* that 'We all loved the reputation for being Christian, but very few the moral virtues'. Conscience is commonly experienced as an 'inner voice' telling us what course of action to follow in particular situations. In describing the characteristics of a virtue C. S. Lewis (1943: 14–15) notes:

> There is one further point about the virtues that ought to be noted. There is a difference between doing some particular just and temperate action

and being a just and temperate man. Someone who is not a good tennis player may now and then make a good shot. What you mean by a good player is the man whose eye and muscles and nerves have been so trained by making innumerable good shots that they can now be relied on. They have a certain tone or quality which is there even when he is not playing, just as a mathematician's mind has a certain habit and outlook which is there even when he is not doing mathematics. In the same way a man who perseveres in doing just actions gets in the end a certain quality of character. Now it is this quality rather than the particular actions which we mean when we talk of the 'virtue' of justice.

We know from many research interventions that religious beliefs and practices are associated with higher life satisfactions, happiness and positive effort, particularly with the virtues of gratitude, kindness, forgiveness, hope and love (see Koenig and Larson, 2001). Character strengths appear to be reinforced by religious practice.

C. S. Lewis (1955: 69) in *Mere Christianity* wrote: 'You cannot make men good by law: and without good men you cannot have a good society. That is why we must go on to think . . . of morality inside the individual.' Character formation must be consciously promoted and we must recognise that institutions play a key role in this character formation. Character formation requires a community of virtuous exemplars who are confident about the kind of character they present to young people. A community that is simply 'open' to a thousand choices will fail in the task of character formation. Can education make us grow wiser – should it be allowed to do this in the public sphere or is this something for the private domain? Is it really possible to accurately judge another person's character – we need to be cautious in our judgements. Learning the virtues involves a kind of practice and habituation. Some are concerned that this is simply some mechanistic training. In regard to character formation we need to give renewed respect to the roles that literature, the arts, history, philosophy, and theology can play in examining the pedagogy, policy, and curriculum for character formation. It is likely that the decline of character education in the 1950s and 1960s was because of its association with Christianity. The power to act deliberately is understood as the will to self-conscious activity. We have mastery over our actions and our intelligence must be our guide. Reason is essential, but should be brought into harmony with our conscience.

The role that literary works play in character formation has become less clear in modern times, but it is clear that exploring literature, in either oral or written, to see how people think and behave must be done within a particular socio-historical context. Reading or listening to stories and poems has been believed to enhance the ability to discern the feelings and intentions of others – it communicates virtues. According to Joan Rockwell (1974: 4):

> My basic premise is that literature neither 'reflects' nor 'arises from' society, but rather is an integral part of it. . . . Fiction is a social product, but also

paradoxically an important element in social change. It plays a large part in the socialisation of infants, in the conduct of politics, and in general gives symbols and modes of life to the population, particularly in those less-easily defined areas such as norms, values and personal and inter-personal behaviour.

It is possible that in the formative nature of literature one could find answers to life's challenges. As Kristjansson (2015: 160) writes, 'Great literature is another much-rehearsed Aristotelian source of critical moral insight, but the snag there is that modernist literature has long since given up on the ideal of moral didactics and, more seriously, postmodernist literature has relinquished altogether the emancipatory impulse for self-knowledge and self-clarification'. He believes that young people today have been weaned off the habit of learning from 'the moral of the story' and that restoring such a habit would be a challenge requiring sustained, systematic and guided practice. Good stories help us understand deeper truths and offer images of virtue in action. They have the power to cultivate virtue by increasing knowledge and the desire for the good. From the Greeks to the present, the virtues expressed in rich literature are seen as leading to the good life and the most important reason for reading about instances of virtue in literature was to become virtuous oneself.

However, there has been a noted decline in the use of virtues within literature as the two studies by Kesebir and Kesebir (2012) demonstrate:

> Study 1 showed a decline in the use of general moral terms such as *virtue*, *decency* and *conscience*, throughout the twentieth century. In Study 2, we examined the appearance frequency of 50 virtue words (e.g. *honesty*, *patience*, *compassion*) and found a significant decline for 74% of them. Overall, our findings suggest that during the twentieth century, moral ideals and virtues have largely waned from the public conversation. Rather than use literature in the classroom to indoctrinate or induce conformity we can use it to spur reflection. It means that stories should be open-ended rather than taught in a didactic way. Instead of 'this man is a hero emulate him', the students recognize who is the hero themselves. McIntyre says (1984: 216) 'Mythology, in its original sense, is at the heart of things. . . . And so too of course is that moral tradition from heroic society to its medieval heirs according to which the telling of stories has a key part in educating us into the virtues.

Character formation is a prominently social process with norms transmitted mostly during childhood. The primary socialisation agents are parents and the family. All the behaviour we consider to be important and which is part of our human nature is learned through socialisation. It gives us our initial system of beliefs, values and norms which are often a reflection of our social status, religion and ethnic group. As Himmelfarb (1995: 11–12) notes:

> 'Values' brought with it the assumption that all moral ideas are subjective and relative, that they are mere customs and conventions, that they have

a purely instrumental, utilitarian purpose, and that they are peculiar to specific individuals and societies. (And, in the current intellectual climate, to specific classes, races, and sexes.) So long as morality was couched in the language of 'virtue', it had a form, resolute character. . . . Values, as we now understand that word, do not have to be virtues; they can be beliefs, opinions, attitudes, feelings, habits, conventions, preferences, prejudices, even idiosyncrasies – whatever any individual, group, or society happens to value, at any time, for whatever reason. One cannot say of virtues, as one can of values, that anyone's virtues are as good as anyone else's, or that everyone has the right to his own virtues.

Material well-being is what the Scottish Enlightenment thinkers wanted. Humanist emphasis on the formation of character – the end result of a humanist education was the better person. There has been a modern crusade for openness and expressiveness in education which has meant that character has moved towards being understood as personality – to an understanding of the open friendly person.

Warnock (1979: 83) stressed that the formation of character entailed presenting pupils with a vision of goodness which inspired them to emulate those who exemplify goodness themselves. As she said: 'In the end, though these are harsh words, a child develops a good character largely by following a good example. This is the only way that virtue can be "taught".' Guroian (1998: 20) makes clear that:

Mere instruction in morality is not sufficient to nurture the virtues. It might even backfire, especially when the presentation is heavily exhortative and the pupil's will be coerced. Instead, a compelling vision of the goodness of goodness itself needs to be presented in a way that is attractive and stirs the imagination. A good moral education addresses both the cognitive and affective dimensions of human nature. Stories are an irreplaceable medium for this kind of moral education – that is, the education of character.

Moreover, the practices and narratives of character formation are not only found in schools, they are found in the communities and contexts in which those schools and teachers live. We have seen in this text many popular ideas and myths about character formation that in one form or the other have been around since antiquity. These include:

1   Children are naturally good and their character formation can be degraded by negative forces in their environment.
2   Parents are entirely responsible for their own children's character formation.
3   Children are born with immoral propensities (original sin) and these need to be eradicated through the imposition of strict discipline if character formation is to stand a chance of being successful.

Contemporary policies and themes 157

4   Peer pressure is a harmful influence on character formation.
5   Character formation is useless as you inherit your character in your DNA.
6   Character formation is simply telling children what virtues they must hold
    and how they should exhibit them in their behaviour.
7   Character formation is mostly influenced by the social and cultural oppor-
    tunities and circumstances in which you find yourself.
8   Character formation is principally influenced by what school you attend.
9   Culture is the chief forger of character through literature, theatre, arts,
    architecture, music.

All of these statements are incompatible with each other as well as being ques-
tionable in themselves.

In the UK the Jubilee Centre for Character and Virtues has developed *A
Framework for Character Education in Schools* (2017) which states particular goals
for character formation:

1   Character is fundamental: it is the basis for human and societal flourishing.
2   Character is largely caught through role-modelling and emotional conta-
    gion: school culture and ethos are therefore central.
3   Character should also be taught: direct teaching of character provides the
    rationale, language and tools to use in developing character elsewhere in
    and out of school.
4   Character is sought freely to pursue a better life.
5   Character is educable: it is not fixed and the virtues can be developed. Its
    progress can be measured holistically, not only through self-reports but also
    more objective research methods.
6   Character depends on building Virtue Literacy.
7   Good character is the foundation for improved attainment, better behaviour
    and increased employability, but most importantly, flourishing societies.
8   Character should be developed in partnership with parents, employers and
    other community organisations.
9   Each child has a right to character education.
10 The development of character empowers students and is liberating.

The Centre claims that these character virtues can be categorised into four
types: *intellectual*, *moral*, *civic*, and *performance* (see Appendix M). These categories
are presented as the aims of education – developing the capacity to think, to act
rightly, to serve and to promote academic excellence.

These character virtues are:

Intellectual virtues: Those virtues that are rational prerequisites for right
    action and correct thinking – for example autonomy, reasoning and perse-
    verance. We want students to think and react in the right way so that they
    do the right thing, and in so doing promote human flourishing for all.

158 Policies and issues

These intellectual virtues are required for the pursuit of knowledge, truth and understanding and include how to interpret, analyse, evaluate, compare and judge – all essential to a well-formed mind that can reason well.

Moral virtues: Those virtues that enable us to respond in ethically sound ways to situations in any area of experience. These are the virtues of courage, self-discipline, compassion, gratitude, justice, humility and honesty, which every child should learn.

Civic virtues: Those virtues necessary for engaged and responsible citizenship. They include service, citizenship and volunteering. These civic virtues assist the flourishing of each person and promote the common good of society. Sometimes civic virtues are seen as a specific subset of the moral ones.

Performance virtues: Those virtues that can be used for both good and bad ends – the qualities that enable us to manage our lives effectively. The virtue most commonly mentioned in this category is resilience – the ability to bounce back from negative experiences. Others include determination, confidence and teamwork. These virtues should derive their ultimate value in being enablers and vehicles of the moral virtues.

Can these virtues make us more human, can they humanise us and form good and virtuous character? The idea of character could be turned to any number of conflicting purposes. Character cannot be reduced to a checklist of moral qualities. As Bondi (1984: 214) defined it: 'character is the self in relation. On this view no private formation of character is possible, even though we work towards a degree of freedom which permit us to claim responsibility for our character.' The Centre's statement also claims that character can be taught, caught and sought. *Taught* is understood broadly as providing educational experiences in and out of school that equip students with the language, knowledge, understanding and skills that enable character formation. *Caught* is when the school community provides the example, culture and inspirational influence in a positive ethos that motivates and promotes character formation. *Sought* is when the student over time makes certain commitments and desires freely to pursue their own character formation.

Berkowitz (1999: 3) claims that character formation is defined as 'the intentional intervention to promote the formation of any or all aspects of the moral functioning of the individual'. The general process of education could be defined as this too with character traits being formed involving moral judgement and assessment. Miller (2013) provides a description of five functional roles of character traits: first, understanding – character traits help us to understand ourselves and other people in various contexts. Second, explanation – character traits provide explanations why people make certain actions and behave in certain ways. Third, prediction – character traits can serve as a prediction of one's behaviour in the future. Fourth, evaluation – character traits are a basis for the estimation and judgement of one's person and finally, fifth, imitation – character traits can become a ground for imitation of a certain person based on his or her positive character traits. This idea of prediction as to how a person will act and behave is central to character, as Hauerwas (1981: 49) writes:

> To emphasise the idea of character is to recognise that our actions are also acts of self-determination; in them we not only reaffirm what we have been but also determine what we will be in the future. By our actions we not only shape a particular situation, we also form ourselves to meet future situations in a particular way. Thus, the concept of character implies that moral goodness is primarily a prediction of persons and not acts, and that this goodness of persons is not automatic but must be acquired and cultivated.

A person's character in this view is behaviour that is reliable, predictable, stable and virtuous.

A common Greek proverb was 'Do not judge a person until he is dead' – since character formation is life-long, the formation of the character of a person cannot be known until after the formative changes stop at death. David Brooks (2015) helps us understand this with a pair of clarifying terms: the 'résumé virtues' and the 'eulogy virtues'. Résumé virtues, he proposes, are those that are valued in the contemporary marketplace: the high test scores achieved by a student and the professional accomplishments achieved. They are the skills that are met with economic success and public approval. Eulogy virtues, on the other hand, are the aspects of character that others praise when a person is not around to hear it: humility, kindness, bravery, faithfulness. Our society exalts the résumé virtues, Brooks argues, but it overlooks the eulogy virtues, which are deeper. He also believes that our schooling system is focused on the résumé virtues which means career success takes priority over developing a profound character. Brooks then divides us into an 'Adam I', who seeks success in the world, and an 'Adam II', who is more deeply committed to character and an inner life. Brooks compares both (2015: X): 'While Adam I wants to conquer the world, Adam II wants to obey a calling to serve the world. While Adam I is creative and savors his own accomplishments, Adam II sometimes renounces worldly success and status for the sake of some sacred purpose . . . While Adam I's motto is "Success", Adam II experiences life as a moral drama. His motto is "Charity, love and redemption".' Brooks believes that society encourages too much self-expression, which he claims leads to self-centeredness, selfishness and pride. What is needed is humility, gratitude and character. Brooks recommends that people ought to find a purpose in life that exceeds a career by developing inner character virtues.

This chapter has surveyed three manifestations of what people believe to be character formation within three different policy contexts. It has contrasted these concrete illustrations of character in reference to different models of character and has further considered other significant character formation themes in contemporary discourse. It demonstrates that character formation continues to depend on an understanding within a cultural context.

Chapter 10

Conclusion

The account developed by this book has attempted to highlight the tension between the ideal presentation of and the actual manifestations that have arisen in character formation throughout history. The examples used from each period of history have attempted to demonstrate that the history of character formation is prone to ambiguity and conceptual confusion. Despite this, I believe that meaningful character formation is fundamental to human flourishing and remains both possible and desirable. We have seen how commentators speak of different categories of character – 'national character', 'moral character', 'virtuous character', 'intellectual character' and 'social character'. These categories are sometimes divided into different types, such as Riesman's (1950) theory of social character, which groups human beings, regardless of nationality or culture, into three major types. Social character is determined by certain kinds of historical society through a process of socialisation. First, with 'tradition-directed' character, people have a strong tendency to follow the traditional customs and practices of their forebearers and is largely rooted in medieval Europe, within highly structured societies coupled with strict class and professional divisions. Second, with 'inner-directed' character, people turn to their inner virtues and standards for guidance and conduct with an internalised set of goals determined largely by the immediate family. This character type includes individuals that are sensitive to the expectations of others. Riesman associates this type with the period from the European Renaissance to the early 20th century. Third, 'other-directed' character is defined through a dependence upon others to provide direction with regards to actions, such as via 'peer groups', particularly those who resemble you in age and social class. This is associated with a rapidly changing society, in technological terms. In each culture, Riesman says, one of these character types predominates. He does not rule out the possibility of other types of character forming, but character is largely instilled by social structure in this theory and therefore appears static with individuals merely conforming to type. While there is little empirical evidence for these character types and the theory is under-developed, his theory provides an insightful lens by which we can view the many dimensions of character that this text has discussed.

Character develops not only from a particular school system or pedagogy, but through family and the influence of larger institutions of socialisation. The family has been, throughout history, the primary location where virtues have been taught and learnt, and this has been essential to the health of society. Culture, particularly a rich culture, significantly affects our capacity to form character. A rich character-building culture once comprised of fellowship, mutual sympathy, relationships and friendships, active membership of community institutions, associations and clubs, our obligations to known neighbours, support structures, networking, role models and volunteering – the essential blocks of a civil society. These building blocks provide us, as members of such a society, with numerous opportunities to build our character and aid our flourishing. However, many are in now decline, particularly in areas of deprivation, and amongst low socio-economic groups (see Murray, 2012, Putnam, 2001). We have seen how previous generations were taught to view the world through the traditions into which they were inculcated, and it was these traditions that provided them with such a conceptual framework of custom and habits as the backdrop to guide their behaviour and character development. Western culture is pluralist, which means there are a multitude of free individuals and groups with different moral, political, religious and other professional interests, which some take to be destructive of a normative character formation, as they believe it leads to chaotic individualism and radical relativism. Perhaps the greatest threat to building character today is the erosion of the traditional civil society. Nevertheless, we have certainly seen that there remains within our culture powerful formative 'social systems' that are increasingly more complex for understanding character formation, such as family, law, education, the market, the media, politics, the academy and health care. To the degree that any one of these falters in its responsibility to such a civil society, so the burden on the others grows.

Defining character formation is no simple task since the concept has been understood, and indeed practised, in various ways throughout time, using different points of emphasis. Different conceptions of character and character formation are contingent on our conception of human nature, our understanding of the purpose of education and how we perceive the relationship between the person and society. It is complex because the meanings we give to character will depend on the philosophy we assume, or explicitly adopt, the psychological theories of motivation, development, emotion, feelings and reasoning we employ, as well as the educational means we learn and teach through. In other words, the way our character is formed, in a Western cultural context, is the primary factor contributing to our understanding of the world and our sense of purpose in being part of it. As Allan Bloom (1991: 351) notes, 'different men see very different things in the world and, although they may partake of a common human nature, they develop very different aspects of that nature; they hardly seem to be of the same species, so little do they agree about what is important in life'. However, we do not form our character by accident and the exercise

162 Policies and issues

of character development can be recognised across a wide range of contexts, activities and circumstances.

Hunter (2001: xiii) makes an argument that the social and cultural conditions that make character development possible in human beings are no longer present in society. He begins with an alarming post mortem in asserting that 'Character is dead. Attempts to revive it will yield little. Its time has passed.' Hunter blames pluralism, diversity and contemporary culture for its death and says that character formation is dependent on a particular set of cultural conditions, which are no longer prevalent in modern Western society. He bemoans the fact there is no common language to talk about character, which is due to the fragmentation of culture – that there is no longer a shared culture. Hunter (2001: 23) reserves his most strident criticisms for psychology, as he believes that character formation needs to be rescued from the 'tyranny of popular psychology' and its pretensions to scientific objectivity. He (2001: XV) summarises his position in arguing that

> we say we want a renewal of character in our day but we don't know what we ask for. To have a renewal of character is to have a renewal of a creedal order that constrains, limits, binds, obligates and compels. The price is too high for us to pay. We want character without conviction; we want strong morality but without the emotional burden of guilt; we want virtue but without particular moral justifications that invariably offend; we want good without having to name evil; we want decency without the authority to insist upon it; we want moral community without any limitations to personal freedom. In short, we want what we cannot possibly have on the terms that we want it.

Hunter references American society in his argument, but his critique can just as well be applied to the modern Western tradition more generally.

Hunter is right to highlight the fact that character formation and the maintenance of its development in the modern context is increasingly problematic. Advanced Western societies exhibit anomic social relations and a rapidly diminishing consensus regarding traditional and contemporary social and ethical norms. Hunter goes so far to conclude that this consensus disappeared a long-time ago, but there has been a recent a revival of interest in virtue and character as moral concepts, and as educational ideals, which has increased dramatically since Hunter wrote his book. McIntyre (1984), who was also pessimistic about the power of modern culture to form character, defined character as the internalisation and embodiment of the values of a social order and that any character, so formed, 'morally legitimates a mode of social existence'. It is certainly the case that the social norms we internalise, consciously or unconsciously through socialisation, contribute significantly to our character formation. However, as we have seen above, it was through enculturation, not schooling, and by broadening one's culture generally, that both children and adults performed culturally prescribed roles. Enculturation in both its explicit and implicit forms is the process of shaping and creating a certain kind of person to function in a community. We begin with certain potentialities and limitations that have been genetically inherited, and then are exposed to the culture one is born into, which emphasises certain character traits as good and others as bad, desired and unwanted, preferred and rejected. This culture is largely socially constructed and learned – it is not innate. In other words, we are not born knowing what our culture entails. Parents and those closest to us during our formative years help to enculturate us into this culture and, as we mature, outside actors aid this enculturation process. When done well, it makes us aware of ourselves as individuals with the capacity to reflect and evaluate the character traits we choose to build. We have seen that the underlying assumptions and reasons for how we think, feel and act remain largely concealed and unconscious. This character formation is also largely non-verbal and is transmitted invisibly, so that the person being formed is generally unaware of the formation, particularly when they are young. The socialisation of virtues is only possible if the culture in which character formation takes place supports said virtues. It is not possible to develop the virtue of courage, for example, within a society where there are no positive exemplars of courage, or where society is governed by authoritarian practices and where the citizens lack freedom. At the same time, if there is no guidance or encouragement given to children, then there can be no successful socialisation. We need to be purposeful in the formation of character, since character is not fixed, but rather something that continues to develop throughout one's life. It is therefore imperative that we take ownership of our responsibilities for developing not only our own character, but that of those in our care as well.

Culture in the West is not homogenous and often has unstated goals with people unaware of their impact on others. Nevertheless, it would be wrong to suggest that enculturation and socialisation are entirely unintentional since both involve deliberate learning with goals that become clearer over an extended period of time. Socialisation, therefore, if it is to be successful in fostering the good, has to be a vital part of the education of people of all ages, but particularly that of children, in how they are shaped and formed, in the pursuit of a purposeful and flourishing life. Education in this book has been understood primarily as a process of active formation and it follows that good education is good character education. Education, therefore, is defined, in part, as the formation of character and in this sense education does not reside solely in the school. We, as educators, need to be attentive to the formative educative work that is happening outside of the school gates, particularly with regards to parenting, child care and occupational roles. There is a multitude of social and educative interactions which contribute to our character formation. These sites of interaction include, but are not limited to, theatres, shops, football stadiums, places of worship, gyms, clubs, as well as the home, school and workplace. In the school, the implicit curriculum or culture is educative through daily routines, expectations, ceremonies, relationships, rituals and the like. Kilpatrick (1992: 26) writes of the implicit curriculum in the following way:

> To the extent that character formation takes place in the school, much of it is accomplished through the spirit and atmosphere of a school, its sports and symbols, its activities and assemblies, its purpose and priorities, its codes of conduct and responsibility – most of all through its teachers and the quality of their example. Ultimately, character education is the responsibility of the school's whole environment. . . . Schools are not the only arena for character education, but schools are a very important arena and are one place to start.

The implicit curriculum in schools is an effective means of character formation, but this does not suggest that such a curriculum is unplanned or random. It is important that it is planned, meaningful and deliberate for it to be effective.

These different formative sites vary in educational intensity, but they are not entirely neutral as they provide experiences which are often 'intentional', even if not always articulated. Intention is understood here as when norms of behaviour are not written down but every member of the community knows what they are, even if they cannot give an articulated account of them. It is when we no longer think about these norms, they are somehow concealed operating under the surface, but are nevertheless understood without being openly expressed. Some may call this intuition, or that they are subjective insights, and by using Pettit's (1999: 253) concept of the 'intangible hand', we can see that the formation of virtuous character in the West is not only largely undetermined, but that there is no clear blueprint of how to re-generate good character where it has more or less ceased to exist. Kroeber and Kluckholm (1952: 157) identified this complex issue when they wrote that

> all cultures are largely made up of overt, patterned ways of behaving, feeling, and reacting. But cultures likewise include a characteristic set of unstated premises and categories ("implicit culture"). . . . Thus, one group unconsciously and habitually assumes that every chain of actions has a goal, and that when this goal is reached tension will be reduced or disappear. To another group, thinking based upon this assumption is by no means automatic. They see life not primarily as a series of purposive sequences but more as made up of disparate experiences which may be satisfying in and of themselves, rather than as means to ends.

Character formation is not the exclusive province of any single entity, but is the province of parents, families, schools, institutions, organisations and even the State.

The best schools will articulate what norms, values and beliefs they wish to instil in their students by establishing a school ethos, values-led culture, and

Conclusion 165

articulating the values, or virtues, that they seek to inculcate in its pupils. This is a slow process as these character norms are not developed in a single act. In such schools, character is also less about academic attainment and more about the commitments we make. We should remember that much of the information children learn in schools is not retained and that only by imparting character qualities are we likely to have a lasting positive impact. McGrath (2018) examines what character education is in school by attempting to devise criteria by which we can authenticate genuine character education programmes. He does not address the culture of the school, nor the extra curricula activities which aid character formation beyond the school. However, he recognises, as does this text, that there is substantial variability in what is meant by character and character education across schools and teachers, which is caused by a diversity of perspectives. Despite this acknowledgement, McGrath lays out some preliminary minimum criteria as an aid to recognising character education programmes in schools. These criteria include that it must be school-based and that it ought to be structured. In addition, in order to be considered as character education, it ought to address specific psychological attributes, identity, moral growth, holistic growth and the development of practical wisdom. His criteria are helpful as a general guide, but he recognises that not all of these criteria are essential for defining what character education is since reasonable differences across character programmes will remain. Kristjansson (2015) argues that in order to be truly successful, any programme of character education needs to satisfy four criteria. It must: (1) align with public perceptions and speak to the dominant anxieties and vulnerabilities of the given context; (2) meet with a relatively broad political consensus and attract political interest, ideally on both the political 'left' and 'right'; (3) be underpinned by a respectable philosophical theory, providing it with a stable methodological, epistemological and moral basis; and (4) be supported by a plausible psychological theory, explaining how the ideals of the educational theory fit into actual human psychology and are generally attainable. In finding a common thread between the criteria that McGrath and Kristjánsson suggest, we can summarise that effective character formation must be integrative, contextual, developmental and positive.

We have seen how literature can be used as one of culture's chief teaching tools in forming character, and that the home has remained the main character forming institution, at least up until late modernity. While the relationship between narrative and the formation of character is complex and forms the topic of numerous debates, it is one of the means by which we are formed – we are formed by stories, as Bondi (1984: 205) observes in describing the power of narrative in shaping our character:

> The power of stories lies not only in their subtle conveyance of truth, but in their ability to teach our hearts, to provide us with reasons of the heart, acquaint us with lives of virtue, offer a focus for the affections and a sense of order and discipline for the passions, and give us the vision necessary to

166 Policies and issues

reinterpret our subjection to the accidents of history. Character and story come necessarily together, then, exactly in their use of a practical language of the well lived life, as we try to take part in the shaping of our character so as to better embody the truth of a story of the good life.

Porter (1990) says the two most important vehicles for character formation are stories and role models. Today, literature often lacks the moral power that classical literature deploys and in that such power has been replaced by literature that is largely amoral and written solely for entertainment purposes. Mass schooling and the rise of social media are two other factors that impact on our character development. It is important for all concerned in the education of character to consider all of the factors and actors in play in a meaningful and careful manner. Although there are arguments to the contrary. Psychologist Robert Plomin goes as far as saying that parents do not make a significant difference in how their children develop morally and that the only important thing that parents pass on to their children is their genes. Everything else in the child's experience is random. This view challenges the idea that character can be shaped significantly, whether by parents, or by our communities. However, it is important for educators of character to hold onto the belief that it is possible to inculcate a desire for self-improvement, similar to that much trumpeted during the Scottish Enlightenment.

Many thinkers in the Western tradition completely reject that there is any normative vision of the person that could be a desired goal of education. They reject the Greek idea that there is an ideal form of humanity that we should all aspire to reach. Education, and thus character education, for them is exclusively identified with the transmission of various nuggets of knowledge and skills that can be learnt and the acquisition of thinking skills germane to a particular subject – not the formation of good character, which they see as an entirely private matter. They equate education with the quantity of the knowledge learned, rather than with the quality of the character the person develops. Aristotle is seen by some through this contemporary lens and is reduced to being viewed as a dead white male who held views that were racist and ethnocentric with understandings of character formation that are, today, outdated and even authoritarian. These cultural prejudices exclude any fair treatment of Aristotle's ideas and philosophy. It ignores that Aristotle's influence on ethics and education has been fundamental to the Western tradition and that this influence was felt beyond Antiquity, and well into the Middle Ages, the Renaissance, Enlightenment, and the modern eras. His thoughts have inspired and captured the imagination of Jewish, Christian, Muslim and secular minds, with Winston Churchill, on reading *Ethics*, declaring: 'Why, this is what I have always thought.' His influence continues today with the rise of virtue theory in the late 20th and early 21st centuries. This text has attempted to demonstrate that Aristotle's contribution to character formation has is not outdated, since his influence, as we have seen, has been acknowledged in every century. Whether we realise it

Conclusion 167

or not, whenever we are talking about character formation, we are often working with ideas that are Aristotelian in origin. This is seen in the categories of character and language that he used – virtue, habituation, traits, dispositions, practical wisdom, to name but a few. Nevertheless, there are many who wish to remove the moral and metaphysical dimensions of character formation rendering it a non-judgemental, therapeutic and wholly instrumental educational approach to education.

Aristotle believed that educators must adopt a clear philosophy in order to effectively teach the young. This book has adopted a broadly theoretical neo-Aristotelian theory that envisions the goals of education as forming people so they can live well and live rightly in a world worth living in. Aristotle, in both his *Ethics* and *Politics*, is directly concerned with 'How to live, in order to live well' as a citizen of a community. His approach is positive, since he places character and virtues in the larger context of human flourishing. His books focus on the excellences of character, how they are acquired and what they are and his focus is on being a good person, rather than on doing good – although the former is not possible without the latter. We must do good things before we can be a good person. He is concerned with the process of formation itself and how learning takes place throughout life, particularly the practical idea of learning by doing, as he believed that character was formed by visible actions. How we think, feel and act are central to his thinking and the young, according to Aristotle, are often not ready for ethics because they lack experience. It is why a person cannot acquire the virtues merely by listening to lectures on ethics. Character can be taught, caught and sought, and it is the interaction between all three that determines the effectiveness of any character forming activities. The chief goal of education is, above all, to form a human being, or to guide them into self-formation so that they can lead a worthy life. Greek discussions of virtue formation were framed around understanding human nature and character formation was seen as a key component to living a flourishing life as a human being in a community of others. Formation is intended to prepare the young to become positive members of their community. The community requires, amongst other things, the participation of people who desire to practice civility and reasoned debate. Character formation is a nurturing process in which positive qualities of character evolve. In order for this to occur, those with any sort of stakes in a child's education need to approach educational activities with some form of understanding of what a human being is so that the educator can provide opportunities for growth in their students – essentially to help them understand what is true, how to develop the means by which one can seek such truths, and to build a capacity to evaluate reality. The outcome of good character formation is the development of virtues, but these can be lost, weakened or strengthened dependent on the type and level of education received. Character formation is not simply about developing the moral virtues in isolation, but requires the intellectual development of the mind, since one cannot be ethically good unless they are also practically wise. Therefore, excellence of mind

168 Policies and issues

is required in building excellence of character, but intelligence alone does not make someone wise. As C. S. Lewis (2009: 24) once wrote: 'I had sooner play cards against a man who was quite sceptical about ethics, but bred to believe that "a gentleman does not cheat", than against an irreproachable moral philosopher who had been brought up as a sharper.'

In the previous chapters, we have seen how character has a paradoxical position in that it is pervasively everywhere in schools and in our culture and yet apparently nowhere. We have also shown how uncertainty about its meaning and appropriate application often arises in different contexts. The notion of character discussed above captures and acknowledges the distinctive and distinguishing features of a person as a result of the multitude of character traits that make up the collection of the elements of character. Moreover, we recognise how character formation cannot be understood as a linear process – a kind of step-by-step process in which one step leads to another, with fluctuations accounted for as developmental regressions. Instead, the formation process should be seen as one in which we progress through stages, usually defined in terms of cognitive development, and these stages overlap and recur in different ways for different people. This formation process is neither simple nor straightforward and becomes increasingly more complex as the child gets older, and more actors affect their development. What we can say is that influence on our character development by anyone is inevitable since it is not possible for us to choose to have no character. The choice is between good character and bad character, and those influencing our development will affect us positively or negatively, or even both. It is not a question about whether we, as educators, can shape the character of students, but rather how we attempt to shape it. Character formation is not something a school chooses to or chooses not to do because it inevitably takes place. We can say that character formation takes time, often a long time and that it starts in early childhood with parents teaching their children to value some actions and disvalue others. The child will gradually move from a consciousness of self to a dimly perceived awareness of right and wrong, which is modelled first by parents and second through the wider family of grandparents and relatives, and by teachers, friends, religious leaders and many others. Character is shaped in classrooms, in clubs, by peer groups and in work settings, all contributing to the process, and building on the start made during early childhood. Yet, ultimately a mature character is not guaranteed, particularly if an individual is experiencing character formation in a random and unplanned manner.

We can say with some confidence that some character qualities or traits appear to be innate – we seem to inherit them, but we are at the same time susceptible to the influence of others and to the environmental and cultural circumstances we find ourselves in. We also know that some of us in the same environments are more disposed to acquire and build certain character traits, habits and moral concepts than others. We know that the richer the culture and environment of learning, the better chance we have of developing good character. That there is an undisputed interaction between nature and nurture and that while the Greeks thought of these two concepts as complementary – two sides of the same coin – since Roman times, the concepts have been seen as separate; nature *versus* nurture. A line from Shakespeare's *The Tempest*, 'a born devil, on whose nature nurture can never stick', illustrates the dualism that arose in Western culture. This pessimistic and largely fatalist stance on character formation continues to pervade much of our culture, but many people continue to believe that character virtues can be taught and acquired through nurture. We can conclude here that while heredity is clearly evident in character formation, it cannot and does not rule out human rationality acting on our environment as a key element in character formation.

The means of forming character are multiple and began within the Western tradition with the Greek stories and myths, later supplemented by the Roman contribution. This Classical tradition was, over time, blended with a second layer of Jewish and Christian theological and ethical traditions and this Classical and theologically inspired literature was believed to develop character simply by teaching it. Formation could also occur through the gradual work of culture, or it could be done in a more conscious and intentional way. Contained within these narrative stories were character models that children and adults were expected to intuitively apply to themselves and others. In so doing, they made concrete what it means to commit to the virtues, and different combinations of the virtues, in life. By the Victorian period, we saw the rise of the novel as a didactic instrument that teaches moral character through a focus on particular virtues. This was particularly successful and was especially seen in the enormous rise in production and popularity of children's stories with a moral theme. These moral stories were considered to be a significant road to the formation and understanding of character. While content and methods of inculcating these stories changed, the goals of character formation remained constant (see Kandel, 1961: 316). However, the use of Classical and theological literary traditions to teach character has since declined enormously in the 20th century and is rarely seen in schools today. The popularity of the didactic moral novel, which in any case through up a whole range of erroneous ideas about what constituted good character, has also declined, which is perhaps the reason why character and virtue words have declined in popular children's literature between 1901 and 2000. Specific character lessons in schools did not exist, but rather character education was infused into the school's ethos, including what and how subjects were taught in the classroom. We have seen how the architecture of schools was thought to shape character, also how sport on the playing fields was thought to develop particular virtues, and how exposure to music could give some quality to one's character. Sport in particular was believed to develop worthwhile and desirable social character traits and qualities such as: working together, maintaining a healthy body, fair play, trust, self-discipline, perseverance, resilience and determination. Whilst these outcomes of participating in sport (team and individual) are still preached in schools today, a focus on the performative elements such as resilience or grit are often emphasised by politicians as important to develop in children for them to become hardened against the effects of failure. By the 1930s, the academic mission of schooling had essentially eclipsed any character forming aims. Self-reliance and self-discipline were beginning to be replaced with an emphasis on personal growth together with self-expression and self-fulfillment, the groundwork of which had already begun in the Scottish Enlightenment of the 18th century.

We have also seen how the example of the relationship between parent and teacher influences a child's character formation, and we have noted the concern that writers on education have consistently shown over the last 2,500 years about selecting teachers who possessed good character. This concern in contemporary education has been reduced to a generalisation of the process by which teachers are selected merely for not having a criminal record, rather than for any positive merits as potential educators of character. Modelling character has been a chief means to form character and is often the teacher's best teaching tool. The ethos or atmospheres of the home and school are other important means by which character is inculcated in the young. We have seen how advocates of character formation claim that instilling virtues in young people has long-lasting positive consequences for the individual and society, including increased academic success; better mental health; healthier lifestyles; enhanced overall well-being; greater life satisfaction; improved behaviour; as well as decreased drug-taking, depression, suicides, violence, vandalism, disciplinary issues and selfishness. Character formation is also associated with greater perceived authenticity; success in the workplace; developing a moral compass; building resilience and confidence; being kind, generous, compassionate, just; being a better partner and friend, finding purpose, and even sleeping better at night. It is easy to see why some educationalists question what character is and whether it is something that can be taught and measured. Cause and effect are not always clear. Critics rightly question whether there is any evidence for its claimed effects. This is why we should not claim more for character formation than the evidence justifies. However, we should have some confidence in advocating for character formation, since we are in a long historical line of eminent thinkers who have done just that: Plato, Aristotle, Averroes, Maimonides, Aquinas, Smith, Kant, Mill and Dewey, to name just a few.

More recently, the language of character has begun to permeate political discourse. Character, for many politicians, is seen as being closely associated with resilience, with politicians viewing it through a lens that is entirely instrumental in approach. This has resulted in many programmes for character formation being focused on building an ability to respond to setbacks, or even on practising 'good manners' as a form of compliance with the rules of the school. Such an approach seeks quick behaviourist outcomes in its participants, rather than the more difficult goal of encouraging students to reflect and commit to character virtues that they can live by and put into action. It forms a modern approach to character formation concerned with rationality, control and

Conclusion   171

efficiency, with a results-orientated approach to training for particular behaviours. The modern usage of the language character creates a disconnection between this results-orientated behaviourist approach and educating with a clear philosophy that leads to the inculcation of virtuous behaviour. Character education is also increasingly used to try and remedy the concerns of the moment – to remediate social deficiencies such as drug-taking, obesity, knife crime and so on. Character formation is not about following rules and commandments, because people are not components of a machine. Some critics seek to align character formation goals, content and methods to either left- or right-wing ideologies. This is not authentic character formation either, in that it degrades the language we use about people; for example, we speak about 'consumers' as opposed to 'people' and about 'voters' rather than 'citizens'. Character formation is life-long and on-going and should not be elusive in school contexts. There is a renewed recognition in the UK that character formation is important for both the individual and society. In early 2019, Ofsted, the English inspection agency for schools, issued its draft guidelines for inspecting schools which, for the first time, contained a requirement for schools to build the character of their students. All 22,000 English schools will be inspected on how they develop the character of their students. In a school culture in which what is not tested or inspected is not taught, this new development will hopefully spur schools on to take character development more seriously, and provision for it more meaningfully.

After 24 centuries, Aristotle's influence on our Western idea of character and character formation remains profound. Aristotle employed the Classical Greek virtues of justice, fortitude, prudence and temperance. The Greeks regarded these virtues as those needed by noble-minded and culturally developed men, and described these modes in their epics as ways of depicting what good behaviours could look like. We should, therefore, read Aristotle within his own time, as it is difficult to disentangle him from the influence of Classical Greek culture and customs. However, that is not to say that his approaches are irrelevant today. Since Aristotle, many people throughout history have taken his words and made them relevant to the society of the time. The Romans saw the virtues as producing firmness in the public man. Jews and Christians saw these Greek and Roman virtues as being implicit in the Bible. Christian notions of the good life evolved from earlier Judaic principles and Christianity added the distinct theological virtues of love, hope and faith. In the Middle Ages, the moral conduct of the chivalrous man was a way of demonstrating to others that he possessed the virtues. During the Middle Ages, a common civilisation with Christianity at the centre was forged, based on character development; in fact, Christianity could be said to have defined the foundation of the Western tradition. Virtues are themselves inherently social qualities, but gradually during the Victorian era they became narrowly associated with behaviour and acquired a utilitarian purpose. Victorian character formation, even when it was presented as a secular entity, was infused with a strong Protestant tone. Excessive moralising does

172 Policies and issues

not constitute character formation because it does not respect the individual. Today, ideas of virtue in elite culture are often seen as old-fashioned and almost 'preachy', despite the steady resurgence in virtue theory.

The Enlightenment, according to McIntyre, was a failed attempt to provide rational justifications for moral character. However, the Enlightenment did give greater emphasis to the civic virtues, but without *a priori* definition of the virtues. Modern ideas of civic virtue are seen through public deliberation, which produce the kinds of civic virtues that are newly defined – in other words it rejects the possibility of *a priori* definitions of virtues. Today, intellectual, moral and civic dimensions of character are advocated for, and seen to go hand-in-hand with each other, but it is clear that the moral dimension to character formation is lagging behind. It is simply taken for granted in our schools and culture that young people can figure it out for themselves, but it is not happening. Instead we have long debates about the nature of character and character formation which range widely from claims that children are born with a blank slate (Locke), to ideas that children are either naturally good (Rousseau), or naturally selfish (Freud). McIntyre believed that contemporary moral theory was of little relevance, since it laid too much emphasis on reason and too little on people and the contexts in which they live their lives. He believed that the decline of virtue theory began during and after the Enlightenment period, since up until then it was generally agreed and accepted that morality was part of the order of things, that it was tied to the virtues and that without developing the qualities of mind and character, one could not lead a virtuous life. MacIntyre believed that an ethics of virtue required an understanding of teleology – end or purpose. This ethics of virtue raised the inevitable question: 'What kind of person ought I be in order to reach my telos?' This question gives direction to acquiring the excellences of character. The rejection of Aristotle's scheme of ethics began to be eroded in the writings of Enlightenment thinkers who isolated the virtues preferring instead a rule-based approach.

We have seen how the question of virtue preoccupied Aristotle and many of his successors for much of the subsequent 2,500 years. The more recent revival of virtue theories in education has largely been a result of the dissatisfaction with non-virtue-based theories of education, particularly those based on Kantian and consequentialist theories. Good character does not suggest that we are seeking perfection, despite the high standards Aristotle set of us in order to achieve good character. Aristotle did not believe that ethics could be codified, nor that young children had the ability to lead a good life, since they had not experienced the practice of the virtues, particularly the intellectual virtues. Aristotle's virtue theory is far from complete and yet, despite its flaws, it provides intelligent guidance in ethical decision-making with its focus on the role of character formation being developed over a life-time. Teachers today are still working out what such a virtue-based theory looks like in the classroom, and there is no single blueprint for its provision, but there is no doubt that character and virtues have come into clearer focus in schools. Aristotle never advocated for the rejection of rules but believed that rules ought to be guided by virtues. Schools clearly have a higher duty to their pupils than simply transmitting academic knowledge, but recourse to a high-flown rhetoric of character formation, without thought or deliberation over goals, content and methods, will simply result in vagueness. There can be no rush to introduce well-intentioned character initiatives without serious thought about how we can educate for the good of the individual to live well.

Character formation is a good in and by itself, rather like the goals of a liberal education, but today there is often no common language or an agreed set of expectations about character formation. However, this book has attempted to bring together the principles that have guided thoughts on character throughout history. First, character formation is not an elitist view of moral agency or education, if one sees all human beings as invested innately with potential. Second, though the process of character formation appears individualistic, one's choices and one's development rests on an interdependence with others. Enhancing the life of human beings means enabling them to acquire moral virtues, understood as dispositions of character. As I have said elsewhere, 'we are not simply economic creatures whose sense of worth and purpose in life is defined by our capacity to secure material well-being. We are not what we do for a living or what we buy, nor are we completely driven by self-interest to maximise our own utility. This reductionist view of human nature can have a powerful and essentially negative impact on character formation from an early age' (Arthur, 2003: 111). In *Gorgias*, Plato made clear that education leads to the transformation of the student since education can never be merely training but ought always to lead to a person's well-being principally through an examination of what it means to live a good life. As I have said character is not fixed for our entire life, but can change for better or worse. We can form our own character, but also the character of others. Character can change over time – it can also be ruined quickly.

Where, how and by whom character formation is conducted are important questions, but for many there is no single model of character formation that would suffice. It is important to stress both the heterogeneity and specificity of the models of character formation employed in different contexts and in the ways in which they are articulated in relation to problems and solutions concerning human character development. Every school ought to have an ideal towards which it strives, the school community may not always live up to that ideal, but the very presence of a clear mission is of supreme importance. Schools must be permeated by opportunities for character formation since character is not formed automatically, it is not a quick fix, but rather needs time and effort, through teaching, example, learning and practice. It requires an intentional positive ethos serving as the background and support for what happens in the school in order that students know, care and act on the virtues that comprise good character. This ethos will also enhance the effectiveness of teaching and learning and that is why we need to be conscious of the goals of education and character formation as being one and the same. While there is no unified definition of character formation Aristotle provides us with one of the most developed and historically inflected conception of character which gives central role to virtue as a normative claim. There is a link between who we are and what we do and therefore education, broadly conceived, ought to teach us the skills to live well so we can answer the classic pair of questions: Who am I? How should I live?

References

Aberback, M. (2009) *Jewish Education and History: Continuity, Crisis and Change*, Routledge: London.

Acland, A. H. D. (1980) The Education of Citizens, in Reeder, D. (ed.) *Educating Our Masters*, Leicester University Press: Leicester.

Addington Symonds, J. (1984) *The Memoirs of John Addington Symonds*, Ed. P. Grosskurth, Random House: New York.

Adler, M. J. (1982) *The Paideia Proposal: An Educational Manifesto*, Simon and Schuster: New York.

Adler, M. J. (1985) *Ten Philosophical Mistakes*, Macmillan: New York.

Ahnert, T. (2015) *The Moral Culture of the Scottish Enlightenment 1690–1805*, Yale University Press: New Haven, CT.

Ahnert, T. and Manning, S. (eds.) (2011) *Character, Self and Sociability in the Scottish Enlightenment*, Palgrave Macmillan: New York.

Ainslie, D. (2007) Character Traits in Human Approaches to Ethics, in Tenenbaum, S. (ed.) *Moral Psychology*, Rodopi: New York.

Allport, G. W. (1921) Personality and Character, *Psychological Bulletin*, 18: 441–55.

Allsop, K. (1965) A Coupon for Instant Tradition, *Encounter*, November, 60–3.

Aloni, N. (2007) *Enhancing Humanity: The Philosophical Foundations of Humanistic Education*, Springer: Dordrecht.

Anderson, P. S. (1956) McGuffey vs the Moderns in Character Training, *The Phi Delta Kappan*, 38 (2): 53–8.

Anderson, R. D. (1995) *Education and the Scottish People 1750–1918*, Clarendon Press: Oxford.

Anderson, S. (1993) *Tainted Souls and Painted Faces: The Rhetoric of Fallenness in Victorian Culture*, Cornell University Press: Ithaca, NY.

Androne, M. (2014) The Influence of the Protestant Reformation on Education, *Procedia – Social and Behavioural Sciences*, 137: 80–7.

Annas, J. (1981) *An Introduction to Plato's Republic*, Clarendon Press: Oxford.

Anscombe, G. E. M. (1958) Modern Moral Philosophy, *Philosophy*, 33 (124): 1–19.

Aries, P. (1962) *Centuries of Childhood*, Jonathan Cape: London.

Armitage, W. H. G. (1952) *Thomas Hughes*, Ernest Benn: London.

Arnold-Brown, A. (1962) *Unfolding Character: The Impact of Gordonstoun*, Routledge Kegan Paul: London.

Arthur, J. (2000) *Schools and Community: The Communitarian Agenda in Education*, Falmer Press: London.

176 References

Arthur, J. (2003) *Education with Character: The Moral Economy of Schooling*, Routledge: London.

Arthur, J. (2005) The Re-emergence of Character Education in British Education Policy, *British Journal of Educational Studies*, 53 (3): 239–54.

Arthur, J. (2014) Traditional Approaches to Character Education in Britain and America, in Nucci, L, Narvaez, D. and Krettenauer, T. (eds.) *Handbook of Moral and Character Education*, Routledge: New York.

Arthur, J. (2016) Convergence on Policy Goals: Character Education in East Asia and England, *Journal of International and Comparative Education*, 5 (2): 59–71.

Arthur, J. (2018) *Policy Entrepreneurship in Education*, Routledge: London.

Arthur, J. (2019) Christianity and the Character Education Movement 1897–1914, *History of Education*, 48 (1): 60–76.

Arthur, J., Davies, I., Wrenn, A., Hadyn, T. and Kerr, D. (2001) *Citizenship Through Secondary History*, Routledge: London.

Artz, F. B. (1966) *Renaissance Humanism 1300–1550*, Kent State University: Kent, OH.

Badley, J. H. (1905) Bedale School, *The Elementary School Teacher*, 5 (5): 257–66.

Bain, A. (1861) *The Study of Character*, Parker Son and Bourn: London.

Baker, B. (1968) Anton Makarenko and the Idea of the Collective, *Educational Theory*, 28: 285–97.

Baker, J. A. and White, M. D. (2016) *Economics and the Virtues: Building a New Foundation*, Oxford University Press: Oxford.

Bamford, T. W. (1967) *The Rise of the Public Schools*, Nelson: London.

Bardsley, J. (1861) *The Formation of English Character*, YMCA: London.

Barnard, H. C. (1961) *History of English Education from 1750*, Hodder and Stoughton: London.

Barnett, M. (2011) *Empire of Humanity: A History of Humanitarianism*, Cornell University Press: Ithaca, NY.

Barnett, S. J. (2003) *The Enlightenment and Religion: The Myths of Modernity*, Manchester University Press: Manchester.

Barrow, R. (2007) *Plato*, Continuum: London.

Barton, J. (2014) *Ethics in Ancient Israel*, Oxford University Press: Oxford.

Beck, F. A. G. (1964) *Greek Education*, Methuen: London.

Becker, L. C. and Becker, C. B. (eds.) (2003) *A History of Western Ethics*, Routledge: New York.

Bell, Q. (1968) *Bloomsbury*, Basic Books: New York.

Bentley, J. H. (1983) *Humanists and Holy Writ: New Testament Scholarship and the Renaissance*, Princeton University Press: Princeton, NJ.

Berkowitz, M. W. (1999) Obstacles to Teacher Training in Character Education, *Action in Teacher Education*, 20 (2): 1–10.

Besser-Jones, L. (2014) *Eudaimonic Ethics: The Philosophy and Psychology of Living Well*, Routledge: London.

Black, R. (1991) Italian Renaissance Education: Changing Perspectives and Continuing Controversies, *Journal of the History of Ideas*, 52 (2): 315–34.

Bland, D. (1998) The Formation of Character in the Book of Proverbs, *Restoration Quarterly*, 40 (4): 221–37.

Bloom, A. (1987) *The Closing of the American Mind*, Simon Schuster: New York.

Bloom, A. (1991) *The Republic of Plato*, Basic Books: New York.

Boland, V. (2007) *St Thomas Aquinas*, Continuum: London.

Bondi, R. (1984) The Elements of Character, *The Journal of Religious Ethics*, 12 (2): 201–18.

Bow, C. B. (2013) The Science of the Applied Ethics at Edinburgh University: Dugald Stewart on Moral Education and the Auxiliary Principles of the Moral Faculty, *Intellectual History Review*, 23 (2): 207–24.

Bowles, S. and Gintis, H. (1976) *Schooling in Capitalist America*, New York: Basic Books.

Bradley, I. (1976) *The Call to Seriousness: The Evangelical Impact of the Victorians*, Lion Books: London.

Bradshaw, D. (2018) Pagan and Christian Paths to Wisdom, in Anton, A. L. (ed.), *The Bright and the Good: The Connection between the Intellectual and Moral Virtues*, Rowman and Littlefield: London.

Broadie, A. (1997) *The Scottish Enlightenment*, Canongate: Edinburgh.

Brooks, D. (2015) *The Road to Character*, Penguin: London.

Butler, J. (1961) *The Analogy of Religion, Natural and Revealed, to the Constitution and Course of Nature*, Ungar: New York.

Cain, P. J. (2007) Empire and the Languages of Character and Virtue in Later Victorian and Edwardian Britain, *Modern Intellectual History*, 4 (2): 249–73.

Callan, E. (1997) *Creating Citizens: Political Education and Liberal Democracy*, Clarendon Press: Oxford.

Carr, D. (2005) On the Contribution of Literature and the Arts to the Educational Cultivation of Mortal Virtues, Feeling and Emotion, *Journal of Moral Education*, 34 (2): 137–51.

Cassirer, E. (1942) Giovanni Rico Della Mirandola, *Journal of the History of Ideas*, 3 (3): 319–46.

Cave, P. (2004) Bukatsudo: The Educational Role of Japanese School Clubs, *Journal of Japanese Studies* 30 (2): 383–415.

Chandos, J. (1984) *Boys Together: English Public Schools, 1800–1864*, Yale University Press: New Haven, CT.

Charlton, K. (1965) *Education in Renaissance England*, Routledge, Kegan and Paul: London.

Chesterton, G. K. (1950) *The Common Man*, Sheed and Ward: London.

Christensen, K. R. (1994) *Politics of Character Development: A Marxist Reappraisal of the Moral Life*, Greenwood: New York.

Clark, R. (1853) *Lectures on the Formation of Character*, Jewett: Boston, MA.

Clarke, F. (ed.) (1938) *Church, Community and Politics*, George Allen and Unwin: London.

Cochrane, E. and Krishner, J. (1986) *The Renaissance: Readings in Western Civilization*, Chicago University Press: Chicago, IL.

Colish, M. L. (1990) *The Stoic Tradition: From Antiquity to the Early Middle Ages*, Brill: New York.

Colish, M. L. (1997) *Medieval Foundations in the Western Intellectual Tradition, 400–1400*, Yale University Press: New Haven, CT.

Collini, S. (1985) The Idea of 'Character' in Victorian Political Thought, *Transactions of the Royal Historical Society*, 5th series 35.

Collini, S. (1991) *Public Moralists: Political Thought and Intellectual Life in Britain 1850–1930*, Clarendon Press: Oxford.

Copleston, F. C. (1993) *A History of Philosophy*, Vol. 1 *Greece and Rome*, Image Books: New York.

Corey, E. (2013) The Aesthetic and Moral Character of Oakeshott's Educational Writings, *Journal of Philosophy of Education*, 47 (1): 86–98.

Croall, J. (1983) *Neill of Summerhill: The Permanent Rebel*, Routledge, Kegan and Paul: London.

Cueva, E. P., Byrne, S. N. and Benda, F. (eds.) (2009) *Jesuit Education and the Classics*, Cambridge Scholars: Cambridge.

Curren, R. R. (2000) *Aristotle on the Necessity of Public Education*, Rowman and Littlefield: London.

Curtis, S. J. and Boultwood, M. E. A. (1965) *A Short History of Educational Ideas*, University Tutorial Press, London.

Curtius, E. R. (1953) *European Literature and the Latin Middle Ages* (tr. W. R. Trask), Princeton University Press: Princeton, NJ.

178 References

Curzon, Lord. (1907) *Frontiers*, Clarendon Press: Oxford.

Dagger, R. (1997) *Civic Virtues, Rights, Citizenship and Republican Liberalism*, Oxford University Press: New York.

Dancey, J. (1963) *The Public School and the Future*, Faber and Faber: London.

Darwin, B. (1929) *The English Public School*, Longmans Green: London.

Davis, C. T. (1965) Education in Dante's Florence, *Speculum: A Journal of Medieval Studies*, 15 (3): 415–35.

Dawson, C. (2010) *The Crisis of Western Education*, Catholic University of America: Washington, DC.

Devettere, R. J. (2002) *Introduction to Virtue Ethics: Insights of the Ancient Greeks*, Georgetown University Press: Washington, DC.

Dewar, D. (1812) *Observations on the Character, Customs and Superstitions of the Irish*, Gale and Curtis: London.

Dewey, J. (1934) *Character Training for Youth, Late Works Vol. 9 of the Complete Works of John Dewey 1882–1953*, Southern Illinois University Press: Carbondale.

Dewey, J. (1944) *Democracy and Education*, The Free Press: New York.

Dishon, G. (2017) Games of Character: Team Sports, Games, and Character Development in Victorian Public Schools 1850–1900, *Paedagogica Historica*, 53 (4): 364–80.

Dishon, G. and Goodman, J. F. (2017) No-excuses for Character: A Critique of Character Education in No-excuses Charter Schools, *Theory and Research in Education*, 15 (2): 182–201.

Dollinger, J. J. I. (1848) *The Reformation and Its Relations with the Schools and Universities and the Education of Youth in the Reformation*, Vol. 1.

Doris, J. M. (2002) *Lack of Character: Personality Moral Behaviour*, Cambridge University Press: Cambridge.

Dover, K. J. (1974) *Greek Popular Morality in the Time of Plato and Aristotle*, University of California Press: Berkley.

Doyal, D. P. (1997) Education and Character A Conservative View, *Phi Deltya Kappen*, 78 (6): 440–3.

Dupre, L. (2008) *Religion and the Rise of Modern Culture*, University of Notre Dame Press: Notre Dame, IN.

Dworkin, R. (1985) *A Matter of Principle*, Harvard University Press: Cambridge, MA.

Elliot, H. S. (1913) The Study of Human Character, *Sociological Review*, a6 (3): 222–35.

Fowers, B. J. (2005) *Virtues and Psychology: Pursuing Excellence in Ordinary Practices*, American Psychological Association: Washington, DC.

Fowers, B. J. (2008) From Continence to Virtue: Recovering Goodness, Character Unity, and Character Types for Positive Psychology, *Theory and Psychology*, 18 (5): 629–53.

Freeman, K. J. (1907) *Schools of Hellas*, Macmillan: London.

Gamble, H. A. (1995) *Books and Reads in the Early Church: A History of Early Christian Texts*, Yale University Press: New Haven, CT.

Garin, E. (1957) *L'educazione in Europa 1400–1600*, Bari.

Gathorne-Hardy, J. (1979) *The Public School Phenomenon*, Harmondsworth: London.

Gemeinhardt, P, Hoof, L. van. and Van Nuffelen, P. van. (2016) *Education and Religion in Late Antiquity*, Routledge: London.

Gerwen, J. Van. (2005) Origins of Christian Ethics, in Schweiker, W. (ed.) *The Blackwell Companion to Religious Ethics*, Blackwell: Oxford.

Gillet, M. S. (1914) *The Education of Character*, Kennedy and Son: New York.

Gilligan, C. (1982) *In a Different Voice: Psychological Theory and Women's Development*, Harvard University Press: Cambridge, MA.

Gimbel, J. (1992) *The Medieval Machine: The Industrial Revolution of the Middle Ages*, Pimlico: London.

Gini, A. and Green, R. M. (2013) *10 Virtues of Outstanding Leaders: Leadership and Character*, Wiley: Chichester.

Giroux, H. A. (1987) Schooling and the Politics of Ethics: Beyond Liberal and Conservative Discourses, *Journal of Education*, 169 (2): 9–33.

Goodman, L. (2018) Moral and Intellectual Virtue from Greek to Arabic Philosophy, in Anton, A. L. (ed.) *The Bright and the Good: The Connection between the Intellectual and Moral Virtues*, Rowman and Littlefield: London.

Grafton, A. and Jardine, L. (1986) *From Humanism to the Humanities: education and the Liberal Arts in Fifteenth and Sixteenth-century Europe*, Duckworth: London.

Green, I. M. (2009) *Humanism and Protestantism: in Early Modern English Education*, Ashgate: Burlington.

Grendler, P. (1989) *Schooling in Renaissance Italy: Literacy and Learning 1300–1600*, John Hopkins University Press: Baltimore, MD.

Grey, J. (2018) *Seven Types of Atheism*, Penguin Books: London.

Griswold, C. L. (1999) *Adam Smith and the Virtues of Enlightenment*, Cambridge University Press: Cambridge.

Grote, G. (1851) *A History of Greece*, John Murray: London.

Guroian, V. (1998) *Tending the Heart of Virtue*, Oxford University Press: New York.

Hadot, P. (1995) *Philosophy as a Way of Life: Spiritual Exercises from Socrates to Foucault*, Blackwell: Oxford.

Hahn, K. (1957) Origins of Outward Bound Trust, in James, D. (ed.) *Outward Bound*, Routledge Kegan Paul: London.

Haley, B. (1978) *The Healthy Body and Victorian Culture*, Cambridge University Press: Cambridge.

Hanley, R. P. (2009) *Adam Smith and the Character of Virtue*, Cambridge University Press: Cambridge.

Hannan, J. (2009) *God's Philosophers: How the Medieval World Laid the Foundations of Modern Science*, Icon Books: London.

Harman, G. (1999) Moral Philosophy Meets Moral Psychology: Virtue Ethics and the Fundamental Aristotelian Error, *Proceedings of the Aristotelian Society*, XCIX (Part 3).

Harris, M. J. (2003) *Divine Command Ethics: Jewish and Christian Perspectives*, Routledge: London.

Hartshorne, H. and May, M. A. (1928–30) *Studies in the Nature of Character*, Macmillan: New York.

Harvey, D. (2005) *A Brief History of Neoliberalism*, Oxford University Press: Oxford.

Hauerwas, S. (1975) *Character and the Christian Life: A Study in Theological Ethics*, Trinity University Press: San Antonio, TX.

Hauerwas, S. (1981) *Visions and Virtues*, Notre Dame University Press, Notre Dame, IN.

Himmelfarb, G. (1995) *The De-Moralization of Society: From Victorian Virtues to Modern Values*, Vintage Books: New York.

Holt, J. (2008) *Public School Literature, Civic Education and Politics of Male Adolescence*, Routledge: London.

Hoof, S. (2006) *Understanding Virtue Ethics*, Acumen: Chesham.

180 References

Howe, D. W. (1975) American Victorianism as a Culture, *American Quarterly*, 27 (5): 507–32.

Howlett, J. (2013) *Progressive Education: A Critical Introduction*, Bloomsbury Academic: London.

Hughes, T. (1957 edition) *Tom Brown's Schooldays*, Macmillan: London.

Hull, E. R. (1911) *The Formation of Character*, B. Herder: London.

Humphreys, R. (1992) *Claims and Achievements of the Charity Organization Society 1869–1890*, Economic History Department Working Papers, London School of Economics: London.

Hunter, J. D. (2001) *The Death of Character: Moral Education in an Age without God or Evil*, Basic Books: New York.

Hunter, J. D. and Nedeliskey, P. (2018) *Science and the Good: The Tragic Quest for the Foundations of Morality*, Yale University Press: New Haven, CT.

Hutchison, H. (1976) An Eighteenth Century Insight into Religious and Moral Education, *British Journal of Educational Studies*, 24 (3): 233–41.

Irwin, T. H. (2003) The Virtues: Theory and Common Sense in Greek Philosophy, in Crisp, R. (ed.) *How Should One Live: Essays on the Virtues* (second edition), Oxford University Press: Oxford.

Jacob, M. C. (2019) *The Secular Enlightenment*, Princeton University Press: Princeton, NJ.

Jaeger, C. S. (1994) *The Envy of Angels: Cathedral Schools and Social Ideals in Medieval Europe 950–1200*, University of Pennsylvania Press: Philadelphia.

Jaeger, W. (1939–45) *Paideia: The Ideals of Greek Culture*, 3 vols. Basil Blackwell: Oxford.

Jamison, A. (1968) F. W. Farrar and Novels of the Public Schools, *British Journal of Educational Studies*, 16 (3): 271–8.

Jarrat, B. (1926) *Social Theories of the Middle Ages 1200–1500*, Ernest Benn Limited: London.

Johnson, H. C. (1987) Society, culture and character development, in Ryan, K., and McLean, G. E. (eds.) *Development in Schools and Beyond,* Praeger: London.

Johnson, R. (1970) Education Policy and Social Control in Early Victorian England, *Past and Present*, 49: 96–119.

Jordan, F. (1886, reprinted 2010) *Anatomy and Physiology in Character*, Kessinger Legacy reprints: New York.

Jordan, F. (1896) *Character as seen in Body and Parentage*, Kegan Paul: London.

Kamteker, R. (2004) Situationism and Virtue Ethics on the Content of Character, *Ethics*, 114 (3): 458–91.

Kandel, I. L. (1961) Character Formation: A Historical Perspective, *Journal of the Educational Forum*, 25 (3): 307–16.

Kass, L. R. (2018) *Leading a Worthy Life: Finding Meaning in Modern Times*, Encounter Books: New York.

Kesebir, P. and Kesebir, S. (2012) The Cultural Salience of Moral Character and Virtue Declined in Twentieth Century America, *Journal of Positive Psychology*, 7 (6): 471–80.

Kidd, O. (2016) The Ferguson Affair: Calvinism and Dissimulation in the Scottish Enlightenment, *Intellectual History Review*, 26 (3): 339–54.

Kilpatrick, W. (1992) *Why Johnny Can't Tell Right from Wrong and What We Can Do About It*, Simon and Schuster: New York.

Kimball, B. A. (1986) *Orators and Philosophers: A History of the Idea of Liberal Education*, Teachers College Press: New York.

Kimball, B. A. (2010) *The Liberal Arts Tradition: A Documentary History*, University Press of America: Lanham, MD.

Kitto, H. (1957) *The Greeks*, Harmondsworth: London.

Klein, L. (1994) *Shaftesbury and the Culture of Politeness: Moral Discourse and Cultural Politics in Early Eighteenth-Century England*, Cambridge University Press: Cambridge.

References 181

Koenig, H. G. and Larson, D. B. (2001) Religion and Mental Health: Evidence for an Association, *International Review of Psychiatry*, 13: 67–78.

Kohlberg, L. (1964) Development of Moral Character and Moral Ideology, in M. L. Hoffman and Hoffman, L. W. (eds.) *Review of Child Development Research*, Russell Sage Foundation: New York.

Kohlberg, L. (1968) The Child as a Moral Philosopher, *Psychology Today*, September: 25–30.

Kohlberg, L. (1984) *The Psychology of Moral Development: The Nature and Validity of Moral Stages*, Harper and Row: New York.

Kohn, A. (1997) How Not to Discuss Character Education, *Phi Delta Kappa*, 429–39.

Korolev, F. F. (1968) The October Revolution and the Education of the New Man, *Soviet Education*, 10 (12): 35–50.

Kreeft, P. (1993) *Saint Thomas Aquinas*, Ignatius Press: San Francisco, CA.

Kristjansson, K. (2012) Positive Psychology and Positive Education: Old Wine in New Bottles, *Educational Psychologist*, 42 (2): 86–105.

Kristjansson, K. (2013) Ten Myths about Character, Virtues and Virtue Education – Plus Three Well-Founded Misgivings, *British Journal of Educational Studies*, 61 (3): 269–87.

Kristjansson, K. (2015) *Aristotelian Character Education*, Routledge: London.

Kroeber, A. L. and Kluckholm, C. (1952) Culture: A Critical Review of Concepts and Definitions, *Papers of the Peabody Museum*, 47: 643–56.

Kultz, C. (2017) *Factories for Learning*, Manchester University Press: Manchester.

Kupperman, J. (1991) *Character*, Oxford University Press: Oxford.

Lakobson, P. M. (1968) Social Psychology and the Problems with Character Education, *Soviet Education*, 10 (6): 19–27.

Langford, P. (2000) *Englishness Identified: Manners and Character 1650–1850*, Oxford University Press: Oxford.

Lapsley, D. K. and Power, F. C. (eds.) (2005) *Character Psychology and Character Education*, University of Notre Dame Press: Notre Dame, IN.

Lauwerys, J. A. and Hans, N. (eds.) (1951) *The Yearbook of Education*, University of London Institute of Education: London.

Lawson, J. and Silver, H. (1973) *A Social History of Education in England*, Routledge: London.

Leming, J. S. (1993) *Character Education: Lessons from the Past, Models for the Future*, Institute of Global Ethics: Camden, ME.

Lewis, C. S. (1943) *Christian Behaviour*, Geoffrey Bles: London.

Lewis, C. S. (1955) *Mere Christianity*, Collins: London.

Lewis, C. S. (1964) *The Discarded Image: An Introduction to Medieval and Renaissance Literature*, Cambridge University Press: Cambridge.

Lewis, C. S. (2009) *The Abolition of Man*, Harper One: New York.

Livingstone, R. (1917) *A Defence of Classical Education*, Macmillan: London.

Livingstone, R. (1941) *The Future in Education*, Cambridge University Press: Cambridge.

Locke, J. (1693) *Some Thoughts Concerning Education*, A and J Churchill at the Black Swann Paternoster-row: London.

Luamer, K. (2009) Moral Education in Japan, *Journal of Moral Education*, 19 (3): 172–82.

Mack, E. C. (1941) *Public Schools and British Opinion 1750–1940*, Methuen: London.

Mahoney, R. H. (2009) Hume's Conception of Character, Thesis PhD, University of Southampton.

Maitland, I. (1997) Virtuous Markets: The Market as School of the Virtues, *Business Ethics Quarterly*, 7 (1): 17–31.

182 References

Mangan, J. A. (1981) *Athleticism in the Victorian and Edwardian Public School: The Emergence and Consolidation of an Educational Ideology*, Cambridge University Press: Cambridge.

Mangan, J. A. (1998) *The Games Ethic and Imperialism: Aspects of the Diffusion of an Ideal*, Frank Cass: London.

Mangan, J. A. and Walvin, J. (eds.) (1987) *Manliness and Morality: Middle-Class Masculinity in Britain and America 1800–1940*, Manchester University Press: Manchester.

Marrou, H. I. (1956) *A History of Education in Antiquity* (1982 edition), University of Wisconsin Press: Madison.

Martin, S. (2018) *The English Public School*, Metro: London.

Marx, K. (1852) *The Eighteenth Brumaine of Louis Bonaparte*, International Publishing: New York (1963).

McCulloch, G. (1991) *Philosophers and Kings: Education for Leadership in Modern England*, Cambridge University Press: Cambridge.

McCunn, J. (1900) *The Making of Character: Some Educational Aspects of Ethics*, Cambridge University Press: Cambridge.

McGrath, R. E. (2018) What Is Character Education: Development of a Prototype, *Journal of Character Education*, 14 (2): 23–36.

McIntyre, A. (1969) Marxism of the Will, *Partisan Review*, 36: 128–33.

McIntyre, A. (1984) *After Virtue* (second Edition), University of Notre Dame Press: Notre Dame, IN.

McIntyre, A. (1998) *A Short History of Ethics*, Routledge: London.

McLoughlin, T. and Halstead, M. (1999) Education in Character and Virtue, in Halstead, M. and McLaughlin, T. (eds.) *Education in Morality*, Routledge: London.

Meilaender, G. C. (1984) *The Theory and Practice of Virtue*, Notre Dame Press: Notre Dame, IN.

Miller, A. (2008) A Critique of Positive Psychology – Or 'The New Science of Happiness', *Journal of Philosophy of Education*, 42 (3–4): 591–608.

Miller, F. D. (1995) *Nature, Justice, and Rights in Aristotle's "Politics"*, Clarendon Press: Oxford.

Mitchell, B. (1980) *Morality: Religious and Secular*, Clarendon Press: Oxford.

Mitchell, M. T. (2019) *The Limits of Liberalism: Tradition, Individualism and the Crisis of Freedom*, University of Notre Dame Press: Notre Dame, IN.

Mittleman, A. L. (2007) *A Short History of Jewish Ethics*, Wiley-Blackwell: Oxford.

Morgan, N. (2017) *Taught Not Caught: Educating for 21st Century Character*, John Catt Educational: Woodbridge.

Morgan, T. (2007) *Popular Morality in the Early Roman Empire*, Cambridge University Press: Cambridge.

Moseley, A. (2007) *John Locke*, Continuum: London.

Muir, J. V. (1982) Protagoras and Education at Thourioi, *Greece and Rome*, 29 (1): 17–24.

Munzel, G. F. (1999) *Kant's Conception of Moral Character*, University of Chicago Press: Chicago, IL.

Murray, C. (2012) *Coming Apart*, Crown Forum: New York.

Murray, H. (1808) *Enquiries Historical and Moral Respecting the Character of Nations and the Progress of Society*, James Ballantyne: Edinburgh.

Musgrave, P. W. (1985) *From Brown to Bunter: The Life and Death of the School Story*, Routledge & Kegan Paul: London.

Naphy, W. G. (2007) *Protestant Revolution*, BBC Books: London.

Nash, R. (1997) *Answering the Virtuecrats: A Moral Conversation on Character Education*, Teachers College Press: New York.

References 183

Neill, A. S. (1960) *Summerhill: A Radical Approach to Child Rearing*, Hart: New York.

Newsome, D. (1961) *Godliness and Good Learning*, John Murray: London.

Nicholson, I. A. M. (1998) Gordon Allport, Character, and the "Culture of Personality," 1897–1937, *History of Psychology*, 1 (1): 52–68.

Noddings, N. (1984) *Caring: A Feminine Approach to Ethics and Moral Education*, University of California Press: Berkeley.

Oakeshott, M. (1962) *Rationalism and Politics and Other Essays*, Methuen: London.

Oakley, F. (1992) *Community of Learning: The American College and the Liberal Arts Tradition*, Oxford University Press: New York.

O'Brien, D. (2018) Hume, Intellectual Virtue, and Virtue Epistemology, in Anton, A. L. (ed.) *The Briight and the Good: The Connection Between Intellectual and Moral Virtues*, Rowman and Littlefield: London.

Ogilvie, R. M. (1964) *Latin and Greek: A History of the Influence of the Classics on English Life 1600–1918*, Routledge Kegan Paul: London.

Orme, N. (1973) *English Schools in the Middle Ages*, Methuen: London.

Orme, N. (2006) *Medieval Schools: From Roman Britain to Renaissance England*, Yale University Press: New Haven, CT.

Orwell, G. (1949) *Nineteen-Eighty Four*, Secker and Warburg: London.

Ott, W. (2006) Aristotle and Plato on Character, *Ancient Philosophy*, 26 (1): 65–79.

Overman, S. J. (2011) *The Protestant Ethic and the Spirit of Sport: How Calvinism and Capitalism Shaped American Games*, Mercer University Press: Mason, GA.

Owen, R. (1813) *A New View of Society: Or, Essays on the Principle of the Formation of the Human Character, and the Application of the Principle to Practice*, Cadell and Davies: London.

Parekh, B. (1993) *Jeremy Bentham: Critical Assessments*, Routledge: London.

Park, R. J. (1987) Biological Thought, Athletics and the Formation of a 'Man of Character', in Mangan, J. A. and Walvin, J. (eds.) *Manliness and Morality: Middle-Class Masculinity in Britain and America 1800–1940*, Manchester University Press: Manchester.

Pear, T. H. (1951) The Training of Character in Some English Schools, in Lauwerys, J. A. and Hans, N. (eds.) *The Yearbook of Education*, University of London Institute of Education: London.

Peck, R. F. and Havighurst, R. J. (1960) *The Psychology of Character Development*, John Wiley: New York.

Perry, A. W. (1920) *Education in England in the Middle Ages*, W. B. Clive: London.

Pertsinidis, S. (2016) *Theophrastus's Characters*, Routledge: London.

Peters, R. S. (1960) Symposium: The Development of Moral Values in Children, *British Journal of Educational Psychology*, 30 (3): 250–8.

Peters, R. S. (1986) *Ethics and Education*, George Allen and Unwin: London.

Peterson, A. (2011) *Civic Republicanism and Civic Education: The Education of Citizens*, Palgrave Macmillan: London.

Peterson, C. and Seligman, M. E. P. (2004) *Character Strengths and Virtues: A Handbook and Classification*, APA Press: Washington, DC.

Pettit, P. (1999) *Republicanism: A Theory of Freedom and Government*, Oxford University Press: Oxford.

Piaget, J. (1932) *The Moral Judgement of the Child*, Kegan Paul, Trench, Trubner and Co: London.

Pieper, J. (1967) *Four Cardinal Virtues: Prudence, Justice, Fortitude and Temperance*, Notre Dame University Press: Notre Dame, IN.

184 References

Pietig, J. (1977) John Dewey and Character Education, *Journal of Moral Education*, 6 (3): 170–80.

Pocock, J. G. A. (1975) *The Machiavellian Moment: Florentine Political Thought and Atlantic Republican Tradition*, Princeton University Press: Princeton, NJ.

Polman, R. (2018) *Blueprint: How DNA Makes Us Who We Are*, Allen Lane: London.

Porter, J. (1990) *The Recovery of Virtue: The Relevance of Aquinas for Christian Ethics*, SPCK: London.

Porter, J. (2005) Trajectories in Christian Ethics, in Schweiker, W. (ed.) *The Blackwell Companion to Religious Ethics*, Blackwell: Oxford.

Porter, J. (2013) The Natural Law and the Normative Significance of Nature, *Studies in Christian Ethics*, 26 (2): 166–73.

Porter, R. (2000) *Enlightenment: Britain and the Creation of the Modern World*, Penguin Press: London.

Pritchard, D. M. (2015) Athens, in Bloomer, W. M. (ed.) *A Companion to Ancient Education*, Wiley Blackwell: Oxford.

Pritchard, I. (1988) Character Education: Research Prospects and Problems, *American Journal of Education*, 96 (4): 469–95.

Puka, B. (1999) Inclusive Moral Education: A Critique and Integration of Competing Approaches, in Leicester, M., Modgil, C. and Modgil, S. (eds.), *Moral Education and Pluralism*, Falmer Press: London.

Putnam, R. (2001) *Bowling Alone*, Simon and Shuster: New York.

Quinlan, M. J. (1941) *Victorian Prelude – History of English Manners 1700–1830*, Columbia University Press: New York.

Randell, J. (1978) *Origins of the Scottish Enlightenment 1707–1776*, Macmillan: London.

Reeves, R. (2007) *John Stuart Mill*, Atlantic Books: London.

Renton, A. (2017) *Stiff Upper Lip: Secrets, Crimes and the Schooling of a Ruling Class*, Weidenfeld and Nicholson: London.

Richards, J. (1988) *Happiest Days: The Public School in English Fiction*, Manchester University Press: Manchester.

Riesman, D. (1950) *The Lonely Crowd: A Study of the Changing American Character*, Yale University Press: New Haven, CT.

Roback, A. (1927) *The Psychology of Character*, Harcourt Brace: Oxford.

Robbins, W. (1959) *The Ethical Idealism of Mathew Arnold*, William Heinemann: London.

Roberts, F. D. (2002) *The Social Conscience of the Early Victorians*, Stanford University Press: Stanford, CA.

Roberts, N. (2004) Character in Mind: Citizenship, Education and Psychology in Britain 1880–1914, *History of Education*, 33 (2): 177–97.

Roberts, K., White, G. E. and Parker, H. J. (1974) *The Character Training Industry: Adventure-Training Schemes in Britain*, David and Charles: Newton Abbott.

Roche, H. (2013) *Sparta's German Children*, Classical Press of Wales: Swansea.

Rockwell, J. (1974) *Fact and Fiction: The Use of Literature in the Systematic Study of Society*, Routledge Kegan Paul: London.

Roick, M. (2017) *Pontano's Virtues: Aristotelian Moral and Political Thought in the Renaissance*, Bloomsbury: London.

Rosenthal, M. (1986) *The Character Factory: Baden Powell's Boy Scouts and the Imperatives of Empire*, Pantheon: New York.

Rothblatt, S. (1976) *Tradition and Change in English Liberal Education: An Essay in History and Culture*, Faber and Faber: London.

Rubenstein, R. E. (2003) *Aristotle's Children*, Harcourt: New York.

Rumsey, J. P. (1989) The Development of Character in Kantian Moral Theory, *The Journal of the History of Philosophy*, 27: 247–65.

Russell, B. (1945) *A History of Western Philosophy*, George Allen and Unwin: London.

Russell, D. (2013) *The Cambridge Companion to Virtue Ethics*, Cambridge University Press: Cambridge.

Rutherford-Harly, T. (1934) The Public School of Sparta, *Greece and Rome*, 3 (9): 129–39.

Ryan, K. and Bohlin, K. E. (1999) *Building Character in Schools: Practical Ways to Bring Moral Instruction to Life*, Jossey-Bass: San Francisco, CA.

Ryle, G. (1975) Can Virtue Be Taught, in Dearden, R. F., Hirst, P. H. and Peters, R. S. (eds.) *Education and the Development of Reason*, Routledge and Kegan Paul: London.

Sadler, M. E., (1908) Introduction, *Moral Instruction and Training in Schools Report of an International Inquiry*, Longmans: London.

Salls, H. S. (2007) *Character Education: Transforming Values into Virtue*, University Press of America: New York.

Sandel, M. (2013) *What Money Can't Buy: The Moral Limits of Markets*, Penguin Press: London.

Sayers, D. (1947) *The Lost Tools of Learning*, GLH Publishing: Louisville, KY.

Schiappa, E. (2003) *Protagoras and Logos*, University of South Carolina Press: Columbia.

Schultz, J. A. (1995) *The Knowledge of Childhood in the German Middle Ages 1100–1350*, University of Pennsylvania Press: Philadelphia.

Schwickerath, R. (1903) *Jesuit Education: Its History and Principles Viewed in the Light of Modern Educational Problems*, Herder: University of Michigan.

Schwartz, B. (1987) *The Battle for Human Nature: Science, Morality and Modern Life*, Norton: New York.

Seeley, J. R. (1885) Our Insular Ignorance, *Nineteenth Century*, 18: 861–72.

Sennett, R. (1998) *The Corrosion of Character: The Personal Consequences of Work in the New Capitalism*, W. W. Norton: New York.

Shahar, S. (1992) *Childhood in the Middle Ages*, Routledge: London.

Shrosbree, C. (1988) *Public Schools and Private Education: The Clarendon Commission 1861–64, and the Public Schools Acts*, Manchester University Press: Manchester.

Siedentop, L. (2014) *Inventing the Individual: The Origins of Western Liberalism*, Allen Lane: London.

Smiles, S. (1871) *Character*, A. L. Burt: New York.

Solomon, W. D. (2018) Early Virtue Ethics, in Snow, N. E. (ed.) *The Oxford Handbook of Virtue*, Oxford University Press: Oxford.

Spencer, H. (1851) *Social Statics*, John Chapman: London.

Spring, G. (1813) *Essays on the Distinguished Traits of Christian Character*, Dodge and Syre: New York.

Stewart, W. A. C. (1972) *Progressives and Radicals in English Education 1750–1970*, Palgrave Macmillan: London.

Stinger, C. L. (1977) *Humanism and the Church Fathers*, New York University Press: New York.

Tannoch-Bland, J. (1997) Dugald Stewart on Intellectual Character, *British Journal for the History of Science*, 30 (3): 307–20.

Tate, N. (2017) *The Conservative Case for Education*, Routledge: London.

Taylor, P. (1964) Moral Virtue and Responsibility for Character, *Analysis*, 2 (5): 17–23.

Thomas, K. (2018) *In Pursuit of Civility: Manners and Civilization in Early Modern England*, Yale University Press: New Haven, CT.

Thompson, J. W. (1963) *Literacy and the Laity in the Middle Ages*, Burt Franklin Research and Source Works Series: New York.

186 References

Tosh, J. (2002) Gentlemanly Politeness and Manly Simplicity in Victorian England, *Transactions of the Royal Historical Society*, 12: 455–72.

Trianosky, G. (1990) Natural Affection and Responsibility for Character, in Flanagan, O. and A. Rorty, A. (eds.) *Identity, Character and Morality*, MIT Press: Cambridge, MA.

Trollope, A. (1865) Public Schools, *Fortnightly Review*, 476–87.

Turner, D. (2015) *Old Boys: The Decline and Rise of the Public School*, Yale University Press: New Haven, CT.

Turner, F. M. (1981) *The Greek Heritage in Victorian Britain*, Yale University Press: New Haven, CT.

Turner, P. (1989) *English Literature 1832–1890*, Clarendon Press: Oxford.

Vail, H. H. (1911) *A History of the McGuffey Readers*, Burrows Brothers: Cleveland, OH.

Vance, R. N. C. (1975) The Ideal of Manliness in the Novels of Charles Kingsley and Thomas Hughes, D. Phil Thesis, University of Oxford.

Victoria Costa, M. (2004) Rawlsian Civic Education: Political Not Minimal, *Journal of Applied Philosophy*, 20 (1): 1–14.

Vitz, P. C. (1986) *Censorship: Evidence of Bias in Children's Books*, Servant Press: Ann Arbor, MI.

Vogt, C. D. (2016) Virtue: Personal Formation and Social Transformation, *Theological Studies*, 77 (1): 181–96.

Walker, A. D. M. (1989) Virtue and Character, *Philosophy*, 64: 349–64.

Walker, R. L. and Ivanhoe, P. J. (2007) *Working Virtue: Virtue Ethics and Contemporary Moral Problems*, Clarendon Press: Oxford.

Warnock, M. (1979) *Education: A Way Ahead*, Blackwell: Oxford.

Watkinson, W. L. (1904) *The Education of the Heart: Brief Essays on Influences That Make Character*, Charles H. Kelly: London.

Watson, F. (1968) *English Grammar Schools to 1660: Their Curriculum and Practice*, Frank Cass: London.

Webber, M. ([1904] 1992) *The Protestant Ethic and the Spirit of Capitalism*, Routledge: New York.

Wenham, J. G. (1892) *The School Manager*, St. Anselm's Press: London.

White, B. (2014) Scapegoat: John Dewey and the Character Education Crisis, *Journal of Moral Education*, 44 (2): 127–44.

White, J. (1990) *Education and the Good Life*, Kogan Paul: London.

Whyte, W. (2003) Building a Public School 1860–1910, *History of Education*, 32 (6): 601–26.

Will, G. F. (1983) *Statecraft as Soulcraft: What Governments Do*, Touchstone: New York.

Wolff, K. H. (ed.) (1993) *From Karl Mannheim*, Routledge: London.

Wooton, D. (2018) *Power, Pleasure and Profit: Insatiable Appetites from Machiavelli to Madison*, The Belknap Press at Harvard University Press: Cambridge, MA.

Wotton, W. (1694) *Reflections Upon Ancient and Modern Learning*, J. Leake for Peter Buck: London.

Wright, N. T. (2010) *After You Believe: Why Christian Character Matters*, Harper One: London.

Wright, S. (2017) *Morality and Citizenship in English Schools: Secular Approaches 1897–1944*, Palgrave: London.

Wright, S. (2018) Educating the Secular Citizen in English Schools 1987–1938, *Cultural and Social History*, 15 (2): 215–32.

Yu, T. (2004) *In the Name of Morality: Character Education and Political Control*, Peter Long: London.

Zhao, F. (1998) *The Strategy for Implementing Character Education*, Qingdao Ocean Press: Qingdao.

Zigler, R. L. (1999) The Formation and Transformation of Moral Impulse, *Journal of Moral Education*, 28 (4): 445–57.

Further Reading
(History and Philosophy)

Anton, A. L. (2018) *The Bright and the Good: The Connection between the Intellectual and Moral Virtues*, Rowman and Littlefield: London.

Armstrong, A. H. (2007) *Cambridge History of Later Greek and Early Medieval Philosophy*, Cambridge University Press: Cambridge.

Arnold, M. (1912) Thoughts on Education from Mathew Arnold, in Huxley, L. (ed.) *Thoughts on Education Chosen from the Writings of Mathew Arnold*, Smith and Elder: London.

Beck, F. A. G. (1975) *Album of Greek Education: The Greeks at School and at Play*, Cheiron Press: Sydney.

Bevir, M. (2017) *Historicism and the Human Sciences in Victorian Britain*, Cambridge University Press: Cambridge.

Black, R. (2004) *Humanism and Education in Medieval and Renaissance Italy*, Cambridge University Press: Cambridge.

Bloomer, W. M. (ed.) (2015) *A Companion to Ancient Education*, Wiley Blackwell: Oxford.

Bonner, S. F. (1977) *Education in Ancient Rome: From the Elder Cato to the Younger Pliny*, University of California Press: Berkley.

Boyd, W. (1950) *History of Western Education*, Adam and Charles Black: London.

Brinton, G. (1959) *A History of Western Morals*, Harcourt Brace and Co: New York.

Browning, R. (2000) Education in the Roman Empire, in Cameron, B. et al. (eds.) *Cambridge Ancient History 11*, Cambridge University Press: Cambridge.

Brunschvig, J. and Lloyd, G. E. R. (eds.) (2000) *Greek Thought: A Guide to Classical Knowledge*, Harvard University Press: Cambridge, MA.

Bryant, J. M. (1996) *Moral Codes and Social Structure in Ancient Greece: A Sociology of Greek Ethics from Homer to Epicureans and Stoics*, State University of New York: New York.

Butts, R. F. (1955) *A Cultural History of Western Education: Its Social and Intellectual Foundations*, McGraw-Hall: New York.

Cameron, B. et al. (eds.) (2000) *Cambridge Ancient History 14*, Cambridge University Press: Cambridge.

Chambliss, J. J. (1987) *Education Theory and a Theory of Conduct from Aristotle to Dewey*, State University of New York Press: New York.

Cook, T. G. (1974) *The History of Education in Europe*, Methuen: London.

Cooper, J. (1990) The Magna Moralia and Aristotle's Moral Philosophy, *American Journal of Philology*, 94 (4): 327–49.

Corno, L. and Anderman, E. M. (eds.) (2016) *Handbook of Educational Psychology*, Routledge: London.

188 Further Reading (History and Philosophy)

Crisp, R. (ed.) (2003) *How Should One Live: Essays on the Virtues* (second edition), Oxford University Press: Oxford.

Cubberley, E. P. (1920) *The History of Education: Educational Practice and Progress Considered as a Phase of the Development and Spread of Western Civilization*, Riverside Press: Cambridge, MA.

Curren, R. R. (1999) Cultivating the Intellectual and Moral Virtues, in Carr, D. and Steutel, J. (eds.) *Virtue Ethics and Moral Education*, Routledge: London.

David, A. (1993) *Virtue, Learning and the Scottish Enlightenment: Ideas of Scholarship in Early Modern History*, Edinburgh University Press: Edinburgh.

Davison, T. (1892) *Aristotle and the Ancients Educational Ideals*, Aeterna Press: New York.

Dooley, P. K. (1991) Correct Habits and Moral Character: John Dewey and Traditional Education, *Journal of Thought*, 26 (3/4): 31–45.

Dove, K. J. (1974) *Greek Popular Morality in the Time of Plato and Aristotle*, Hackett Publishing: Cambridge.

Downey, G. (1957) Ancient Education, *Classical Journal*, 52 (8): 337–45.

Ducat, J. (2006) *Spartan Education: Youth and Society in the Classical Period*, Classical Press of Wales: Swansea.

Eby, F. (1940) *The History and Philosophy of Education, Ancient and Medieval*, Prentice-Hall: New York.

Ferguson, J. (1958) *Moral Values in the Ancient World*, Routledge: London.

Foot, P. (2001) *Natural Goodness*, Oxford University Press: New York.

Frankena, W. (1965) *Three Historical Philosophies of Education*, Scott, Foresman and Co: Chicago, IL.

Freeman, M. (2011) From 'Character-Training' to 'Personal Growth': The Early History of Outward Bound 1941–1965, *History of Education*, 40 (1): 21–43.

Gagarin, M. (1987) Morality in Homer, *Classical Philology*, 82 (4): 285–306.

Gangel, K. O. and Benson, W. S. (2002) *Christian Education: Its History and Philosophy*, Wipf and Stock Publishers: Eugene, OR.

Gill, C. (1983) The Question of Character-Development: Plutarch and Tacitus, *The Classical Quarterly*, 33 (2): 469–87.

Gill, C. (2003) The School in the Roman Imperial Period, in Inwood, B. (ed.) *The Cambridge Companion to the Stoics*, Cambridge University Press: Cambridge.

Golden, M. (1990) *Children and Childhood in Classical Athens*, John Hopkins University Press: Baltimore, MD.

Goldie, M. (1991) The Scottish Catholic Enlightenment, *Journal of British Studies*, 30 (1): 20–62.

Good, H. G. (1961) *A History of Western Education*, Macmillan: New York.

Goodlad, L. M. E. (ed.) (2003) *Victorian Literature and the Victorian State: Character and Governance in a Liberal Society*, Mark Hopkins University: Baltimore, MD.

Goodlad, L. M. E. (2017) Moral Character, in Bevir, M. (ed.) *Historicism and the Human Sciences in Victorian Britain*, Cambridge University Press: Cambridge.

Gordon, P. and White, J. (2010) *Philosophers and Educational Reform: The Influence of Idealism on British Educational Thought*, Routledge: London.

Graves, F. P. (1909) *A History of Education Before the Middle Ages*, Macmillan: New York.

Greaves, R. L. (1969) *The Puritan Revolution and Educational Thought*, Rutgers University Press: New Brunswick, NJ.

Greenleaf, B. K. (ed.) (1978) *Children Through the Ages: A History of Childhood*, Noble Books: New York.

Gutek, G. L. (1997) *Historical and Philosophical Foundations of Education*, Prentice-Hall: Upper Saddle River, NJ.

Further Reading (History and Philosophy) 189

Hamilton, L. (1989) *Towards a Theory of Schooling*, Falmer Press: London.

Herman, A. (2002) *The Scottish Enlightenment: The Scots' Invention of the Modern World*, Fourth Estate: London.

Herman, G. (2006) *Morality and Behaviour in Democratic Athens: A Social History*, Cambridge University Press: Cambridge.

Hudson, S. D. (1986) *Human Character and Morality: Reflections from the History of Ideas*, Routledge, Kegan and Paul: London.

Hunt, A. (1999) *Governing Morals: A Social History of Moral Regulation*, Cambridge University Press: Cambridge.

Hutcheon, P. D. (1999) *Building Character and Culture*, Praeger: Westport, CT.

Hutchinson, D. S. (1986) *The Virtues of Character*, Routledge: London.

Jeffreys, M. V. C. (1946) *Education Christian or Pagan*, University of London Press: London.

Jenks, C. (2005) *Childhood: Critical Concepts in Sociology*, Routledge: Abingdon.

Jeynes, W. (ed.) (2012) Character Instruction in Protestant Education Throughout History, in *International Handbook of Protestant Education* Vol. 6: 3–34, *International Handbook of Religion and Education*, Springer: Dordrecht.

Johansen, K. F. (1998) *A History of Ancient Philosophy: From the Beginnings to St. Augustine*, Routledge: London.

Karras, R. M. (2003) *From Boys to Men: Formations of Masculinity in Late Medieval Europe*, University of Pennsylvania Press: Philadelphia.

Kemmis, S. and Edward-Groves, C. (2018) *Understanding Education: History, Politics and Practice*, Springer: Singapore.

Kennell, N. M. (1995) *The Gymnasium of Virtue: Education and Culture in Ancient Sparta*, University of North Carolina Press: Chapel Hill.

Kenny, A. (2006) *Ancient Philosophy: A New History of Western Philosophy* (Vols. 1–4, Vol. 1), Oxford University Press: New York.

Kretzmann, N., Kenny, A. and Pinborg, J. (eds.) (1982) *The Cambridge History of Later Medieval Philosophy: From the Rediscovery of Aristotle to the Disintegration of Scholasticism, 1100–1600*, Cambridge University Press: Cambridge.

Lakoff, G. (2002) *Moral Politics: How Liberals and Conservatives Think*, University of Chicago Press: Chicago, IL.

Lascarides, V. C. and Hinitz, B. F. (2000) *History of Early Childhood*, Flamer: London.

Lockwood, T. C. (2013) Habituation, Habits, Character in Aristotle's Nicomachean Ethics, in Sparrow, T. and Hutchinson, A. (eds.) *A History of Habit from Aristotle to Bourdieu*, Lexington Books: New York.

Lord, C. (1982) *Education and Culture in the Political Thought of Aristotle*, Cornell University Press: Ithaca, NY.

Lord, C. (1996) Aristotle and the Idea of Liberal Education, in Hedrick, C. and Ober, J. (eds.) *Demockratia: A Conversation on Democracy, Ancient and Modern*, Princeton University Press: Princeton, NJ.

Lord, F. (1926) *Man and His Character*, Kingsgate Press: London.

Lynch, J. (1972) *Aristotle's School: A Study of a Greek Educational Institution*, University of California Press: Berkley.

Mack, P. (2011) William Smellie's Dreams: Character and Consciousness in the Scottish Enlightenment, in Ahnnert, T. and Manning, S. (eds.) *Character, Self, and Sociability in the Scottish Enlightenment*, Palgrave Macmillan: London.

Mackenzie, J. M. (ed.) (1986) *Imperialism and Popular Culture*, Manchester University Press: Manchester.

190 Further Reading (History and Philosophy)

MacKillop, I. (2010) *The British Ethical Societies*, Cambridge University Press: Cambridge.

McClellan, B. E. (1992) *Schools and the Shaping of Character: Moral Education in America 1607-Present*, ERIC: Bloomington, IN.

Meyer, A. (1965) *An Educational History of the Western World*, McGraw-Hill: New York.

Miller, A. (2008) A Critique of Positive Psychology – or 'The New Science of Happiness', *Journal of Philosophy of Education*, 42 (3–4): 591–608.

Miller, F. D. (1995) *Nature, Justice, and Rights in Aristotle's "Politics"*, Clarendon Press: Oxford.

Montmargquet, J. (2003) Moral Character and Social Science Research, *Philosophy*, 78 (305) 355–68.

Muirhead, J. ([1908] 2008) The Religious Foundation of Moral Instruction, in Sadler, M. E. (ed.) Introduction, *Moral Instruction and Training in Schools Report of an International Inquiry*, Longman: London.

Nejemy, J. M. (2004) *Italy in the Age of the Renaissance 1300–1550*, Oxford University Press: Oxford.

Neuberg, V. (1971) *Popular Education in Eighteenth Century England*, Welbourne Press: London.

Nicholas, D. (1992) *The Evolution of the Medieval World 312–1500*, Longman: London.

Ober, J. (1989) *Mass and Elite in Democratic Athens*, Princeton University Press: Princeton, NJ.

Patteson, J. B. (1827) *On the National Character of the Athenians*, Waugh and Innes: Edinburgh.

Powell, A. (ed.) (2018a) *A Companion to Sparta*, Wiley-Blackwell: Oxford.

Powell, A. (2018b) Sparta and the Imperial Schools of Britain, in Powell, A. (ed.) *A Companion to Sparta*, Wiley-Blackwell: Oxford.

Purpel, D. E. (1997) The Politics of Character Education, in Molnart, A. (1997) *The Construction of Children's Characters*, Chicago University Press: Chicago, IL.

Rawson, B. (2003) *Children and Childhood in Roman Italy*, Oxford University Press: Oxford.

Raymont, T. (1937) *A History of the Education of Young Children*, Longmans, Green, Land and Co: London.

Reed, P. A. (2012) Motivating Hume's Natural Virtues, *Canadian Journal of Philosophy*, 42 (1): 134–47.

Reed, P. A. (2017) Hume on the Cultivation of Character, *Philosophia*, 45 (1): 299–315.

Reeves, R. (2007) *John Stuart Mill*, Atlantic Books: London.

Reydams-Schils, G. (2011) Authority and Agency in Stoicism of the Roman Imperial Era, *Oxford Review of Education*, 36: 561–74.

Richer, M. (2018) Spartan Education, in Powell, A. (ed.) *A Companion to Sparta*, Wiley-Blackwell: Oxford.

Ringer, F. (1979) *Education and Society in Modern Europe*, Indiana University Press: Bloomington.

Roberts, J. (1989) Aristotle on Responsibility for Action and Character, *Ancient Philosophy*, 9 (1): 23–6.

Rorty, A. O. (1998) *Philosophy of Education: New Historical Perspectives*, Routledge: London.

Roseth, C. J. (2016) Character Education, Moral Education and Moral-Character Education, in Corno, L. and Anderman, E. M. (2016) (eds.) *Handbook of Educational Psychology*, Routledge: London.

Rousmaniere, K., Dehli, K. and de Coninck-Smith, N. (eds.) (1997) *Discipline, Moral Regulation and Schooling: A Social History*, Garland Publishing: New York.

Sayer, A. (2005) *The Moral Significance of Class*, Cambridge University Press: Cambridge.

Schmitter, P. (1975) Compulsory Schooling at Athens and Rome, *American Journal of Philology*, 96 (3): 276–89.

Schnapp, A. (1997) Images of Young People in the Greek City-State, in Levi, G. and Schmitt, J. C. (eds.) *A History of Young People in the West*, Vol. 1: 12–50, Harvard University Press: Cambridge, MA.

Further Reading (History and Philosophy)   191

Schneewind, J. B. (1998) *A History of Moral Philosophy*, Cambridge University Press: Cambridge.

Schwartz, A. (1979) Aristotle on Education and Choice, *Educational Theory*, 29 (2): 97–107.

Schwickerath, R. (1903) *Jesuit Education: Its History and Principles Viewed in the Light of Modern Education Problems*, Herder: St. Louis, MO.

Searle, G. R. (1971) *The Quest for National Efficiency: A Study in British Politics and Political Thought 1899–1944*, University of California Press: Berkley.

Searle, G. R. (2004) *A New England?: Peace and War 1886–1918*, Clarendon Press: Oxford.

Shahar, S. (1992) *Childhood in the Middle Ages*, Routledge: London.

Sherman, N. (1989) *The Fabric of Character: Aristotle's Theory of Virtue*, Clarendon Press: Oxford.

Simon, B. and Bradley, I. (eds.) (1975) *The Victorian Public School*, Gill and Macmillan: London.

Simon, J. (1966) *Education and Society in Tudor England*, Cambridge University Press: Cambridge.

Snow, N. E. (ed.) (2018) *The Oxford Handbook of Virtue*, Oxford University Press: Oxford.

Sparrow, T. and Hutchinson, A. (2013) *A History of Habit from Aristotle to Bourdieu*, Lexington Books: New York.

Stewart-Robertson, J. C. (1981) The Well-Principled Savage, or the Child of the Scottish Enlightenment, *Journal of the History of Ideas*, 42 (3): 503–25.

Stock-Morton, P. (1988) *Moral Education in a Secular Society: The Development of Moral Laique in 19th Century France*, State University of New York Press: New York.

Stone, L. (1964) The Educational Revolution in England 1540–1640, *Past and Present*, 28: 71–8.

Wardle, D. (1970) *English Popular Education 1780–1970*, Cambridge University Press: Cambridge.

Warren, W. A. (1998) The Shift from Character to Personality in Mainline Protestant Thought 1935–1945, *Church History*, 67 (3): 537–55.

Watz, M. (2011) An Historical Analysis of Character Education, *Journal of Enquiry and Action in Education*, 4 (2): 34–53.

Weidmann, T. (1989) *Adults and Children in the Roman Empire*, Yale University Press: New Haven, CT.

Woodward, W. H. (reprinted 1996) *Victtorino da Feltre and other Humanist Educators*, University of Toronto Press: Toronto, ON.

Wynne, E. A. (1986) The Great Tradition in Education: Transmitting Moral Values, *Educational Leadership*, 43 (4): 4–9.

Ascham, R. (1570) The Schoolmaster.

Burgh, J. (1747) Thoughts on Education.

Elyat, T. (1531) The Governor.

Ferguson, A. (1764) History of Civil Society.

Hume, D. (1739) Treatise on Human Nature.

Hutchinson, R. (1725) Systems of Moral Philosophy.

Miller, J. (2013) The Origins of the Distinction of Ranks.

Reid, T. (1764) Enquiry into Human Nature.

Smith, A. (1759) The Theory of Moral Sentiments.

Reid, T. (1788) Essays on the Active Powers of the Human Mind on the Principles of Common Sense.

Appendices

A selection of extracts from different teaching materials that were widely known and used within Western culture and in the school curriculum from the 3rd century BC to the 20th-first century is provided in these appendices. Philosophers and teachers have for centuries given serious attention to basic questions such as what to teach, how to teach and how to improve teaching, but these questions were not generally reduced to school teaching, but rather a concern for culture seen as educator. Inevitably my choice of teaching materials in this list is selective. What these texts were really teaching in terms of how students should be and how they should see the world was determined largely by their understanding within the context in which they were enculturated. These selected documents are intended to prompt discussion about the history of forming character and an excellent and detailed study of the kinds of materials used in different historical periods can be found in Bruce Kimball's *The Liberal Arts: A Documentary History* (2010).

Extracts List

Homer's *Iliad*
Theophrastus *Characters* (2nd/3rd century BC)
Juvenal's *Satires* (2nd century)
Colloquy of Aelfric (10th century)
The Imitation of Christ by Thomas a Kempis (1418)
Dialogues of Juan Luis Vives (1539)
Joseph Hall's *Characters of Virtues and Vices* (1608)
Shorter Catechism of the Scottish Church (1648)
L. Bates's *Story Lessons on Character Building (Morals) and Manners* (1900)
F. J. Gould's *The Children's Plutarch* (1910)
William J. Hutchins, *The Children's Morality Code* (1918)
Hitler Youth Year Books 'Jungen-Eure Welt' 1937 and 1939.
Jubilee Centre for Character and Virtues *Secondary Character Programme of Study* (2016)

Appendix A

Extracts from Homer's *Iliad*.

Nothing can be more exact than the distinctions he has observed in the different degrees of virtues and vices. The single quality of courage is wonderfully diversified in the several characters of the Iliad. That of Achilles is furious and intractable; that of Diomede forward, yet listening to advice, and subject to command; that of Ajax is heavy and self-confiding; of Hector, active and vigilant: the courage of Agamemnon is inspirited by love of empire and ambition; that of Menelaus mixed with softness and tenderness for his people: we find in Idomeneus a plain direct soldier; in Sarpedon a gallant and generous one.

(Theodore Alois Buckley, Introduction to
Pope's Iliad, p. iii)

Here are some of the many virtue related lines in the *Iliad*:

For sure such courage length of life denies,
And thou must fall, thy virtue's sacrifice.
Greece in her single heroes strove in vain;
Now hosts oppose thee, and thou must be slain.

(The Meeting of Hector and Andromache,
Book VI, p. 201)

Appendix B

This is an extract from Theophrastus *Characters* which is one of 30 stories he wrote and used as a teaching aid.

II. *The Flatterer* (i)

Flattery may be considered as a mode of companionship degrading but profitable to him who flatters.

The Flatterer is a person who will say as he walks with another, 'Do you observe how people are looking at you? This happens to no man in Athens but you. A compliment was paid to you yesterday at the Stoa. More than thirty persons were sitting there; the question was started, Who is our foremost man? Everyone mentioned you first, and ended by coming back to your name.' With these and the like words, he will remove a morsel of wool from his patron's coat; or, if a speck of chaff has been laid on the other's hair by the wind, he will pick it off; adding with a laugh, 'Do you see? Because I have not met you for two days, you have had your beard full of white hairs; although no one has darker hair for his years than you.' Then he will request the company to be silent while the great man is speaking, and will praise him, too, in his hearing, and mark his approbation at a pause with 'True'; or he will laugh at a frigid joke, and stuff his cloak into his mouth as if he could not repress his amusement. He will request those whom he meets to stand still until 'his Honour' has passed. He will buy apples and pears, and bring them in and give them to the children in the father's presence; adding, with kisses, 'Chicks of a good father.' Also, when he assists at the purchase of slippers, he will declare that the foot is more shapely than the shoe. If his patron is approaching a friend, he will run forward and say, 'He is coming to you'; and then, turning back, 'I have announced you.' He is just the person, too, who can run errands to the women's market without drawing breath. He is the first of the guests to praise the wine; and to say, as he reclines next the host, 'How delicate is your fare!' and (taking up something from the table) 'Now this – how excellent it is!' He will ask his friend if he is cold, and if he would like something more; and, before the words are spoken, will wrap him up. Moreover he will lean towards his ear and whisper with him; or will glance at him as he talks to the rest of the company. He will take the cushions from the slave in the theatre, and spread them on the seat with his own hands. He will say that his patron's house is well built, that his land is well planted, and that his portrait is like.

[In short the Flatterer may be observed saying and doing all things by which he conceives that he will gain favour.]

Appendix C

Extract from the *Satires*, a collection of satirical poems by the Latin author Juvenal written in the early 2nd century AD and used in schools from Roman times until the present. Juvenal criticises the actions and beliefs of many of his contemporaries, providing insights into questions of morality and conduct. It was also used to teach Latin.

Satire II: Hypocrites are intolerable

I get an itch to run off beyond the Sarmatians and the frozen sea, every time those men who pretend to be old-time paragons of virtue and live an orgy, dare to spout something about morals.

Vltra Sauromatas fugere hinc libet et glacialem Oceanum, quotiens aliquid de moribus auden qui Curios simulant et Bacchanalia uiuunt (2.1–3)

Satire XIV: Avarice is not a family value

Although youths imitate the other vices of their own free will, they are commanded to practice only avarice unwillingly. For this vice deceives with the appearance and shape of a virtue, since it has a grim bearing and a severe surface and exterior, the miser is lauded as if he were frugal without hesitation – as if he were a sparing man, and a sure guardian of his own possessions, better than if the Serpent of the *Hesperides* or the one from the *Black Sea* guarded those same fortunes.

sponte tamen iuuenes imitantur cetera, solam inuiti quoque auaritiam exercere iubentur. fallit enim uitium specie uirtutis et umbra, cum sit triste habitu uultuque et ueste seuerum,
nec dubie tamquam frugi laudetur auarus, tamquam parcus homo et rerum tutela suarum certa magis quam si fortunas seruet easdem Hesperidum serpens aut Ponticus. . . . (14.107–14)

Satire XV: People without compassion are worse than animals

But these days there is greater concord among snakes.
A savage beast spares another with similar spots.
When did a stronger lion rip the life from another lion?
In what forest did a wild boar perish under the tusks of larger boar?

sed iam serpentum maior concordia.
Parcit cognatis maculis similis
fera. quando Leoni fortior eripuit
uitam leo? quo nemore umquam
expirauit aper maioris dentibus apri
(15.159–162)

Appendix D

Extract from the *Colloquy of Aelfric* – Aelfric is believed to have been a monk in Oxfordshire about the end of the 10th and the beginning of the 11th centuries. He took boy pupils and wrote his colloquy (or dialogue) in Anglo Saxon and Latin to teach them the Latin language. It is written in the form of question and answer between the teacher and various workers.

BOYS: We do not want to be wise, since a man who deceives himself with pretence is not wise.

TEACHER: How do you want to be wise?

BOYS: We want to be simple men without hypocrisy, and wise so that we can refrain from doing evil by doing good. You reason more deeply than we can understand at our age, but tell us in your own language and not so profoundly.

TEACHER: I shall do as you ask. You, boy, what did you do, today?

BOY: I have done many things – last night, when I heard the alarm, I rose from my bed, went out to the church and sang evensong with the brothers, then we sang about all the sacred offices and morning praises, after those, prime and seven psalms with the litany and first mass of the day. After that, we sang the sixth service, and then we ate, drank and slept, and then again, we got up and sang nones. And so, here we are with you, and we are ready to listen to what you have to say.

TEACHER: When do you want to sing Vespers and Compline?

BOY: When the time comes.

Appendix E

Extract from *The Imitation of Christ* by Thomas à Kempis (1380–1471) first published in 1418 and read all over Europe. While it is a devotional work it provides the moral example of how to live as demonstrated by Jesus Christ. It would have been used in grammar schools alongside Bible study.

The second chapter

Having a humble opinion of self

EVERY man naturally desires knowledge; but what good is knowledge without fear of God? Indeed a humble rustic who serves God is better than a proud intellectual who neglects his soul to study the course of the stars. He who knows himself well becomes mean in his own eyes and is not happy when praised by men.

If I knew all things in the world and had not charity, what would it profit me before God Who will judge me by my deeds?

Shun too great a desire for knowledge, for in it there is much fretting and delusion. Intellectuals like to appear learned and to be called wise. Yet there are many things the knowledge of which does little or no good to the soul, and he who concerns himself about other things than those which lead to salvation is very unwise.

Many words do not satisfy the soul; but a good life eases the mind and a clean conscience inspires great trust in God.

The more you know and the better you understand, the more severely will you be judged, unless your life is also the more holy. Do not be proud, therefore, because of your learning or skill. Rather, fear because of the talent given you. If you think you know many things and understand them well enough, realize at the same time that there is much you do not know. Hence, do not affect wisdom, but admit your ignorance. Why prefer yourself to anyone else when many are more learned, more cultured than you?

If you wish to learn and appreciate something worth while, then love to be unknown and considered as nothing. Truly to know and despise self is the best and most perfect counsel. To think of oneself as nothing, and always to think well and highly of others is the best and most perfect wisdom. Wherefore, if you see another sin openly or commit a serious crime, do not consider yourself better, for you do not know how long you can remain in good estate. All men are frail, but you must admit that none is more frail than yourself.

The fourth chapter

Prudence in action

DO NOT yield to every impulse and suggestion but consider things carefully and patiently in the light of God's will. For very often, sad to say, we are so weak that we believe and speak evil of others rather than good. Perfect men, however, do not readily believe every talebearer, because they know that human frailty is prone to evil and is likely to appear in speech.

Not to act rashly or to cling obstinately to one's opinion, not to believe everything people say or to spread abroad the gossip one has heard, is great wisdom.

Take counsel with a wise and conscientious man. Seek the advice of your betters in preference to following your own inclinations.

A good life makes a man wise according to God and gives him experience in many things, for the more humble he is and the more subject to God, the wiser and the more at peace he will be in all things.

Avoiding idle talk

SHUN the gossip of men as much as possible, for discussion of worldly affairs, even though sincere, is a great distraction inasmuch as we are quickly ensnared and captivated by vanity.

Many a time I wish that I had held my peace and had not associated with men. Why, indeed, do we converse and gossip among ourselves when we so seldom part without a troubled conscience? We do so because we seek comfort from one another's conversation and wish to ease the mind wearied by diverse thoughts. Hence, we talk and think quite fondly of things we like very much or of things we dislike intensely. But, sad to say, we often talk vainly and to no purpose; for this external pleasure effectively bars inward and divine consolation.

Therefore we must watch and pray lest time pass idly.

When the right and opportune moment comes for speaking, say something that will edify.

Bad habits and indifference to spiritual progress do much to remove the guard from the tongue. Devout conversation on spiritual matters, on the contrary, is a great aid to spiritual progress, especially when persons of the same mind and spirit associate together in God.

Appendix F

Extract from the *Dialogues* of Juan Luis Vives (1492–1540), in England called *Tudor School Boy Life*, which was used in many grammar schools in the late Middle Ages and early Renaissance.

XXV Praecepta educationis – *The Precepts of Education*

BUDAEUS, GRYMPHERANTES

There are three parts to this dialogue: Exordium, Narratio, and Epilogus.

I. Introductory (Exordium)

BUD. What is this so great and so sudden a change in you? It might be included in Ovid's *Metamorphoses*.

GRYM. Is it a change for the better or the worse?

BUD. For the better, in my opinion, at least, if one may argue and estimate as to the goodness of a mind from outward countenance, bearing, words, and actions.

GRYM. Can you then, my most delightful friend, congratulate me?

BUD. I do indeed congratulate you and exhort you to go on, and I pray God and all the saints, that you may have just increase day by day of such fruitfulness. But please don't grudge so dear a friend as I am, to impart the art so distinguished and glorious, which could in so short a time infuse so much virtue in a man's heart.

II. The Exposition (Narratio)

GRYM. The art and the fountain of this stream is that 235very man who is so fruitful in goodness – Flexibulus, if you know him.

BUD. Who does not know the man? He, as I have heard from my father and my cousins, is a man of great wisdom and experience of things, not only known to this city, but also generally beloved and honoured as only few are. Oh, fortunate that you are! to have heard him more closely and to have conversed with him familiarly, and thereby to have gained so great a fruit in the forming of manliness!

GRYM. By so much the happier art thou, to have had all this born with you in your home, as they tell me, and to be able, not once and again as I, but every day, as often as you pleased, to listen to such a father, holding forth wisely on the greatest and most useful topics.

BUD. Stop this, please, and let the conversation proceed, with which we started, about thee and Flexibulus.

GRYM. Let us then be silent with regard to your father since this is your desire: let us return to Flexibulus; nothing is sweeter to me than his discourse, nothing more sagacious than his counsels, nothing more weighty than his precepts, or more holy. So by this foretaste of himself which he has provided me, the thirst has been stimulated and increased in a wonderful degree, to draw further from that sweet fountain of wisdom. Those who describe the earth tell us that the streams are of wonderful formation and nature; some inebriate, others take away 236drunkenness; some send stupor, others sleep. I have experienced that this fountain has the property of making a man of a brute, a useful person of a wastrel, and of a man an angel.

BUD. Might I not be able also to draw something from this fountain, though it be with the tip of my lips?

GRYM. Why shouldst thou not? I will show you the house where he dwells.

BUD. Another time! But do thou, whilst we are walking along (or let us sit down, if you like), tell me something of his precepts, those which thou considerest to be his best and most potent.

The Precepts

GRYM. I will gladly recall them to memory as far as I am able if it will give you pleasure and be of use. First of all he taught me that no one ought to think highly of himself, but moderately or, more truly, humbly; that this was the solid and special foundation of the best education, and truly of society. Hence to exercise all diligence to cultivate the mind, and to adorn it with the knowledge of things by the knowledge and exercise of virtue. Otherwise, that a man is not a man but as cattle. That one should be interested in sacred matters and regard them with the greatest attention and reverence. Whatsoever on those matters you either hear, or see, to regard it as great, wonder-moving, and as things which surpass your power of comprehension. That you should frequently com237mend yourself to Christ in prayers, have your hope and all your trust placed in Him. That you should show yourself obedient to parents, serve them, minister to them and, as each one has power, be good and useful to them. That we should honour and love the teacher even as the parent, not of our body but (what is greater) of our mind. That we should revere the priests of the Lord, and show ourselves attentive to their teaching, since they are to us in place of the Apostles and even of the Lord Himself. That we should stand up before the old, uncovering our heads, and attentively listen to them, from whom, through their long experience of life, wisdom may be gathered. That we should honour magistrates, and that when they order anything we should listen to what they say – since God has committed us to their care. That we should look for, admire, honour, and wish all good to, men of great ability, of great learning, and to honest men, and seek the friendship and intimacy of those from whom so great fruits can be obtained, and that we attend to it especially that we turn out like them. And in the last place, that reverence is due to those who are in places of dignity, and therefore it should be given freely and gladly. What do you say as to these precepts?

BUD. So far as I can form a judgment regarding them, they are taken out from some rich storehouse of wisdom. But tell me if many people do not come to honour, who don't deserve it, *e.g.*, 238priests who don't act in accordance with so great a title, depraved magistrates, and foolish and delirious old men? What is the opinion of Flexibulus of these? Are they to be honoured as greatly as the more capable men?

GRYM. Flexibulus knew very well that there are many such, but he did not allow that those of my age could judge in matters of this kind. We had not yet obtained such insight and wisdom, that we could judge with regard to them. That forming of opinion in these matters must be left over to wise men, and to those who are placed in authority over us.

BUD. Therein he was right, as it seems to me.

GRYM. He used to add: that a youth ought not to be slow in baring his head, in bending his knee, nor in calling any one by his most honoured titles, nor remiss in pleasant and modest discourse. Nor does it become him to speak much amongst his elders or superiors. For it would not otherwise agree with the reverence due from him. Silent himself, he should listen to them, and drink in wisdom from them, knowledge of varied kinds, and a correct and ready method of speaking. The shortest way to knowledge is diligence in listening. It is the part of a prudent and thoughtful man to form right judgments about things, and in every instance of that about which he clearly knows. Therefore a youth ought not to be tolerated, who speaks hastily and judges hastily, nor one who is inclined to asserting and deciding 239hastily; that he ought to be reluctant to argue and judge on even small and slight questions of any kind, or, at any rate, rather timid, *i.e.*, conscious of his own ignorance. But if this is true in slight matters, what shall we say of literature, of the branches of knowledge? of the laws of the country, of rites, of the customs and institutions of our ancestors? Concerning these, Flexibulus said, it was not permissible in the youth to urge an opinion or

204 Appendix F

to dispute or to call in question; not to cavil, nor to demand the grounds, but quietly and modestly, to obey them. He supported his opinion by the authority of Plato, a man of great wisdom.

BUD. But if the laws are depraved in their morality, unjust, tyrannical?

GRYM. As to this Flexibulus expressed himself as he had done with regard to old men. "I know full well," said he, "there are many customs in the state which are not suitable, that whilst some laws are sacred, some are unjust, but you are unskilled, inexperienced in the affairs of life, how should you form an opinion? Not as yet have you reached that stage in erudition, in the experience of things, that you should be able to decide. Perchance, such is your ignorance or licence of mind, you would judge those laws to be unjust which are established most righteously and with great wisdom. But who could render manifest those laws which should be abrogated without inquiring, discussing, and 240deciding on points one by one? For this, you are not yet capable."

BUD. That is clearly so. Go on to other points.

III. Epilogue

GRYM. No ornament is more becoming or pleasing in the youth than modesty. Nothing is more offensive and hateful than impudence. There is great danger to our age from anger. By it we are snatched to disgraceful actions, of which afterwards we are most keenly ashamed. And so we must struggle eagerly against it, until it is entirely overcome, lest it overcome us. The leisurely man, badly occupied, is a stone, a beast; a well-occupied man is in truth a man. Men, by doing nothing, learn to do evil. Food and drink must be measured by the natural desire of hunger and thirst, not by gluttony, and not by brute-lust of stuffing the body. What can be more loathsome to be said than that a man wages war on his own body by eating and drinking, which strip him of his humanity, and hand him over to the beasts, or make him even as it were a log of wood. The expression of the face and the whole body show in what manner the mind within is trained. But from the whole exterior appearance, no mirror of the mind is more certain than the eyes, and so it is fitting that they should be sedate and quiet, not elated nor dejected, neither mobile nor stiff, and that the face itself should not be drawn into severity or ferocity, but into a cheer241ful and affable cast. Sordidness and obscenity should be far absent from clothing, nurture, intercourse, and speech. Our speech should be neither arrogant nor marked by fear, nor (would he have it by turns) abject and effeminate, but simple and by no means captious; not twisted to misleading interpretations, for if that happens, nothing can be safely spoken, and a noble nature in a man is broken, if his speech is met by foolish and inane cavils. When we are speaking, the hands should not be tossed about, nor the head shaken, nor the side bent, nor the forehead wrinkled, nor the face distorted, nor the feet shuffling. Nothing is viler than lying, nor is anything so abhorrent. Intemperance makes us beasts; lying makes us devils; the truth makes us demigods. Truth is born of God; lying of the Devil, and nothing is so harmful for the communion of life. Much more ought the liar to be shut out from the concourse of men than he who has committed theft, or he who has beaten another, or he who has debased the coinage. For what intercourse in the affairs or business of life or what trustful conversation can there be with the man, who speaks otherwise than as he thinks? With other kinds of vices, this may be possible; but not with lying. Concerning companions and friendship of youths he said much and to the purpose, that this was not a matter of slight moment to the honesty or else the shame of our age, that the manners of 242our friends and companions are communicated to us as if by contagion, and we become almost such as those are, with whom we have intimate dealings; and therefore in that matter, there should be exercised great diligence and care. Nor did he permit us to seek friendships and intimacies ourselves, but that they should be chosen by parents or teachers or educators, and he taught that we should accept them, and honour them as they were recommended. For parents, in choosing for us, are guided by reason, whilst we may be seized by some bad desire or lust of the mind. But if, by any chance, we should find ourselves in useless or harmful circumstances, then it behoves us as soon as possible to seek advice from our superiors, and to lay our cares before them. He said, from time to time, indeed, very many other weighty and admirable things, and these things also he explained with considerable fullness and exactness. But these points which I have already stated were, on the whole, the most important on the subject of the right education of youth.

Appendix G

Extract from Joseph Hall's *Characters of Virtues and Vices* published in 1608 – this text was adapted from Theophrastus' *Characters* for Christian teaching purposes and used in schools.

Of the honest man.

HE looks not to what he might do, but what he should. Justice is his first guide: the second law of his actions is expedience. He had rather complain than offend: and hates sin more for the indignity of it than the danger. His simple uprightness works in him that confidence which ofttimes wrongs him, and gives advantage to the subtle, when he rather pities their faithlessness than repents of his credulity. He hath but one heart, and that lies open to sight; and, were it not for discretion, he never thinks aught whereof he would avoid a witness. His word is his parchment, and his yea his oath; which he will not violate for fear or for loss. The mishaps of following events may cause him to blame his providence, can never cause him to eat his promise: neither saith he, 'This I saw not,' but, 'This I said.' When he is made his friend's executor, he defrays debts, pays legacies; and scorneth to gain by orphans or to ransack graves: and therefore will be true to a dead friend, because he sees him not. All his dealings are square and above the board: he bewrays the fault of what he sells, and restores the overseen gain of a false reckoning. He esteems a bribe venomous, though it come gilded over with the colour of gratuity. His cheeks are never stained with the blushes of recantation, neither doth his tongue falter, to make good a lie with the secret glosses of double or reserved senses: and when his name is traduced, his innocency bears him out with courage: then, lo, he goes on the plain way of truth, and will either triumph in his integrity or suffer with it. His conscience overrules his providence: so as in all things, good or ill, he respects the nature of the actions, not the sequel. If he see what he must do, let God see what shall follow. He never loadeth himself with burdens above his strength, beyond his will; and once bound, what he can he will do; neither doth he will but what he can do. His ear is the sanctuary of his absent friend's name, of his present friend's secret: neither of them can miscarry in his trust. He remembers the wrongs of his youth, and repays them with that usury which he himself would not take. He would rather want than borrow, and beg than not pay. His fair conditions are without dissembling: and he loves actions above words. Finally, he hates falsehood worse than death: he is a faithful client of truth; no man's enemy; and it is a question, whether more another man's friend or his own. And if there were no heaven, yet he would be virtuous.

Appendix H

An extract from the *Shorter Catechism* of the Scottish Kirk of 1648 that every Scot's child would have known by heart and recited. This catechism was the principal teaching tool for young people and those of 'weaker capacity'. It comprised 107 questions and answers and was written as a manual of instruction. The following are extracts from the catechism.

Q. 40. *What did God at first reveal to man for the rule of his obedience?*
A. The rule which God at first revealed to man for his obedience, was the moral law.[b]
[b] Rom. 2:14,15. Rom. 10:5.

Q. 41. *Where is the moral law summarily comprehended?*
A. The moral law is summarily comprehended in the ten commandments.[c]
[c] Deut 10:4. Matt. 19:17.

Q. 42. *What is the sum of the ten commandments?*
A. The sum of the ten commandments is, To love the Lord our God with all our heart, with all our soul, with all our strength, and with all our mind; and our neighbour as ourselves.[d]
[d] Matt. 22:37–40.

Q. 43. *What is the preface to the ten commandments?*
A. The preface to the ten commandments is in these words, *I am the Lord thy God, which have brought thee out of the land of Egypt, out of the house of bondage.*[e]
[e] Exod. 20:2.

Q. 44. *What doth the preface to the ten commandments teach us?*
A. The preface to the ten commandments teacheth us, That because God is the Lord, and our God, and Redeemer, therefore we are bound to keep all his commandments.[f]
[f] Luke 1:74,75. 1 Pet. 1:15–19.

Q. 63. *Which is the fifth commandment?*

A. The fifth commandment is, *Honour thy father and thy mother; that thy days may be long upon the land which the Lord thy God giveth thee.*[v]

[v] Exod. 20:12.

Q. 64. *What is required in the fifth commandment?*

A. The fifth commandment requireth the preserving the honour, and performing the duties, belonging to every one in their several places and relations, as superiors,[w] inferiors,[x] or equals.[y]

[w] Eph. 5:21.

[x] 1 Pet. 2:17.

[y] Rom. 12:10.

Q. 65. *What is forbidden in the fifth commandment?*

A. The fifth commandment forbiddeth the neglecting of, or doing any thing against, the honour and duty which belongeth to every one in their several places and relations.[z]

[z] Matt. 15:4–6. Ezek. 34:2–4. Rom. 13:8.

Q. 66. *What is the reason annexed to the fifth commandment?*

A. The reason annexed to the fifth commandment, is a promise of long life and prosperity (as far as it shall serve for God's glory and their own good) to all such as keep this commandment.[a]

[a] Deut. 5:16. Eph. 6:2,3.

Q. 67. *Which is the sixth commandment?*

A. The sixth commandment is, Thou shalt not kill.[b]

[b] Exod. 20:13.

Q. 68. *What is required in the sixth commandment?*

A. The sixth commandment requireth all lawful endeavours to preserve our own life,[c] and the life of others.[d]

[c] Eph. 5:28,29.

[d] 1 Kings 18:4.

Q. 69. *What is forbidden in the sixth commandment?*

A. The sixth commandment forbiddeth the taking away of our own life, or the life of our neighbour unjustly, or whatsoever tendeth thereunto.[e]

[e] Acts 16:28. Gen. 9:6.

Q. 70. *Which is the seventh commandment?*

A. The seventh commandment is, *Thou shalt not commit adultery.*[f]

[f] Exod. 20:14.

210 Appendix H

Q. 71. *What is required in the seventh commandment?*

A. The seventh commandment requireth the preservation of our own and our neighbour's chastity, in heart, speech, and behaviour.[g]

[g] 1 Cor. 7:2,3,5,34,36. Col. 4:6. 1 Pet. 3:2.

Q. 72. *What is forbidden in the seventh commandment?*

A. The seventh commandment forbiddeth all unchaste thoughts, words, and actions.[h]

[h] Matt. 15:19. Matt. 5:28. Eph. 5:3,4.

Q. 73. *Which is the eighth commandment?*

A. The eighth commandment is, *Thou shalt not steal.*[i]

[i] Exod. 20:15.

Q. 74. *What is required in the eighth commandment?*

A. The eighth commandment requireth the lawful procuring and furthering the wealth and outward estate of ourselves and others.[k]

[k] Gen. 30:30. 1 Tim. 5:8. Lev. 25:35. Deut. 22:1–5. Exod. 23:4,5. Gen. 47:14,20.

Q. 75. *What is forbidden in the eighth commandment?*

A. The eighth commandment forbiddeth whatsoever doth or may unjustly hinder our own or our neighbour's wealth or outward estate.[l]

[l] Prov. 21:17. Prov. 23:20,21. Prov. 28:19. Eph. 4:28.

Q. 76. *Which is the ninth commandment?*

A. The ninth commandment is, *Thou shalt not bear false witness against thy neighbour.*[m]

[m] Exod. 20:16.

Q. 77. *What is required in the ninth commandment?*

A. The ninth commandment requireth the maintaining and promoting of truth between man and man,[n] and of our own and our neighbour's good name,[o], especially in witness-bearing.[p]

[n] Zech. 8:16.

[o] 3 John 12.

[p] Prov. 14:5,25.

Q. 78. *What is forbidden in the ninth commandment?*

A. The ninth commandment forbiddeth whatsoever is prejudicial to truth, or injurious to our own or our neighbour's good name.[q]

[q] 1 Sam. 17:28. Lev. 19:16. Ps. 15:3.

Appendix H 211

Q. 79. *Which is the tenth commandment?*

A. The tenth commandment is, *Thou shalt not covet thy neighbour's house, thou shalt not covet thy neighbour's wife, nor his man-servant, nor his maid-servant, nor his ox, nor his ass, nor any thing that is thy neighbour's.*[r]

[r] Exod. 20:17.

Q. 80. *What is required in the tenth commandment?*

A. The tenth commandment requireth full contentment with our own condition,[s] with a right and charitable frame of spirit toward our neighbour, and all that is his.[t]

[s] Heb. 13:5. 1 Tim. 6:6.

[t] Job 31:29. Rom. 12:15. 1 Tim. 1:5. 1 Cor. 13:4–7.

Q. 81. *What is forbidden in the tenth commandment?*

A. The tenth commandment forbiddeth all discontentment with our own estate,[v] envying or grieving at the good of our neighbour,[w] and all inordinate motions and affections to any thing that is his.[x]

[v] 1 Kings 21:4. Esther 5:13. 1 Cor. 10:10.

[w] Gal. 5:26. James 3:14,16.

[x] Rom. 7:7,8. Rom. 13:9. Deut. 5:21.

Appendix I

Extracts from Bates, L. (1900) *Story Lessons on Character Building (Morals) and Manners* a text used in homes and schools to teach character.

III. Loyalty

7. Rowland and the apple tart

Perhaps you have never heard the word Loyalty before, and maybe Rowland had not either, but he knew what it meant, and tried to practise it.[11]

Rowland was not a very strong little boy, and he could not eat so many different kinds of food as some children can, for some of them made him sick. Among other things he was forbidden to take pastry. His mother, who loved him very dearly, had one day said to him, "Rowland, my boy, I cannot always be with you, but I trust you to do what I wish," and Rowland said he would try always to remember.

One time he was invited to go and stay with his cousins, who lived in a fine old house in the country. They were strong, healthy, rosy children, quite a contrast to their delicate little cousin, and perhaps they were a little rough and rude as well.

There was a large apple tart for dinner one day, and when Rowland said, "I do not wish for any, Auntie, thank you," his cousins looked at him in surprise, and the eldest said scornfully, "I am glad that **I** am not delicate," and the next boy remarked, "What a fad!" while the third muttered "Baby". This was all very hard to bear, and when his Aunt said, "I am sure a little will not hurt you," Rowland felt very much inclined to give in, but he remembered that his mother trusted him, and he remained true to her wishes.

This is Loyalty, doing what is right even when there is no one there to see.

(Blackboard) Be True or Loyal when no eyes are upon you.

IV. Truthfulness. (DIRECT UNTRUTH)

8. Lucy and the jug of milk

"Lucy," said her mother, "just run to the dairy and fetch a pint of milk for me, here is the money; and do remember, child, to look where you are going, so that you do not stumble and drop the jug." I am afraid Lucy was a little like another girl you will hear of (*Story Lesson 103*); she was too fond of staring about, and perhaps rather careless.

However, she went to the dairy and bought the milk, and had returned half-way home without any mishap, when she met a flock of sheep coming down the road, followed by a large sheep-dog. Lucy stood on the pavement to watch them pass; it was such fun to see the sheep-dog scamper from one side to the other, and the timid sheep spring forward as soon as the dog came near them. So far the milk was safe; but, after the sheep had passed, Lucy thought she would just turn round to have one more peep at them, and oh, dear, her foot tripped against a stone, and down she fell, milk, and jug, and all, and the jug was smashed to pieces.

Lucy was in great trouble, and as she stood there and looked at the broken jug, and the milk trickling down the gutter, she cried bitterly.

A big boy who was passing by at the time, and had seen the accident, came across the road and said to her: "Don't cry, little girl, just run home and tell your mother that the sheep-dog bounced up against you and knocked the jug out of your hand; then you will not be punished".[13]

Lucy dried her eyes quickly, and gazed at the boy in astonishment. "Tell my mother a **lie**!" said she; "**no**, I would rather be punished a dozen times than do so. I shall tell her the truth," and she walked away home. Lucy was careless, but she was not untruthful; surely the boy must have felt ashamed!

You remember the Fairy Queen said that **Truth** was the foundation of our beautiful Temple (*Story Lesson 1*), and the building will all tumble down in ruins if we do not have a strong foundation, so we must be brave to bear punishment (as Lucy was) if we deserve it, and be sure to

(Blackboard) Tell the truth whatever it costs

Appendix J

Extract from F. J. Gould's *The Children's Plutarch*, first published in 1910 by Kessinger Publishing of London but reproduced in 2017 by Yesterday's Classics for use for nine-year-olds and above. Gould collected thousands of stories, of which 'The Just Man' is but one, to help children develop character through narrative.

The just man

The judges sat in the court of justice, and before them stood two men, one of whom was accusing the other of a wrong done to him. The [17] name of the accuser was Aristides (*Ar-is-ty-deez*).

"We have heard what you say, Aristides," said one of the judges, "and we believe your story, and we shall punish this man – "
"No, no, not yet," cried Aristides.
"Why not?"
"You have not heard what he has to say for himself. Even though he is my enemy, I wish him to have fair play."

And because he was always so honest and fair to others, the people of Athens called him Aristides the Just.

When the Persians came over to Greece with a very great army, the men of Athens went out to meet them at Marathon, 490 B.C. Only ten thousand against twelve times that number of Persians! But the men of Athens had more than swords and spears and daggers – they had stout hearts to fight for their homes and their fatherland against the tyrant forces of Persia. The Greeks chose several generals, each taking command for one day. When it came to the turn of Aristides to command, he gave way to a better captain than himself, for he thought more of the good of Athens than of his own glory; and under this other captain the Greeks gained the victory.

After the battle, when the Persians fled in haste and terror, and much spoil was left behind [18] tents, clothes, gold, silver, etc. – the Greeks left Aristides to look after all these treasures while they pursued the foe; for they knew his honesty, and they knew he would touch nothing, but keep the booty to be shared by all. How differently he acted from the Athenian who was known as the Torch-bearer. A Persian, who lay hiding in a lonely place after the battle, saw the Torch-bearer approach, his long hair being fastened by a band. Seeing this band round his head, the Persian supposed him to be a prince, and he knelt before him in homage; and then he rose and offered to show the Greek a concealed treasure. It was a heap of gold which he had put down a well. Now, the Torch-bearer knew he ought to acquaint Aristides of this store; but, instead of doing so, he slew the Persian, and kept the gold for himself. The Torch-bearer thought of his own pleasure more than of doing his duty to Athens.

Once a year the people of Athens were asked if there were any persons whom they wished to banish, so that the country might be set free from any men that were disliked and dangerous. Each citizen voted by writing on a shell or bit of broken pottery the name of the man he wished to send into exile. As Aristides passed along the street he met a man who held out a shell.

"Sir," said the stranger, "can you write?"
"Yes."
[19] "Well, I cannot; and I should be glad if you would write a name for me on this shell – the name of a man whom I would like to banish."
"Yes; what is the name?"
"Aristides."
"Has he ever done you any harm?"
"No; but it vexes me to hear people always calling him the Just. I think he must be a vain and stuck-up person."

Aristides wrote his own name on the shell, and walked away. The man took the shell, and threw it into a part of the market-place railed round for the purpose. The shells and potsherds were counted, and I am sorry to say that more than six thousand bore the name of Aristides. For while many Athenians admired him, many others thought he was too strict and old-fashioned. But three years afterward, when an immense fleet of Persian ships was coming against the coasts of Greece, the Athenians sent for Aristides to come back; and he returned in time to take part in the battle on sea, in which the Persians were utterly beaten.

During this war the city of Athens had been almost deserted by its people, who had fled to safer places; and the Persians had blackened its houses by fire, and made its walls into broken heaps. After the sea-fight the Persian general of the land forces sent a letter to the Athenians, prom- [20] ising to build their city again, and to give them much money, and to make Athens the leading town in Greece, if only they would agree not to oppose him any more. He sent the letter by messengers, who waited some days for an answer. When the Spartans heard of the letter coming to Athens, they also sent messengers to Athens. They

216 Appendix J

said they hoped the Athenians would not yield; they would take care of the women and children of Athens, if the men would fight on against the Persians. Aristides was in the city, and the people agreed to give answers thus:

To the messengers from Sparta he said:

> "We do not wonder at the Persians expecting us to yield up our liberty in return for gold and silver. But the Spartans are Greeks like ourselves. We wonder that they should be afraid lest we should sell ourselves for the gifts of the Persians. No, the people of Athens will not give up their freedom for all the gold above ground or under ground."

He replied to the Persian messengers, as he lifted his hand and pointed to the sun:

> "As long as that sun flames in the sky, so long will we carry on war with the Persians, who have laid waste our land and burned our holy temples."

On another occasion one of the chief captains of Athens spoke to the people of Athens at a public meeting, and said:

> [21] "I have thought of a most useful thing which might be done for the good of this city; but it cannot be told to you all, as that would hinder its being done."
> "Then," cried the people, "tell it only to Aristides, for he is a just man."

The captain came to Aristides, and whispered to him in such a way that no one else could hear:

> "This is my plan. The other tribes of Greece have brought their ships into our harbor. If we set fire to these ships, Athens alone will have a fleet, and Athens will then be leader of all Greece."

Aristides went to the people, and spoke thus:

> "My friends, the plan which has been told me would, perhaps, be useful to the city of Athens; but it would be wicked."
> "Then," exclaimed the people, "whatever it is, it shall not be carried out."

So you see that, though they had once banished Aristides, the citizens now thought very well of him, and followed his advice.

You remember the Torch-bearer who was so eager to get the gold from the well. He was a kinsman of Aristides, and was the richest man in Athens. When, one day, certain enemies accused him of some offence, they tried to make out before the judges what a bad, cruel character he had. So they said:

"This Torch-bearer is a kinsman of the good [22] man Aristides. He is very rich, and Aristides is very poor. Look at Aristides; how poor are his clothes; he is not warmly clad in cold weather like his kinsman; his wife and children have but a poor dwelling. And here is this hard-hearted Torch-bearer; he has plenty of money, and he will not help his friend."

Aristides was called to the court.

"Is this true?" the judges asked, after these tales had been told over again to him.

"No," said Aristides. "It is not the fault of my kinsman that I am poor. It is my own choice. I have few things belonging to me; I want no more. It is very easy to be good when a man is rich. I would sooner try to be honest and just when I am poor; and therefore I glory in my poverty."

The persons in the court thought to themselves: "We would sooner be the poor man Aristides than the rich Torch-bearer."

When Aristides died, he was still so poor that there was not enough money in the house to pay for a proper funeral. Though he had been a captain in the army of Athens, a leader of ships in the great sea-fight, and a magistrate over the people, yet he had never taken pains to pile up riches. Therefore, the Athenians buried him at the public cost, and also paid for the building of a monument, so that all who passed by might see [23] it and keep the noble Aristides in memory. And so well did the folk of Athens love the remembrance of this Just Man that they gave large gifts of money to each of his daughters at their marriage, and to his son they gave a sum of silver and a plot of land well planted with trees. And for years afterward persons who belonged to his family received kind treatment from the city.

In this way the good deeds of a man remain after he is dead, and make the world happier.

Only the actions of the just
Smell sweet and blossom in the dust.

Appendix K

'The Children's Morality Code' was widely adopted by schools in the USA in the 1920s and 1930s and became influential as a codification of virtues that were intended to build the character of American children. William Hutchins was the author and it appeared in the *Journal of the National Education Association* XIII (1924), 292. Teachers used it to help form the character of their pupils in school.

The children's morality code

WILLIAM J. HUTCHINS

Boys and girls who are good Americans try to become strong and useful, that our country may become ever greater and better. Therefore, they obey the laws of right living which the best Americans have always obeyed.

I. The law of self-control

Good Americans Control Themselves
  Those who best control themselves can best serve their country.

1   I will control my tongue, and will not allow it to speak mean, vulgar or profane words.
2   I will control my temper, and will not get angry when people or things displease me. Even when indignant against wrong and contradictory falsehoods. I will keep my self- control.
3   I will control my thoughts, and will not allow a foolish wish to spoil a wise purpose.
4   I will control my actions. I will be careful and thrifty, and insist on doing right.
5   I will not ridicule nor defile the character of another; I will keep my self-respect, and help others to keep theirs.

Appendix K   219

II. The law of good health

The welfare of our country depends upon those who are physically fit for their daily work. Therefore:

1   I will try to take such food, sleep, and exercise as will keep me always in good health.
2   I will keep my clothes, my body and my mind clean.
3   I will avoid those habits which would harm me, and will make and never break those habits which will help me.
4   I will protect the health of others, and guard their safety as well as my own.
5   I will grow strong and skilful.

III. The law of kindness

Good Americans Are Kind.

In America those who are different must live in the same communities. We are of many different sorts, but we are one great people. Every unkindness hurts the common life, every kindness helps. Every unkindness hurts the common life, every kindness helps the common life. Therefore:

1   I will be kind in all my thoughts. I will bear no spites or grudges. I will never despise anybody.
2   I will be kind in my speech. I will never gossip nor will I speak unkindly of anyone. Words may wound or heal.
3   I will be kind in my acts. I will not selfishly insist on having my own way. I will be polite: rude people are not good Americans. I will not make unnecessary trouble for those who work for me, nor forget to be grateful. I will be careful of other people's feelings. I will do my best to prevent cruelty, and will give help to those who are in need.

IV. The law of sportsmanship

Good Americans Play Fair

Strong play increases and trains one's strength and courage. Sportsmanship helps one to be a gentlemen, a lady. Therefore:

1   I will not cheat; I will keep the rules, but will play the game hard, for the fun of the game, to win by strength and skill. If I should not play fair, the loser would lose the fun of the game, the winner would lose his self-respect, and the game itself would become a mean and often cruel business.
2   I will treat my opponents with courtesy and trust them if they deserve it. I will be friendly.

220 Appendix K

3   If I play in a group game, I will play, not for my own glory, but for the success of my team.
4   I will be a good loser or a generous winner.
5   And in my work as well as in my play, I will be sportsmanlike – generous, fair, honourable.

V. The law of self-reliance

Good Americans Are Self-Reliant
Self-conceit is silly, but self-reliance is necessary to boys and girls who would be strong and useful.

1   I will gladly listen to the advice of older and wiser people; I will reverence the wishes of those who love and care for me, and who know life and me better than I. I will develop independence and wisdom to choose for myself, act for myself, according to what seems right and fair and wise.
2   I will not be afraid of being laughed at when I am right. I will not be afraid of doing right when the crowd does wrong.
3   When in danger, trouble, or pain, I will be brave. A coward does not make a good American.

VI. The law of duty

Good Americans Do Their Duty
The shirker and the willing idler live upon others, and burden fellow-citizens with work unfairly. They do not do their share for the country's good. I will try to find out what my duty is, what I ought to do as a good American, and my duty I will do, whether it is easy or hard. What it is my duty to do I can do.

VII. The law of reliability

Good Americans Are Reliable
Our country arrows great and good as her citizens are able more fully to trust each other.
Therefore:

1   I will be honest in every act, and very careful with money. I will not cheat, nor pretend, nor sneak.
2   I will not do wrong in the hope of not being found out. I cannot hid the truth from myself. Nor will I injure the property of others.
3   I will not take without permission what does not belong to me. A thief is a menace to me and others.
4   I will do promptly what I have promised to do. If I have made a foolish promise, I will at once confess my mistake, and I will try to make good

Appendix K 221

any harm which my mistakle may have caused. I will so speak and act that people will find it easier top trust each other.

VIII. The law of truth

Good Americans Are True

1   I will be slow to believe suspicions lest I do injustice; I will avoid hasty opinions lest I be mistaken as to facts.
2   I will hunt for proof, and be accurate as to what I see and hear. I will learn to think, that I may discover new truth.
3   I will stand by the truth regardless of my likes and dislikes, and scorn the temptation to lie for myself or friends, nor will I keep the truth from those who have a right to it.

IX. The law of workmanship

Good Americans Try to Do the Right Thing in the Right Way

The welfare of our country depends upon those who have learned to do in the right way the work that makes civilisation possible. Therefore:

1   I will get the best possible education, and learn all that I can as a preparation for the time when I am grown up and at my life work. I will invent and make things better if I can.
2   I will take real interest in work, and will not be satisfied with slipshod, lazy, and merely passable work. I will form the habit of good work and keep alert; mistakes and blunders cause hardships (sometimes disaster) and spoil success.
3   I will make the right thing in the right way to give it value and beauty, even when no one else sees or praises me. But when I have done my best, I will not envy those who have better, or have received larger reward. Envy spoils the work and the worker.

X. The law of teamwork

Good Americans Work in Friendly Co-operation with Fellow-Workers

One alone could not build a city or a great railroad. One alone would find it hard to build a bridge. That I may have bread, people have sowed and reaped, people have made plows and threshers, have built mills and mined coal, made stoves and kept, stores. As we learn better how to work together, the welfare of our country is advanced.

1   In whatever work I do with others, I will do my part and will encourage others do their part, promptly, quickly.

2   I will keep in order the things which we use in our work. When things are out of place, they are often in the way, and sometimes they are hard to find.
3   In all my work with others, I will be cheerful. Cheerlessness depresses all the workers and injures all the work.
4   When I have received money for my work, I will be neither a miser nor a spendthrift. I will save or spend as one of the friendly workers of America.

XI. The law of loyalty

Good Americans Are Loyal

If our America is to become ever greater and better, her citizens must he loyal, devotedly faithful, in every relation of life full of courage and regardful of their honor.

1   I will be loyal to my family. In loyalty I will gladly obey my parents or those who are in their place and show them gratitude. I will do my best to help each member of my family to gain strength and usefulness.
2   I will be loyal to my school. In loyalty I will obey and help other pupils u> obey those rules which further the good of all.
3   I will be loyal to my town, my State, my country. In loyalty I will respect and help others to respect their laws and their courts of justice.
4   I will be loyal to humanity. In loyalty I will do my best to help the friendly relations of our country with every other country, and to give to everyone in every land the best possible chance.

If I try simply to be loyal to my family, I may be disloyal to my school. If I try simply to be loyal to my school, I may be disloyal to my town, my State and my country. I may be disloyal to humanity. If I try simply to be loyal to my town, State and country, I may be disloyal to humanity. I will try above all things else to be loyal to humanity; then I shall surely be loyal to my country, my State and my town, to my school and to my family. And those who obey the law of loyalty obey all the other ten laws of the Good American.

Appendix L

Extracts from the *Hitler Youth Yearbooks* for 1937 and 1939 as contained in Lewin, H. S. (1947) Hitler Youth and the Boy Scouts of America: A Comparison of Aims, *Human Relations*, 1 (2): 206–27. These extracts (a series of maxims) below would have been drilled into members of the Hitler Youth (Hitler Jugend). The character formation in these extracts is presented with great emotional fervour forming beliefs and attitudes in conformity with Nazi ideology that each member accepts, spreads and enacts. This character formation was largely an attempt to create a 'new man' for the totalitarian regime. It involved sacrifice, hardship, comradeship, discipline, extreme loyalty, service, absolute authority, devotion, and obedience. Semi-military principles and techniques are emphasised along the lines of Sparta and the worship of the healthy perfect body is predominant in the Yearbooks to promote racial superiority. They fit with the militaristic model of character formation.

Character education must stand in the foreground of Hitler Youth education. Trustworthiness, self-subordination to the welfare of the community and silent devotion to duty are virtues demanded in a national socialist State.

Absolute honesty is a pre-condition for being a Hitler Youth member.

Only the selfless may follow the flag of the Hitler Youth.

By his appearance must the Hitler Youth member convince his folk comrades that he is a carrier of a great ideal.

Happy is he who has done his duty to his fatherland.

The fostering of sound and healthy bodies is the first aim of education. Physical perfection is fundamental for racial preservation.

Your body belongs to the nation.

He who vacillates, he who cannot stand the din of battle, does not belong to our ranks.

The Hitler Youth member must be able to stand hardship of any kind.

Blind obedience of the individual makes it possible that the decision of the group succeeds.

Cowards cannot win the freedom of their nation.

The spirit of comradeship must pervade all Hitler Youth activities.

Service in the Hitler Youth is honor service for the German people.

224 Appendix L

The members of the Hitler Youth shall be ready at ant time for service to their community.

The best Hitler Youth member is the one who is totally imbued with the national socialist view of life.

The Hitler Youth is the youth of the Fuehrer.

The religious youth organisation has no place in our time.

The Hitler Youth member must acquire at least elementary knowledge and practical experience of the practices of the German Army.

Appendix M

Below is an abstract from the Character Education Programme of Study (2016) produced by the Jubilee Centre for Character and Virtues at the University of Birmingham. It represents a contemporary take on how to form character. The full programme is available at www.jubileecentre.ac.uk

Sample lesson 2 – an intelligence virtue: good sense

Session 1: Virtue knowledge

Good sense

The virtue of 'good sense' forms part of every other virtue. It moulds, informs and transforms our basic desires, emotions, instincts and impulses into morally good decisions. These decisions strengthen our virtues and tackle our vices. 'Good sense' is like a lighthouse that illuminates what we have to do to realise or practise the virtues. It is a moral compass that steers us towards the more virtuous decisions, and away from the less virtuous ones. It takes a lifetime of practice, experience and reflection to calibrate this compass correctly.

Developing and acting with 'good sense' gives us freedom – being thoughtful and vigilant about what we are doing, why we are doing it and what we hope to achieve for ourselves and others through doing it. On this reading, to be 'free', means to have the freedom that the practised musician, artist, or sportsman enjoys: they have all the basic and advanced movements, quite literally at their fingers, and are able to weave them together almost intuitively, like second nature, as they respond to the demands of a situation. This is what 'good sense' does – it pulls together and balances out all the necessary virtues to cope with what the situation demands.

Living with 'good sense' sets out the ways and means of realising the good in the down to earth, concrete realities of any given situation. When it is well practised, it enables suppleness in the face of the complexities of the ethical life. It is the essence of a life well lived.

226 Appendix M

1. What can those who have this virtue do particularly well?

The person who lives with good sense is able to order their lives well.

- They know what the point and purpose of human life is (to flourish as a human being, rather than to wither; to build character, rather than to erode or destroy it).
- Those with 'good sense' know how to suit their actions to that very goal. All that the person with good sense does will turn out well.
- To live with good sense is to be able to direct all human action to the goal of human flourishing, or happiness.

Good sense directs emotions and actions to their proper goal, or end. This direction is first of all a work of reason and moral intuition, or perception. It requires:

- Foresight to realise what is and is not required to do this. This foresight is based upon a remembrance of past experience and a correct estimate of the present conditions and circumstances. It enables us to direct our actions to their goal, thoughtfully.

Perhaps the best way to think of 'good sense' is to think through what 'bad sense' might look like.

It is bad sense, for example, to live unfairly, or exploitatively, to live and act with cowardice, or rashness, or to live an overly indulgent lifestyle. Acting in such ways will not count as flourishing as a human, neither will it make us genuinely happy.

Those with good sense are able to decide or determine which act or acts will attain the goal of human flourishing in any situation. The chief act of this virtue is to command.

Task 1

- Put the above definition of 'good sense' into your own words.
- When have you had to act with 'good sense'?

Discuss

- Think of a person from real life, or literature who you think has demonstrated particularly 'bad sense'. Explain your answer in a short paragraph.

2. What are the benefits of acting out this virtue?

As we develop the habit of acting well, we will develop the habits of thinking well, or of perceiving what is required, or demanded by the situation and the circumstances we are in.

Appendix M   227

Without good sense we will target goals that fail to satisfy, or find ourselves trapped in unbecoming desires and satisfactions. Without 'good sense' there is no virtue. Living without 'good sense' can make us timorous, small-minded and rather selfish about our own selves and anxieties, not to mention foolish. It is 'bad sense' to be unfair, cowardly or overly indulgent!

Living with 'good sense' enables us to live vigorously and decisively, with vitality and a touch of moral nobility.

Task 2

* Define 'timorous'.
* Talk about a person who you think has displayed particularly noble moral qualities. Explain what those qualities were, and how they acted with good sense.

3. When might I have to practise this virtue?

Whenever we are called to practise any virtue at all, the virtue of good sense will form part of that other virtue. It assists us in perceiving what kind of response the situation calls for, and how to reconcile the virtues, if and when they collide, or point towards contradictory actions. It forms the deliberation and evaluation part of every other virtue.

For example:

* Adam borrows £50 from Baruch. The virtue of justice demands that each person gets what they deserve. Justice demands, therefore, that Baruch reimburses Adam to the tune of £50.

But how and when shall it be paid back?

* If Adam lacked good sense, then he would never pay it back. He would simply not have the foresight or resolution to set aside the appropriate funds. Instead, he might delay the reimbursement until he had inherited some money, or go for an easy gain by gambling at the races.
* If Adam lacked good sense, he may also pressurise himself to pay it back too quickly, on terms that were personally disadvantageous.
* Alternatively, if he had good sense, then Adam would be able to reimburse according to his ability, and as soon as possible, to an agreed timeframe. He may, for instance, deposit £5 a week in a bank, with a view to paying the loan back as soon as possible. And, having determined that this is the just thing to do (which indeed it is), he would see his actions through until Baruch is reimbursed. It is also worth mentioning that Adam would have had the 'good sense' only to borrow what he could afford to pay back, and for things that were worth having.

228 Appendix M

Task 3

- Show how 'good sense' can be used to help Adam decide whether he should borrow the money in the first place. What sorts of things will he need to consider?

4. Which desires or emotions may be alerting me to practise this virtue?

Every desire, emotion, or passion is an invitation to practise 'good sense'. It is good sense that moulds, transforms, and educates the emotions towards morally right actions.

For example:

My emotions, instincts, impulses and desires tell me that:

- I am angry because I sense unfairness is at work here. But, I want to be a fair person, giving each what they deserve; I don't want to be harsh and cruel in doing this, neither do I want to be a 'push over'. Acting with good sense will transform my anger into fairness, guiding me in how to be fair in the situation.
- I am afraid because I sense danger is at work here. But I want to be a brave person, overcoming internal and external obstacles to being a fair person; I want to overcome my fears and do the right thing, without being reckless. I don't want to be a coward, neither do I want to be foolhardy, or rash. Acting with good sense will transform my fear, guiding me to choose the ways and things I have to do to be brave in whatever situation I am in.
- I am craving because I sense my appetites for food, knowledge, things (e.g. shoes or video games) and pleasure need fulfilling. But I want to live with self-control – I don't want to consume more than my share, or use others as ends to my own pleasure, neither do I want to starve to death. Acting with good sense will transform my instinctual cravings, guiding me to choose the ways and things that will lead me to strengthen self-control in whatever situation I am in.
- It helps us to weigh up the situation, the activity that is required in the situation and transform this into a decision that we can carry out to realise the good of human flourishing. Good sense guides and educates our emotions towards the roads that lead to this flourishing, to the building up of character, rather than the undermining of it.

Task 4

- Choose one of the emotions (anger, fear, craving) listed above, or another emotion that you have experienced. Explain how practising the virtue of 'good sense' led you to act reasonably, educating your emotions. How did the situation turn out for you?

Task 5

- Think of a situation when you have acted with 'bad sense'. Explain it to yourself in a short piece of writing.
- What was the situation?
- What did you do, or say?
- What should you have said, or done to have improved the situation?

Index

Abelard, Peter 60
Acland, Arthur 117
Act for Setting Schools (1696) 91
Adam I/II characters 159
Addison, Joseph 91
Adler, Mortimer 88
Advisory Committee on Character 144
Advisory Council for Education 127
Aesop's Fables 41–2, 73
after-school activities 128–9, 147
Agamemnon 44
agape 61
Ahnert, T. 89
Aids to Reflection in the Formation of Character (Coleridge) 104
Ailred of Rievaulx, Abbot 59
Alberti, Leon Battista 70–1
All Parliamentary Committee 143
Allsop, K. 102
Aloni, N. 47–8
Ambrose, St. 58–9
Ancient City, The (Fustel de Coulangs) 39
Anglican schools 117
Annas, J. 48
Anscombe, G. E. M. 149–50
Antidosis (Isocrates) 46
Antipodes (Isocrates) 52
Aquinas, Thomas 64–8, 112
Aries, P. 62
Aristophanes 46
Aristotle: Boethius's commentary on 60; character and 12–13, 47, 49–50, 171; character formation and 3–7, 9, 13–14, 49–53, 132, 149, 171, 174; children's reasoning skills related to activities/ programs and 132; contemplative life and 93; education and 4–5, 8, 51–2, 167; ethics of 14, 21, 33, 48, 76, 87,

166, 172; flourishing of humans and 16, 50, 60, 65–6; Greek culture and 43; human nature and, assumptions about 93; humans as social animals and 66; intellectual virtues and 50–1; law and 56; modesty and 50; moral conduct and 49; moral virtues and 49; music and 41–2; philosophy of 43, 79; prudence and 87; purpose in life and 51; science and 95; Sophists and 47; Stewart's ideas and 97; Stoicism and 54; supreme good of humans and 60, 65–6; virtue ethics and 33–4; virtues and 16–17, 33, 50–1; *see also specific work*
Arnold-Brown, A. 17
Arnold, Thomas 101, 104–6
Arthur, J. 6
Artz, F. B. 72
Ascham, Roger 77
Asian schools 146–7
Athenian character formation 9, 41–5
Augustine, St. 58, 60–1, 90, 152
Austen, Jane 108
authority 88–9
autonomy 9, 11, 125
Averroes 68
Axial Age 8

Backhouse, W. H. 128
Bacon, Francis 81
Baden-Powell, ? 31
Badley, John Haden 31
Bain, Alexander 28, 93, 116
Bamford, T. W. 105, 110
Barclay, James 86
Barnett, M. 69, 114
Barrow, R. 40
Basil the Great 59

Index   231

Battle of the Books, The 73–4
Becker, C. B. 79–80
Becker, L. C. 79–80
Bell, Quentin 116
Bentham, Jeremy 83
Berkowitz, M. W. 158
Bernard of Chartres 79
Bible/biblical tradition 55–7, 68, 77, 171
Bloom, Alan 152, 161
Board of Education Circular (1910) 126
Board of Education's Handbook (1937) 127
boarding schools 128
Boethius 42, 60
Bohlin, K. E. 152
Bondi, R. 12, 158, 165–6
Bosanquet, Bernard 119
Bosanquet, Helen 119
Bow, C. B. 97
Boy Detective serial 124
Boys Brigade 126
Boy Scouts 126
Boy's Own Paper serial 124
Bradley, G. G. 107, 109
Bradshaw, D. 67–8
brainwashing 30
Braithwaite, Richard 78
Brooks, David 159
Building of Character (Miller) 122–3
Burgh, James 92
Burke, Edmund 95
Butler, Joseph 81
Butler, Samuel 78, 103, 104

Callan, E. 22, 151–2
Calvinism 91, 95–7, 115
Calvin, John 76
Carr, D. 152
Cassirer, E. 72
Catholicism 23, 58, 68, 78, 90, 126
Cato the Elder 53
Chandos, J. 102, 110
character: ambiguity about 5; Aristotle
   and 12–13, 47, 49–50, 171; autonomy
   and 11; change and 10, 173; classical
   foundations and 45–52; components of
   10–11; concept of 2–3, 10; conduct and
   10–11; continent 29; culture and 11;
   diverse ideas about 5–6; etymology of 10;
   expression and, regularity of 11; features/
   qualities of 13–14, 158–9; Greek idea
   of, ancient 45–52, 68; incontinent
   29; inner-directed 160; intellectual

160; interpretations of 9; Kass and 33;
   language of 110, 122–5, 149, 162, 170–1,
   173; measuring/quantifying, difficulty of
   1; militaristic 30; moral 18, 32, 66–7, 114,
   160; national 160; other-directed 160;
   paradoxical position of 168; personality
   and 9–10; Peters's idea of 1–2;
   principles/convictions and 11; science
   and 93–4; social 160; term of 9; themes,
   significant 149–59; tradition-directed
   160; types of 29; vicious 29; virtuous 29,
   160; will power and 11
Character (Smiles) 115–16
character education *see* character formation;
   education
Character Education Enquiry, The, report
   129–30
character education movement 129
Character Education Programme of Study
   157–8, 225–9
Character Education Promotion Act
   (2015) 148
character formation: Aristotle and 3–7,
   9, 13–14, 49–53, 132, 149, 171, 174;
   background information 8–9; benefits of
   170, 173; Christian culture and 58–68;
   community of virtuous exemplars and
   154; complexity of 2, 168; curriculum in
   schools and 163–4; education and 1, 5,
   8–9, 15–16, 65, 125, 163–5, 173; failed
   efforts in Britain 134; goal of 16, 167;
   historical context and 2–3, 7, 169–72;
   ideas about, popular 156–7; importance
   of 171; intangible hand and 164;
   intellectual judgements and, sound 152;
   knowledge transmission and 8; life-long
   159; myths about 156–7; as nurturing
   process 167; outcome of good 167;
   overview 2–3, 5–7, 169–70, 173–4; Plato
   and 10, 44–5, 51–2; process 17, 155–6,
   159, 167–8; resiliency of concept over
   time 8; as social process 155–6; term of
   5; threat to, current 161; true 17; *see also*
   definition of character formation; models
   of character formation; *specific historical
   period/foundation/influence*
*Characteristics of Men, Manners, Opinions,
   Times* (Cooper) 85
character policy *see* contemporary character
   policies/themes
Character and Resiliency Manifesto (Hinds)
   143

232 Index

Characters (Theophrastus) 51, 194–5
Character as seen in Body and Parentage (Jordan) 32
Character and Studies Befitting a Free-Born Youth (Vergerio) 73
Characters of Virtues and Vices (Hall) 78, 206–7
Charity Organization Society 119
charter schools 141
Chaucer, Geoffrey 62–3
Chesterton, G. K. 9
children's books 103
'Children's Morality Code, The' 218–22
Children's Plutarch, The (Gould) extract 214–17
children's reasoning skills related to activities/programs 132
Chinese character policies 148–9
Chinese Communist Party 148
choice 11
Christensen, Kit 18
Christian Education of Youth, The (Pius XI) 67
Christian ethics 58
Christianity, rise of 54
Christian model: Abelard and 60; Ambrose and 58–9; Aquinas and 64–7; Augustine and 58, 60–1; biblical tradition/Bible and 55–7, 68; Christian culture and 58–68; classical foundations and 55; Clement of Alexandria and 59; converts and 63; education and 62–4; examples of, numerous 20; good life and, notions of 171; Jesuits and 20–1; Jesus and 20; Lombard and 60; love and 60–1; pagan literature/myth and 60–1; *paideia* and 58; revelation and 60–1; Victorian character formation and 113–14
Church of England 117, 127
Churchill, Winston 166
Cicero 52–3, 58–60, 68
Citizens Growing Up paper (1949) 127
civic virtues 158
Clarenden Commission 107
Clarke, Fred 127
Clark, Rufus 116
classical foundations: Athenian character formation 9, 41–5; background information 39–40; character and 45–52; Christian model and 55; cultural context 43–5; models of character formation and 54; overview 6, 171; Rome/Roman Empire 52–4, 150, 171; Sophists 42,

46–7, 151; Spartan character formation 9, 30, 40–1; *see also* Greece, ancient
Classification of Character Strengths and Virtues framework (VIA) 140
Clement of Alexandria, Archbishop 59
Clinton, Bill 139
Clouds, The (Aristophanes) 46
Code for Successful Workers 24
cognitive psychology 131
Coleridge, Samuel Taylor 104, 152
Colish, M. L. 52, 69–70
Collini, Stefan 105, 110–11
Colloquy of Aelfric 63, 198
Communist Party 19, 148
Confucianism 146–9
conscience 153–4
consciousness 151
conservatism 27
conservative model 26–8
Conservative Party Conference (2018) 144
contemplative life 93
contemporary character policies/themes: absurdity of not teaching virtues 152; Chinese 148–9; civic virtues 158; Clinton and 139; coercion of individuals, liberal opposition to 152; conscience 153–4; criticism of character education in schools and 151; eulogy virtues 159; *Framework for Character Education in Schools, A* 157; ideas about character formation and, popular 156–7; indoctrination 151–2; intellectual virtues 157–8; international dimensions 146–9; IPEN and 141; Japanese 146–7; KIPP and 141–2; language of character 149; liberal education 153; literary works, role of 154–5; models of character formation 139; moral virtues 158; myths about character formation 156–7; negative view of human nature and 150; OFSTED Education and Inspection Framework 144–6; overview 7, 139, 159; performance virtues 158; PERMA teaching approach 140–1; positive education 139–42; predictable behaviour 158–9; résumé virtues 159; significant 149–50; Singaporean 148; South Korean 147–8; stock of characters in society 152–3; UK policy on character education 142–6; Vietnamese 149; virtue theory, return of

149–50; vision of goodness 156; West's cultural tradition 153
continent character 29
Conventional Morality 132
Cooper, Lord Anthony Ashley (Earl of Shaftesbury) 85, 104
Copleston, F. C. 14
corporal punishment 54, 70, 106, 117, 151
Corrosion of Character, The 25
Council of Rome (853) 62
Counter-Reformation 78
Creating Your Best Life (Miller) 140
Crede (Pierce the Ploughman) 64
Creed 64
culture 11, 161–2
Curzon, Lord 124

Dagger, R. 24
Dancey, John 128
Darwin, Charles 109, 116
Dawson, Christopher 3
definition of character formation: Aristotle's 13; background information 8–9; Berkowitz's 158; Bloom's 161–2; Bondi's 12, 158, 165–6; broad 13; complexity of 2, 5, 161–2; conflicting 9–15; Goethe's 12; Harman's 14; Hunter's 162; Kamteker's 11–12; Kristjansson's 14–15; Kupperman's 17; McIntyre's 162; Marx's 12; multiple 1; overview 6; Peters's 1–2; Russell's 14; Spencer's 15; Taylor's 12; theoretical approaches and 2; Trianosky's 14
Democracy and Education (Dewey) 130
De Pueris (*The Liberal Education of Children*) (Erasmus) 75
Descartes, Rene 81
descriptive statements 88
'Development of Moral Thinking and Choices in years 10–16' (Kohlberg) 132
Devettere, R. J. 47, 51
Dewar, Daniel 92
Dewey, John 33, 130–1
dialectics 64
Dialogues (Vive) 64, 201–5
Dickens, Charles 97
discipline 17
Dishon, G. 141–2
Dollinger, J. J. I. 77
Doris, J. M. 34
Dupre, L. 69
Dworkin, Ronald 144

earnestness 105
Edinburgh Review 102, 104
Educating Christians (Grech) 128
education: in Anglican schools 117; Aquinas and 65; Aristotle and 4–5, 8, 51–2, 167; in Asian schools 146–7; autonomy and 9, 125; in boarding schools 128; character formation and 1, 5, 8–9, 15–16, 65, 163–5, 173; in charter schools 141; Christian attitude toward 58; Christian model of character formation and 62–4; conservative 27–8; criticism of character education in schools and 151; curriculum in schools and character formation 163–4; defining 163; elite 105; goal of 3; in Greece, ancient 8, 13, 39, 41; intentional experiences and 164; Kristjansson's views of character formation and 165; liberal 74–5, 107, 134, 153; liberal arts 74; Locke and 82; McGrath's views of character formation and 165; mass schooling and 166; medieval 62–4; modern foundations and 71–80; in neo-liberal ideology 26; Plato and 47–8, 51–2, 112, 173; positive 139–42; in preparatory schools 30; progressive 31–3, 134; Renaissance 70–80; in Renaissance 71–7; in Roman Empire 53–4; Scottish Enlightenment foundations and 93; State's role in, increasing 127; in Synagogue schools 55–6; Trollope and 101–2; USA influences on British 130; Victorian 84, 114–15; *see also specific school*
Education Act (1496) 90
Education Act (1633) 91
Education Act (1646) 91
Education Act (1870) 117
Education Act (1944) 127
Education with Character (Arthur) 6
Education of Character, The (Gillet) 126
Education of Character, The (Mountford) 127
Education Inspection Framework (OFSTEAD) 144–6
Elementarie (Mulcaster) 77
Elementary School Teacher, The (Badley) 31
elite schooling 105
Elliot, H. S. 83–4
Elyat, Thomas 77
enculturation 162–3

234 Index

English public school character formation: Arnold and 101, 104–6; background information 101; Bradley and 107; children's books and 103; Clarendon Commission and 107; Darwin and 109; in early 19th century 102–3; earnestness and 105; Eton School and 107; evangelicalism and 104, 109–10; Farrar and 107; Fraser and 106; games-playing and 108; Harrow School and 102–3, 114; heroes who were religious and 109; Hughes and 106; language of character and 110; manliness and 104–5; in mid-19th century 103–5; mind and 109; models of character formation 110; morality and 109–10; novels about 103–4; overview 6; Protestantism and 109; Qundle School and 103; Rugby School and 104–6; sexual promiscuity and 102–3; social environment 107; socialisation and 108; sports and 108; Taunton Commission and 107; themes, common 102; Trollope and 101–2; Warre and 107

Enlightenment 172; *see also* Scottish Enlightenment foundations

Enlightenment liberalism 22

Enlightenment Project 94–5

Enquiries Historical and Moral (Murray) 92

Entwistle, Dorothy 125

Erasmus 75

Erikson, Eric 131

Essays on a Liberal Education (Farrar) 107

ethical instruction 121–2

ethical relativism 130

Ethics (Aristotle) 29, 48, 166–7

ethics: of Aristotle 14, 21, 33, 48, 76, 87, 166, 172; Christian 58; relativism and 130; Victorian instruction on 121–2; virtue 33–5, 46, 59–60, 79, 172

Ethology 120

Eton School 107

eudaimonic character 51; *see also* flourishing of humans

Eugenics Education Society (EES) 122

eulogy virtues 159

Eusebius of Caesarea 58

evangelicalism 104, 109–10

Excellence in Schools (White Paper) 142

Fables of Aesop 41–2, 73

failure, personal 119

family 161

family love 44, 71, 87

Farrar, F. W. 103–4, 107

Feltre, Vittorino da 73

Ferguson, Adam 86, 89

First Book of Discipline 91

flourishing of humans 16, 18, 50, 60, 65–6, 160

Fordyce, David 86

Formation of Character, The (Hull) 126

Fourth Lateran Council (1215) 62

Fowers, Blaine 29

Framework for Character Education in Schools, A (2017) 157–8, 225–9

Fraser, George McDonald 106

free personality 127

free will 120, 151

Fry, T. C. 103

Fundamental Law on Japanese Education (2006) 147

Further Education and Skills Inspection Handbook under Personal Development 145

Fustel de Coulanges 39

Galton, Francis 32, 122

Gamble, Richard 153

games-playing 108, 123–4, 128, 169–70

Garin, E. 71–2

Gathorne-Hardy, J. 101

genetics 114, 122, 168–9

Gerwen, J. Van 59

Gillet, Martin S. 67, 126

Gilligan, Carol 132–3

Gini, A. 21

Girl Guides 126

Goethe, Johann Wolfgang von 12

Golden Rule 55, 81

Goodman, J. F. 141–2

Goodman, L. 68

Gordon, General 109

Gorgias (Plato) 173

gothic influences 111–12

Governor (Elyat) 77

Grafton, A. 72

Grech 128

Greece, ancient: Athenian character formation 9, 41–5; character and 45–52, 68; culture 43–5, 111; education and 8, 13, 39, 41; Jews and 57; liberal arts and 74; *paideia* concept and 39, 58, 73;

Sophists and 42, 46–7; Spartan character formation 9, 30, 40–1
Green, I. M. 68
Green Papers 135, 142
Green, R. M. 21
Green, Thomas Hill 114, 121
Gregory the Great, Pope 153
Grendler, P. 72
Grey, J. 95
Griswold, C. L. 87
Grote, G. 47
Guroin, V. 156

habits of industry 115
Hadley, J. A. 28
Hadot, P. 39
Hahn, Kurt 108
Haley, B. 123
Hall, Joseph 78
Halstead, Mark 150
Handbook of Suggestions for Consideration of Teachers and others concerned in the work of Public Elementary Schools 125
Hardie, Keir 121
Harman, G. 14, 52
Harm Principle 84
Harris, M. J. 57
Harrow School 102–3, 114
Hartshorne, Hugh 129–30
Harvey, D. 24
Hauerwas, S. 10, 159
Havighurst, R. J. 133
Hawthorne, Nathaniel 103
health and character formation 108
Hegel, F. 114
hegemonic model 18–20
Himmelfarb, Gertrude 111, 116, 155–6
Hinds, Damian 143–4
History of Philosophy (Copleston) 14
Hitler Youth Yearbooks extracts 223–4
Hobbes, Thomas 81
Holt, J. 114
Homer 41, 44–5, 53
Hoof, S. 34
Howe, D. W. 111
Hughes, Thomas 106
Hull, Ernest 126
humanism 20, 70, 156
humans: flourishing of 16, 18, 50, 60, 65–6, 160; nature of, assumptions about 93; as social animals 66; supreme good of 60, 65–6

Hume, David 86–8, 90–2, 113
humility, promotion of 147
Hunter, J. D. 31–2, 140, 142–3, 162
Hutcheson, Francis 86, 89

ignorance 66
Iliad (Homer) 41, 44, 193
Imitation of Christ (Thomas à Kempis) 63, 199–200
incontinent character 29
Independent Labour Party 121
individuality 70
indoctrination 72, 139, 150–2
industry, habits of 115
inner-directed character 160
Institute of Education 128
Institutes (Quintilian) 52–3
intangible hand 164
intellectual character 160
intellectual judgements, sound 152
intellectual virtues 50–1, 157–8
intelligence/intuition (*sophia*) 50
international dimension of character policy 146–9
International Positive Education Network (IPEN) 141
interpersonal relations 147
Introduction to the Education Code (1905 and 1905) 125
intuition 164
Irwin, T. H. 47
Isocrates 46, 52
Italian Renaissance *see* Renaissance
Ivanhoe, P. J. 34

Jacob, M. C. 90
Jaeger, C. S. 41, 43
Japanese character policies 146–7
Jardine, L. 72
Jarrat, B. 64, 67
Jerome 59
Jesuits 20–1
Jesus 20
Jewish model 55–7
Jordan, Furneaux 32
Jubilee Centre for Character and Virtues 6, 144, 157–8, 225
Judaeo-Christian tradition 113–14, 121, 171
Julius II, Pope 80
justice, virtue of 154
Justinian, Emperor 61

236 Index

Kamteker, R. 11–12
Kant, Immanuel 83
Kass, Leon 3, 33
Kesebir, P. 155
Kesebir, S. 155
Kilpatrick, W. 164
Kimball, B. A. 74, 80
Kingsley, Charles 103
KIPP (Knowledge is Power Programme)
    141–2
Kluckholm, C. 164
knowledge transmission 8; *see also* education
Knox, John 76
Kohlberg, Lawrence 131–2
Kohn, A. 151
Kristjansson, Kristjan 14–15, 141, 155,
    165
Kroeber, A. L. 164
Kupperman, J. 17

Langord, P. 91
language of character 110, 122–5, 149, 162,
    170–1, 173
Lapsley, D. K. 29
Laws (Plato) 51
Laws of Lycurgus 41
laws and virtues 27, 56, 154
lay morality 72
learning 15, 65, 154; *see also* education
Lecky, William 103
Lectures on the Formation of Character (Clark)
    116
Leming, James 130
Letter of Aristeas, The 57
Letters (Pliny) 53
Lewis, C. S. 153–4, 168
liberal arts 74
liberal education 74–5, 107, 134, 153
liberal model 22–3
liberal Protestantism 134
life, meaningful 3
literacy 75–6
literary works 154–5, 165–6, 169; *see also*
    specific title
Lives of Aristides and Cato (Plutarch) 53
Livingstone, Sir Richard 109, 112, 128, 153
Locke, John 82
Lombard, Peter 60
love 20–1, 44, 60–1, 63, 66, 71, 87, 133,
    171; *see also* Golden Rule
Loyola, Ignatius 20
Luther, Martin 75–7

Mackenzie, John 122
Mack, Henry Fielding 103, 107
Mahoney, R. H. 87
Maimonides 57, 68
Maitland, I. 26
Makarenko, Anton 19
Making of Character, The (McCunn) 122
Mangan, J. A. 107–8
manliness 104–5
manners 91, 113
Mannheim, Karl 27
Marrou, H. I. 42, 45
Marshall, Alfred 119–20
Martin of Braga, St. 59
Marx, Karl 12
Mason, Charlotte 117
mass schooling 166
May, Mark 129–30
McClelland, Alan 128
McCulloch, G. 101
McCunn, John 122
McGrath, R. E. 165
McGuffey, William Homes 123
McIntyre, A. 5, 36, 95, 150, 152–3, 155,
    162, 172
McLaughlin, Terry 150
medieval foundations: background
    information 55–7; Christian culture and
    58–68; education in medieval period and
    62–4; Jewish model and 55–7; models
    of character formation and 68; modern
    foundations and 70–1; overview 6, 171;
    Renaissance and 69; *see also* Christian
    model
Meilaender, G. C. 4
Mere Christianity (Lewis) 154
Mew Educational System 147–8
militaristic character 30
Miller, Caroline 140
Miller, John 86
Mill, John Stuart 10, 83–4, 116, 120–1
mind 109, 167–8
Ministry of Education 127
Mirandola, Giovanni Pico Della 72
Mitchell, Basil 134
Mitchell, M. T. 76
Mittleman, A. L. 56
models of character formation: classical
    foundations and 54; conservative
    26–8; contemporary policies/
    themes 139; in English public school
    period 110; hegemonic 18–20;

liberal 22–3; in medieval period 68; neo-liberal 24–6; no single model of 173; overview 8–9, 17–18, 35–6; progressive sub-model 31; psychological 28–9; radical 29–33; Republican-liberal 23–4; in Scottish Enlightenment period 97; theological 20–1; in Victorian period 124; virtue ethics 33–5; *see also specific type*

modern foundations: Alberti and 70–1; background information 69; Bentham and 83; Bible/biblical tradition and 77; Counter-Reformation and 78; education and 71–80; Erasmus and 75; Hobbes and 81; humanism and 70; intellectual figures and, key 80–4; Kant and 83; liberal arts and 74; literacy and 75–6; Locke and 82; Luther and 75–7; medieval foundations and 70–1; Mill and 83–4; Mirandola and 72; modernity process and 69; More and 75; non-religious curriculum and 77–8; overview 6; *paideia* concept and 73; Protestant Reformation and 76; Quarrel of the Ancients and Moderns and 73–4; Renaissance and 70, 79; Rousseau and 82–3; Scholasticism and 71–2; *see also* Renaissance

modesty 50

monkish virtues 90

moral behaviour/conduct 49, 115

moral character 18, 32, 66–7, 114, 160

moral development theory 132

moral examples 87, 154, 156, 166, 170

Moral Instruction League (MIL) 121–2, 125–6

morality 72, 87–9, 109–10

moral judgement 85, 105

moral philosophy 142

moral theory 172

moral truths 27

moral virtues 49, 67, 158

Morant, Sir Robert 125

More, Hannah 118–19

More, Thomas 54, 75

Morgan, Nicky 43, 143, 146

Mosley, A. 82

Mountford, E. A. 127

Muirhead, John 122

Mulcaster, Richard 77

Murray, Hugh 92

music 41–2

narratives 154–5, 165–6, 169

Nash, R. 134–5

national character 160

National Character Awards 144

National Curriculum Statement of Values, Aims and Purposes 142

National Efficiency movement 114

National Institute for Moral Instruction 24

National Political Education Institutes 30

National Secular Society 117, 121

National Vigilance Association 119

nature versus nurture concept 168–9

Nazi Germany and character training 129

Nedeliskey, P. 31–2, 140

Neil, A. S. 32–3

neo-liberal model 24–6

Newsome, David 105

Newsom Report (1963) 133

New View of Society, A (Owens) 118

Nichomachean Ethics (Aristotle) 60

1984 (Orwell) 25

Noddings, Nel 133

novels 154–5, 165–6, 169; *see also specific title*

Oakeshott, Michael 27

Oakley, F. 79

obedience 40–1

O'Brien, D. 88

Odyssey, The (Homer) 41, 44

OFSTEAD 144–6

Ogilvie, R. M. 112

'On Being Conservative' (Oakeshott) 27

On the Education of Boys and their Moral Culture (Feltre) 73

On the Education of Children (Plutarch) 53

On Liberty (Mill) 10, 120–1

'On National Character' (Hume) 92

On the Teacher (Aquinas) 65

Open Letter to Christian Nobility of the German Nation, An (Luther) 76

Oration on the Dignity of Man (Mirandola) 72

Orwell, George 25

other-directed character 160

out-of-school field courses 129

Overbury, Thomas 78

Overman, S. J. 96

Ovid 77

Owen, Robert 107, 117–18, 120

238 Index

pagan myths 61
paideia concept 39, 58, 73
Panathinaikos (Isocrates) 46
parents 166, 170
Parents National Education Union 117
Park, R. J. 108
Pastoralia (Gregory the Great) 153
Paternoster 64
patristic theology, revival of 79
Pear, T. H. 128
Peck, R. F. 133
performance virtues 158
Pericles 44
PERMA (positive, emotions, relationships,
   meaning, achievement) teaching
   approach 140–1
personal failure 119
personal growth 134, 170
personality 9–10, 127, 152
persuasion 151
Peterson, C. 23, 140
Peters, R. S. 1–2
Pettit, P. 164
Piaget, Jean 131–2
Pieper, J. 76, 151
Pierce the Ploughman 64
Pius XI, Pope 67
Plato: character formation and 10, 44–5,
   51–2; education and 47–8, 51–2,
   112, 173; Greek culture and 43; moral
   conduct and 49; music and 41–2;
   persuasion and 151; Stoicism and 54;
   virtues and 10, 33, 47, 51, 97; *see also
   specific work*
Platonic Academy 61
Pliny 53
Plomin, Robert 166
Plowden Report (1969) 133
Plutarch 52–3
politics 90–3
Politics (Aristotle) 48, 53, 167
popular psychology 28, 162
Porter, J. 79, 166
Porter, R. 93
Positions (Mulcaster) 77
positive education 139–42
positive ethos 173–4
positive psychology 140
Post-Conventional Morality 132
poverty/poor 58, 114, 119
Power, F. C. 29
Pre-Conventional Morality 132

preparatory schools 30
Prescriptions Against Heretics
   (Tertullian) 59
Prime of Miss Jean Brodie 151
private schools 128
Problems of Men (Dewey) 130
progressive education 31–3, 134
progressive sub-model 31
proscriptive statements 88
Protagoras (Plato) 44–5, 47
Protestantism 76, 91–2, 95–6, 109, 112–13,
   117, 134
Protestant Reformation 76, 91
Protestant virtues 76, 96
Proverbs 56
prudence/practical wisdom (*phronesis*)
   50, 87
Psalms 56
psychological model 28–9
psychology 28–9, 131, 140, 162
public schools 101, 141; *see also* English
   public school character formation
Puka, B. 36

quadravivium 64
Quaestions disputatae de veritate 65
Quarrel of the Ancients and Moderns 73–4
Quintilian 52–3
Qundle School 103

radical model 29–33
Ratio Studiorum 20, 78
Rawls, John 23
Readers for American elementary schools
   (McCuffey) 123
reason 88–90
Reddie, Cecil 31
Reflections Upon Ancient and Modern Learning
   (Wotton) 74
Reformation 76, 91
Reid, Thomas 86, 89
relativism, ethical 130
religion versus virtues 85
religious consciousness, transformative 114
Religious Education (1924) 129
Renaissance: Artz and 72; Dewey's
   recommendation of attention to child's
   interests/experiences and 131; education
   in 70–80, 71–7; Garin and 72; Grendler
   and 72; humanists in 20; inner-directed
   character and 160; liberal arts and 74;
   medieval foundations and 69; modern

foundations and 70, 79; patristic theology and, revival of 79; *see also* modern foundations

Report of the Consultative Committee on the Primary School (1926) 126–7

Republic (Plato) 10, 48, 151

Republican-liberal model 23–4

respectability 111

résumé virtues 159

revelation 60–1

Revised Code for Scotland (1879) 113

rhetoric 42; *see also* language of character

Richards, J. 102

Riesman, D. 160

Riots, Communities and Victims Panel 143

Roback, A. 28

Robbins, W. 121

Robert Elsmere (Ward) 114

Roberts, Kenneth 128

Roche, Helen 30

Rockwell, Joan 154–5

role modelling 87, 154, 156, 166, 170

Rome/Roman Empire 52–4, 150, 171

Rosenthal, M. 30–1

Rothblatt, Sheldon 108

Rousseau, Jean-Jacques 82–3

Royal Prussian Cadet Corp. 30

Rugby School 104–6

Rupert of Deutz, Abbot 59

Russell, Bertrand 14

Rutherford-Harly, T. 30

Ryan, K. 152

Ryle, Gilbert 134

Sadler, Michael 126

Sandel, M. 25

Satires (Juvenal) 196–7

Sayers, D. 64

Scholasticism 64, 70–2, 79

School of Athens, The painting (Raphael) 80

School HMIs 115

schooling *see* education; *specific school*

School and Life report (1947) 127

Schoolmaster (Ascham) 77

Schools: Achieving Success (White Paper) 142

Schools: Building on Success (Green Paper) 142

Schools Establishment Act (1616) 91

Schwartz, B. 142

science 92–5, 140

scientific knowledge (*episteme*) 50

Scottish Education Department 127

Scottish Enlightenment foundations: authority and 88–9; background information 85–6; Burke and 95; Calvinism and 91, 95–7; Catholicism and 90; civic optimism and 92; contradictions and, internal 91; Education Acts (19633 and 1646) and 91; education and 93; Enlightenment as cultural process and 85–6; Enlightenment Project and 94–5; Hume and 87–8, 90–2; interpretation of period, continuous 86; manners and 91; material well-being and 156; models in 97; national improvement and 89, 93; orthodox religious faith versus 89–90; overview 6, 172; politics and 90–3; Protestantism and 91–2, 95–6; reason and 88–90; science and 92–4; self-improvement and 97; Smith and 86–7, 90–1; social sciences and 95; Stewart and 97; utilitarianism and 91–2; Weber and 95

Scotus, Duns 60

Secular Education League 122

secularism 113, 116–7, 134, 171–2

Seeley, J. R. 105

self-assertion 94

self-determination 120, 159

self-discipline 170

self-discovery 134

self-formation 94

self-fulfilment 94

Self-Help (Smiles) 115

self-help policies 117

self-improvement 28, 94, 97

self-reflection 85

self-reliance 170

Seligman, Marty 140

Seneca 53, 59, 68

Sennett, R. 25

'Seven Cardinal Virtues of the Protestant Ethic' (Overman) 96

Shaftesbury, Earl of 85, 104

Shakespeare, William 169

Shorter Catechism (Scottish Kirk) 89, 208–11

Short History of Ethics, A (McIntyre) 5

Siedentop, L. 39, 70, 90

Singaporean character policies 148

Smiles, Samuel 115–16

240 Index

Smith, Adam 26, 86–7, 90–1
Smith, Sydney 102
social character 160
social conditions/environments 107, 118, 162
social interactions 88
socialisation 18, 88, 108, 161, 163
social media 166
social sciences 95
Society for the Reformation of Manners 119
Society for the Suppression of Vice 119
Socrates 45–8
soft virtues 13
Solomon, W. D. 94
Sophists 42, 46–7, 151
South Korean character policies 147–8
Soviet Russian character formation 19–20, 129
Spartan character formation 9, 30, 40–1
Spencer, Herbert 15
Spens Report on Secondary Education 127
Spinoza, Baruch 81
sports 108, 123–4, 128, 169–70
Spring, G. 112
'Step By Step Character Leads to Success' (1929) 131
Stephen, Fitzjames 104
Stewart, Dugald 97
Stoicism 54
stories 154–5, 165–6, 169; *see also specific title*
Story Lessons on Character Building (Bates) extracts 157, 212–13
Strength of the People, The (Helen Bosanquet) 119
Summerhill School 32
Sunday School Movement 125
Symonds, John Addington 102–3
Synagogue schools 55–6
System of Logic (Mill) 120

tabula rosa theory 82
Taught Not Caught (Morgan) 143
Taunton Commission 107
Taylor, P. 12
teaching 65; *see also* education
technical skills (*techne*) 50
teleology 67, 94, 172
Tempest, The (Shakespeare) 169
Ten Commandments 64, 115
Tertullian 59

Thelwall, John 152
theological model 20–1; *see also* Christian model
theological virtues 20, 63, 66, 171
Theophrastus 51
Theory of Moral Sentiments, The (Adam Smith) 86
Third Lateran Council (1179) 62
Thomas, K. 78–9
Thomas à Kempis 63
Thompson, J. W. 78
Thring, Edward 107
Tom Brown's School Days (Hughes) 106
Tosh, J. 105
To Young Men, On How They Might Derive Profit from Pagan Literature (Basil the Great) 59
tradition-directed character 160
Treatise on Human Understanding (Hume) 88
Trianosky, G. 14
Trollope, A. 101–2
Turner, P. 110
20th-century influences: after-school activities and 128–9; boarding schools and 128; character education in 2000 and, similarities of 135; 'Character Education Enquiry' report and 129–30; character training in schools and 128; Christian books 125–6; Church of England conference and 127; *Citizens Growing Up* paper (1949) and 127; cognitive psychology 131–2; Dewey and 130–1; Education Act (1944) and 127; Erikson and 131; ethical relativism and 130; Gilligan and 132–3; *Introduction to the Education Code* and 125; Kholberg and 131–2; Moral Instruction League and 125–6; Nash and 134–5; Newsom Report (1963) and 133; Noddings and 133; overview 7; personal growth 134; Piaget 131–2; Plowden Report (1969) and 133; private schools and 128; *Report of the Consultative Committee on the Primary School* and 126–7; Ryle and 134; Sadler and 126; *School and Life* report (1947) and 127; secularism 134; self-discovery 134; Spens Report on Secondary Education and 127; 'Step by Step Character Leads to Success' and 131; Sunday School Movement and 125; values clarification and 133–4; *Young*

Citizens at School document (1950) and 127–8; youth policies and 129
Twigg, Stephen 143

UK policy on character education 142–6
Union of Ethical Societies 121
University of Chicago 131–2
University of Glasgow 86
University of Oxford 124
University Society of America 131
utilitarianism 91–2
Utopia (More) 54

Vail, H. H. 123
values 155–6; *see also* virtues
Values in Action (VIA) 140
values clarification 133–4
Vance, R. N. C. 104
Vergerio, Pier Paolo 73
Vergerius, Petrus Paulus 73
vicious character 29
Victorian character formation: background information 111–12; books about 122–3; Bosanquet (Helen) and 119; character and, concept of 111; character training and 117; Christian model and 113–14; Church of England and 117; Education Act (1870) and 117; education and 84, 114–15; ethical instruction and 121–2; evolution theory and 113; games-playing and 123–4; genetics and 114, 122; gothic influences and 111–12; Greek culture and 111; Green and 114; habits of industry and 115; health and, mental and physical 114; as high point in character education 117–18; ideas running parallel to each other 113; industrialisation and 113; language of character and 122–4; McGuffey and 123; manners and 113; Marshall and 119–20; Mill and 120–1; mixture of traditional beliefs and modern science 118–19; models of character formation and 124; moral character and 114; moral conduct and 115; moral movement and 119; More (Hannah) and 118–19; overview 6, 171–2; Owens and 117–18, 120; poor and 112–13, 119; Protestantism and 112–13, 117; respectability and 111; secularism and 113, 116–17, 171–2;

self-help policies and 117; Smiles and 115–16; social environment and 118; societal developments shifting concept of citizenship and 113; societies suppressing immorality and 119; State as organiser of domestic public policy and 113; working-class children and 124; Young Men's Christian Association and 116
Victorian moralism 114
Vietnamese character policies 149
virtue ethics 33–5, 46, 59–60, 79, 172
virtues: absurdity of not teaching 152; Aquinas and 66–7; Aristotle and 16–17, 33, 50; Cicero and 58; civic 158; conservative 26; corruption and 87; cultural perspectives of 171; defining 4, 16–17; eulogy 159; Greek teaching of 13; Hume and 87; intellectual 50–1, 157–8; of justice 154; justice 154; laws and 27, 56, 154; learning 154; monkish 90; moral 49, 67, 158; performance 158; Plato and 10, 33, 47, 97; privilege and 29; Protestant 76, 96; religion versus 85; Republican-liberal 23; résumé 159; Smith and 86–7; socialisation of 163; Socrates and 47; soft 13; theological 20, 63, 66, 171; theory 149–50, 172
virtue theory, return of 149–50
virtuous behaviour 89
virtuous character 29, 160
Vive, Jean Luis 64
voluntary after-school clubs in Japan (*Bukatsudo*) 147
'Vospitania' 19

Walker, R. L. 34
Walvin, J. 108
Ward, Mrs. Humphrey 114
Warnock, M. 156
Warre, Edward 107
weakness 66
Wealth of Nations, The (Adam Smith) 86
Weber, Max 95–6
Welldone, J. E. C. 114
Western character formation 162–7
White Papers 135, 142
Wilberforce, William 119
Will, G. F. 27
William of Auxerre 60
William of Ockham 64

242 Index

William of Wykeham 64
will power 11, 66, 109
Wilson, J. M. 103
Wittgenstein, L. 6
Wooton, D. 87
working-class children 124
Wotton, W. 74
Wright, N. T. 21

Yearbook of Education (1951) 128
Young Citizens at School document (1950)
127–8
Young Men's Christian Association
(YMCA) 116
Yu, T. 29–30

Zola, Emile 114